Grose's Classical Dictionary of the Vulgar Tongue

FRANCIS GROSE, ESQ.
F.R.S. & A.S.

GROSE'S

Classical Dictionary

OF THE

VULGAR TONGUE,

REVISED AND CORRECTED,

With the Addition of numerous

SLANG PHRASES,

COLLECTED FROM *TRIED* AUTHORITIES.

BY PIERCE EGAN,

Author of "Boxiana," "Picture of the Fancy," "Sporting Anecdotes," &c.

"A kind of *cant* phraseology is current from one end of the Metropolis to the other, and you will scarcely be able to move a single step, my dear JERRY, without consulting a *Slang* Dictionary, or having some friend at your elbow to explain the strange expressions which, at every turn, will assail your ear."

Corinthian Tom—LIFE IN LONDON.

LONDON:

PRINTED FOR SHERWOOD, NEELY, AND JONES,

PATERNOSTER-ROW.

1823.

KK.

MARCHANT, Printer, Ingram-Court, Fenchurch-Street.

PREFACE

TO THE

FIRST EDITION.

The great approbation with which so polite a nation as France has received the Satirical and Burlesque Dictionary of Monsieur Le Roux, testified by the several editions it has gone through, will, it is hoped, apologize for an attempt to compile an English Dictionary on a similar plan; our language being at least as copious as the French, and as capable of the witty equivoque; besides which, the freedom of thought and speech arising from, and privileged by, our constitution, gives a force and poignancy to the expressions of our common people, not to be found under arbitrary governments, where the ebullitions of vulgar wit are checked by the fear of the bastinado, or of a lodging during pleasure in some gaol or castle.

The many vulgar allusions and cant expressions that so frequently occur in our common conversation and periodical publications, make a work of this kind extremely useful, if not absolutely necessary, not only to foreigners, but even to natives resident at a distance from the Metropolis, or who do not mix in the busy world: without some such help, they might hunt through all the ordinary Dictionaries, from Alpha to Omega, in search of the words, "black legs, "lame duck, a plumb, malingeror, nip cheese, "darbies, and the new drop," although these are all terms of well-known import at Newmarket, Exchange-alley, the City, the Parade, Wapping, and Newgate.

The fashionable words, or favourite expressions of the day, also, find their way into our political and theatrical compositions: these, as they generally originate from some trifling event, or temporary circumstance, on falling into disuse, or being superseded by new ones, vanish without leaving a trace behind. Such were the late fashionable words, *a bore* and *a twaddle*, among the great vulgar; *maccaroni* and *the barber*, among the small: these, too, are here carefully registered.

The Vulgar Tongue consists of two parts; the first is the Cant Language, called sometimes Pedlars French, or St. Giles's Greek; the second, those burlesque phrases, quaint allusions, and nick-names for persons, things, and places, which, from long uninterrupted usage, are made classical by prescription.

Respecting the first, that is, the canting language, take the account given of its origin, and the catastrophe of its institutor, from Mr. Harrison's Description of England, prefixed to Hollingshead's Chronicle; where, treating of beggars, gypsies, &c. he says, "It is not yet fifty "years sith this trade began: but how it hath "prospered sithens that time, it is easy to judge; "for they are now supposed, of one sexe and "another, to amount unto above ten thousand "persons, as I have harde reported. More-"over, in counterfeiting the Egyptian roges, they "have devised a language among themselves,

" which they name Canting, but others Pedlars " French, a speache compact thirty years since " of English, and a great number of odde " words of their own devising, without all order " or reason; and yet such it is, as none but " themselves are able to understand. The first " deviser thereof was hanged by the neck, as a " just reward, no doubt, for his desartes, and a " common end to all of that profession.

" A gentleman (Mr. Thomas Harman) also " of late hath taken great paines to search out the " secret practizes of this ungracious rabble; and, " among other things, he setteth down and de- " scribeth twenty-two sorts of them, whose names " it shall not be amisse to remember, whereby " each one may gather what wicked people they " are, and what villany remaineth in them."

For this list see the word Crew.—This was the origin of the cant language; its terms have been collected from the following Treatises:—

The Bellman of London, bringing to light the most notorious villanies that are now practised in the kingdom. Profitable for gentlemen, lawyers, merchants, citizens, farmers, masters of households, and all sorts of servants, to marke, and delightfull for men to reade.—Lege, Perlege, Relege.—1608.

Thieves falling out, true men come by their goods.—1615.

English Villanies, seven severall times prest to death by the printers; but (still reviving againe) are now the eighth time (as the first) discovered by lanthorne and candle-light: and the help of a new cryer, called O-per-se O; whose loud voyce proclaims, to all that will hear him, another conspiracy of abuses lately plotting together, to hurt the peace of the kingdom; which the bell-man (because he ther went stumbling i'th'dark) could never see till now; and because a company of rogues, cunning canting gypsies, and all the scumme of our nation, fight under their tattered colours. At the end is a canting dictionary to teach their language, with canting songs. A booke to make gentlemen merry, citizens warie, countrymen carefull; fit for justices to reade over, because it is a pilot by whom they may make strange discoveries.—London, 1638.

Bailey's and the new Canting Dictionary have also been consulted, with the History of Bamfield More Carew, the Sessions Papers, and other modern authorities. As many of these terms are still professionally used by our present race of free-booters of different denominations, who seem to have established a systematical manner of carrying on their business, a knowledge of them may therefore be useful to gentlemen in the commission of the peace.

The second part, or burlesque terms, have been drawn from the most classical authorities; such as soldiers on the long march, seamen at the capstern, ladies disposing of their fish, and the colloquies of a Gravesend-boat.

Many heroic sentences, expressing and inculcating a contempt of death, have been caught from the mouths of the applauding populace, attending those triumphant processions up Holborn-hill, with which many an unfortunate hero till lately finished his course; and various choice flowers have been collected at executions, as well those authorised by the sentence of the law, and performed under the direction of the sheriff, as those inflicted under the authority and inspection of that impartial and summary tribunal, called the Mob, upon the pickpockets, informers, or other unpopular criminals.

In the course of this work many ludicrous games and customs are explained, which are not to be met with in any other book: the succession of the finishers of the law, the abolition of the triumph or ovation of Holborn-hill, with the introduction of the present mode of execution at Newgate, are chronologically ascertained; points of great importance to both the present and future compilers of the Tyburn Chronicle.

To prevent any charge of immorality being brought against this work, the Editor begs leave to observe, that when an indelicate or immodest word has obtruded itself for explanation, he has endeavoured to get rid of it in the most decent manner possible; and none have been admitted but such as either could not be left out without rendering the work incomplete, or in some measure compensate by their wit for the trespass committed on decorum. Indeed, respecting this matter, he can with great truth make the same defence that Falstaff ludicrously urges in behalf of one engaged in rebellion, viz. that he did not seek them, but that, like rebellion in the case instanced, they lay in his way, and he found them.

The Editor likewise begs leave to add, that if he has had the misfortune to run foul of the dignity of any body of men, profession, or trade, it is totally contrary to his intention; and he hopes the interpretations given to any particular terms that may seem to bear hard upon them, will not be considered as his sentiments, but as the sentiments of the persons by whom such terms were first invented, or those by whom they are used.

PREFACE

TO THE

SECOND EDITION.

The favourable reception with which this Book was honoured by the Public has encouraged the Editor to present a second edition, more correctly arranged, and very considerably enlarged. Some words and explanations in the former edition having been pointed out as rather indecent or indelicate, though to be found in Le Roux, and other Glossaries of the like kind, these have been omitted, softened, or their explanations taken from books long sanctioned with general approbation, and admitted into the seminaries for the education of youth—such as Bailey's, Miege's, or Philips's Dictionaries; so that it is hoped this work will now be found as little offensive to delicacy as the nature of it would admit.

A list is here added of such books as have been consulted for the additions.

A

CAVEAT

FOR

COMMON CURSETORS,

VULGARLY CALLED

VAGABONES;

SET FORTH BY

THOMAS HARMAN, Esquier,

FOR THE

Utilitie and Proffyt of hys Naturall Countrye.

Newly Augmented and Imprinted, Anno Domini M.D.LXVII.

Viewed, Examined, and Allowed according unto the Queen's Majestye's Injunetions.

Imprinted at London, in Flete-street, at the Signe of the Faulcon, by William Gryffith; and are to be solde at his Shoppe in Saynt Dunstone's Churche Yarde, in the West.

THE

CANTING ACADEMY;

OR,

VILLANIES DISCOVERED:

WHEREIN ARE SHEWN

The Mysterious and Villanous Practices of that Wicked Crew, commonly known by the Names of

HECTORS, TRAPANNERS, GILTS, &c.

With several NEW CATCHES and SONGS.

ALSO A

COMPLEAT CANTING DICTIONARY,

BOTH OF

Old Words, and such as are *now most in Use*.

A Book very useful and necessary (to be known, but not practised) for all People.

THE SECOND EDITION.

LONDON;

Printed by F. Leach, for Mat. Drew; and are to be sold by the Booksellers.

N.B. The Dedication is signed R. Head.

HELL UPON EARTH;

OR THE MOST PLEASANT AND DELECTABLE

HISTORY

OF

WHITTINGTON'S COLLEDGE;

OTHERWISE (VULGARLY) CALLED

NEWGATE.

Giving an Account of the HUMOURS of those COLLEGIANS who are strictly examined at the OLD BAILY, and take their highest Degrees near HYDE PARK CORNER.

Being very useful to all Persons, either Gentle or Simple, in shewing them the Manner of the ROBBERIES and CHEATS, committed by Villains on the Nation; whereby they may be the more careful of being wronged by them for the future.

LONDON:
PRINTED IN THE YEAR 1703.

THE

SCOUNDREL'S DICTIONARY;

OR, AN

EXPLANATION

OF THE

CANT WORDS used by THIEVES, HOUSE-BREAKERS, STREET ROBBERS, and PICKPOCKETS about Town.

TO WHICH ARE PREFIXED

Some Curious Dissertations on the ART of WHEEDLING,

AND A

Collection of their FLASH SONGS, with a PROPER GLOSSARY.

The whole printed from a *Copy taken on one of their Gang,* in the late Scuffle between the Watchmen and a Party of them on Clerkenwell Green; which Copy is now in the Custody of one of the Constables of that Parish.

LONDON:

Printed for J. Brownnell, in Pater-noster-row.

M.DCC.LIV.

[Price Sixpence.]

PREFACE

TO THE

THIRD EDITION.

Few, if any, remarks, I trust, will be deemed necessary, after the preceding Prefaces, in which the utility of such a Dictionary has been so clearly pointed out; and, after the care observed, in every instance, towards expunging *coarse* and *broad* expressions, where it could be done, without *frittering* away the spirit of the work. In the present edition, for myself, I have strongly to re-echo the sentiments of the former editors, namely, that I have neglected no opportunity of excluding indelicate phrases, which might have been adopted by my predecessors, nor of *softening* down others, where propriety pointed out such a course as not only necessary, but, perhaps, essential to render palatable this CLASSICAL DICTIONARY OF THE VULGAR TONGUE. At all events, if any apology is requisite, the subject in question must be viewed as a *compilation* of sentences collected from the lower walks of society, in which a scrupulous attention to *nicety* of expression is neither expected nor looked for; the persons alluded to, from whose lips they have escaped, not being "*partiklar* as to a *shade*" in colouring their *lingo*, or in displaying their *taste* for *erudition* —their only object being *effect*.

The above argument has been so well handled by a celebrated poet,* and is so *a-propos*, that I cannot elucidate the subject better than by quoting his remarks:—"With respect to that "peculiar language, called *Flash* or *St. Giles's* "*Greek*, in which Mr. CRIB's Memorial and the "other articles in the present volume are written, "I beg to trouble the reader with a few observa- "tions. As this expressive language was origi- "nally invented, and is still used, like the

* Thomas Moore.

" cipher of the diplomatists, for purposes of " secrecy, and as a means of eluding the vigi- " lance of a certain class of persons, called, " *flashicé*, *Traps*, or in common language, Bow- " Street-Officers, it is subject of course to con- " tinual change, and is perpetually either alter- " ing the meaning of old words, or adding new " ones, according as the great object, secrecy, " renders it prudent to have recourse to such in- " novations. In this respect, also, it resembles " the cryptography of kings and ambassadors, " who, by a continual change of cipher, contrive " to baffle the inquisitiveness of the *enemy*. But, " notwithstanding the Protean nature of the " *Flash* or *Cant* language, the greater part of " its vocabulary has remained unchanged for " centuries, and many of the words used by the " Canting Beggars in Beaumont and Fletcher, " and the Gipsies in Ben Jonson's Masque, are " still to be heard among the *Gnostics* of Dyot- " street and Tothill-fields. To *prig* is still to " steal; to *fib*, to beat; *lour*, money; *duds*, " clothes; *prancers*, horses; *bouzing-ken*, an " alehouse; *cove*, a fellow; a *sow's baby*, a pig, " &c. &c. There are also several instances of "the same term, preserved with a totally diffe-"rent signification. Thus, to *mill*, which was "originally 'to rob,' is now 'to beat or fight;' "and the word *rum*, which, in Ben Jonson's "time, and even so late as Grose, meant *fine* "and *good*, is now generally used for the very "opposite qualities; as, 'he's but a *rum* one,' "&c. Most of the Cant phrases in Head's "English Rogue, which was published, I believe, "in 1666, would be intelligible to a *Greek* of "the present day; though it must be confessed "that the Songs which both he and Dekker have "given would puzzle even that 'Graiæ gentis "decus,' Caleb Baldwin, himself. For in-"stance, one of the simplest begins,

"Bing out, bien Morts, and towre and toure,
"Bing out, bien Morts, and toure;
"For all your duds are bing'd awast;
"The bien Cove hath the loure.

"To the cultivation, in our times, of the "science of Pugilism, the *Flash* Language is "indebted for a considerable addition to its "treasures. Indeed, so impossible is it to de-"scribe the operations of THE FANCY without

" words of proportionate energy to do justice " to the subject,—that we find Pope and Cowper, " in their translation of the *Set-to* in the Iliad, " pressing words into the service which had " seldom, I think, if ever, been enlisted into " the ranks of poetry before. Thus Pope,

> "'Secure this hand shall his whole frame confound,
> " *Mash* all his bones and all his body *pound*.

" Cowper, in the same manner, translates κοψε " δε . . . . . . παρηιον, '*pash'd* him on the cheek;' " and, in describing the wrestling-match, makes " use of a term, now more properly applied to " a peculiar kind of blow,* of which Mendoza " is supposed to have been the inventor.

> "'Then his wiles
> " Forgat not he, but on the ham behind
> " *Chopp'd* him."

As this work is a *classical* one, I hope Mr. Hazlitt will not be offended by my quoting his opinions upon the subject. " What we under-

* " A *chopper* is a blow struck on the face with the back " of the hand."—*Boxiana*, vol. ii. p. 20.

"stand by *cant* or *slang* phrases.—To give an "example of what is not very clear in the gene- "ral statement, I should say that the phrase "*To cut with a knife*, or *To cut a piece of wood*, "is perfectly free from vulgarity, because it is "perfectly common: but to *cut an acquaintance* "is not quite unexceptionable, because it is not "perfectly common or intelligible, and has hard- "ly yet escaped out of the limits of slang "phraseology. I should hardly therefore use "the word in this sense without putting it in "italics as a license of expression, to be received "*cum grano salis*. All provincial or bye-phrases "come under the same mark of reprobation—all "such as the writer transfers to the page from "his fire-side or a particular *coterie*, or that he "invents for his own sole use and convenience. "I conceive that words are like money, not the "worse for being common, but that it is the "stamp of custom alone that gives them circula- "tion or value."—"The proper force of words "lies not in the words themselves, but in their ap- "plication. A word may be a fine-sounding "word, of an unusual length, and very imposing "from its learning and novelty, and yet in the "connection in which it is introduced, may be "quite pointless and irrelevant. It is not pomp "or pretension, but the adaptation of the ex-"pression to the idea that clenches a writer's "meaning:—as it is not the size or glossiness "of the materials, but their being fitted each to "its place, that gives strength to the arch; or as "the pegs and nails are as necessary to the sup-"port of the building as the larger timbers, and "more so than the mere showy, unsubstantial "ornaments. I hate any thing that occupies "more space than it is worth. I hate to see a "load of band-boxes go along the street, and I "hate to see a parcel of big words without any-"thing in them."*

So do I, Mr. Hazlitt; but, unfortunately for me, the instance that I shall quote to support the assertion is from the vulgar tongue. However, as some slight balance in its favour, it has none of the *emptiness* of the band-box about it; on the contrary, it is one of the shortest, if not the most emphatic sentences in the English language. The *Classic*, in *toasting* it over his champagne,

* Second Volume of Table Talk: "*On familiar Style.*"

might shrug up his shoulders, and make wry faces, with contempt, at its vulgarity, and let the force of it die away upon his lips; but to hear it from the *chaffer* of a rough and ready costard-monger, *ogling* his POLL from her *walker* to her *upper crust*, with a pot of *heavy* in his *morley*, and drinking to her, with a leary, wanton nod, "*Here's* LUCK!" then the beauty and conciseness of the expression, added to the emphasis, character, and effect of laconic phraseology, must be felt beyond all doubt: indeed, it is a volume in itself; and even the *learned* might admit it to be *multum in parvo*. The *slang* language, in many other instances, is very emphatic—videlicet, *Pigs*, meaning TRAPS, otherwise *thief-takers*; the etymology of which phrase stands good in the *rookeries*, although such sort of derivation might be in danger of being *queered* by the M.A.'s at the UNIVERSITIES.—The meaning is, that, as the *pigs* root up the ground with their snouts, so the *traps*, being *down* to the haunts of the thieves, root up the *prigs* when they want them. A more elegant illustration cannot be met with even in the work on the "SUBLIME and BEAUTIFUL." The *flash lingo* has, also, its *synonomies*—for money, the numerous terms are applied, the *blunt*, the *lour*, *kelter*, *steeven*, *mopusses*, *stuff*, *cole*, *rhino*, *need-ful*, *bit*, *ready*, *bustle*, &c. &c.

In order to throw as much light upon this *classi-cal* subject as I can, and as there is nothing like authorities to proceed upon, I feel induced to make the following poetic quotation from a little ingenious work* connected with the argument:—

"But many of my readers may not know
What 'tis the FANCY means, so I'll explain it.
I hope the *very* LEARNED will not *throw*
Stones on my explanation, and *disdain* it;
The best *of* language can but be so, so,—
Tho' BERKELEY *breed* it, and tho' BARCLAY *brew* it.
I struggle all I can,—I do my best;
The *thing* is *difficult*,—but let that rest.

"FANCY'S a term for every blackguardism,—
A term for favourite men and favourite cocks,—
A term for gentlemen who make a schism
Without the lobby, or within the box;
For the best rogues of *polish'd* VULGARISM,
And those who deal in scientific knocks;
For bull-dog breeders, badger-baiters,—all
Who *live* in gin and jail, or not at all!

* The FANCY: a Selection from the Poetical Remains of the late Peter Corcoran, of Gray's Inn, student-at-law.

The subject is so inexhaustible, and travels out to such an extent, that it would be a waste of time to pursue it any further, in order to point out more authorities by way of elucidation; suffice it to observe, that every exertion has been made to collect and arrange, under their proper heads, all the new phrases which have occurred since the last edition. To improve, not to degrade mankind; to remove *ignorance*, and put the UNWARY on their guard; to arouse the *sleepy*, and to keep them AWAKE; to render those persons who are a *little* UP, more FLY: and to cause every one to be *down* to those tricks, manœuvres, and impositions practised in life, which daily cross the paths of both young and old, has been the sole aim of the Editor; and if he has succeeded in only one instance in doing good, he feels perfectly satisfied that his time has not been misapplied.

PIERCE EGAN.

December 1, 1822.

BIOGRAPHICAL SKETCH

OF

FRANCIS GROSE, ESQ.

Mr. Grose, an eminent antiquary, was the son of a jeweller, at Richmond, in Surrey, who fitted up the coronation crown for George II. He was born in 1731, and having a taste for heraldry and antiquities, his father procured him a place in the College of Arms, which, however, he resigned in 1763. By his father he was left an independent fortune, which he was not of a disposition to add to or even to preserve. He early entered into the Surrey Militia, of which he became adjutant and paymaster; but so much had dissipation taken possession of him, that, in a situation which, above all others, required attention, he was so careless as to have for some time (as he used pleasantly to tell) only two books of accounts, viz. his right and left hand pockets. In the one he received, and from the other paid; and this, too, with a want of circumspection which may be readily supposed from such a mode of book-keeping. His losses on this occasion roused his latent talents: with a good classical education he united a fine taste for drawing, which he now began again to cultivate; and, encouraged by his friends, he undertook the work from which he derived both profit and reputation: his Views of Antiquities in England and Wales, which he first began to publish, in numbers, in 1773, and finished in 1776. The next year he added two more volumes to his English Views, in which he included the islands of Guernsey and Jersey, which were completed in 1787. This work, which was executed with accuracy and elegance, soon became a favourite with the public at large, as well as with professed antiquaries, from the neatness of the embellishments, and the succinct manner in which he conveyed his information, and, therefore, answered his most sanguine expectations; and, from the time he began it to the end of his life, he continued without intermission to publish various works, generally to the advantage of his literary reputation, and almost always to the benefit of his finances. His wit and good humour were the abundant source of satisfaction to himself and entertainment to his friends. He visited almost every part of the kingdom, and was a welcome guest wherever he went. In the summer of 1789 he set out on a tour in Scotland; the result of which he began to communicate to the public in 1790, in numbers. Before he had concluded this work, he proceeded to Ireland, intending to furnish that kingdom with views and descriptions of her antiquities, in the same manner he had executed those of Great Britain; but, soon after his arrival in Dublin, being at the house of Mr. Hone there, he suddenly was seized at table with an apoplectic fit, on the 6th of May, 1791, and died immediately. He was interred in Dublin.

"His literary history," says a friend, "respectable as it is, was exceeded by his good-humour, conviviality, and friendship. Living much abroad, and in the best company at home, he had the easiest habits of adapting himself to all tempers; and, being a man of general knowledge, perpetually drew out some conversation that was either useful to himself, or agreeable to the party. He could observe upon most things with precision and judgement; but his natural tendency was to humour, in which he excelled both by the selection of anecdotes and his manner of telling them: it may be said, too, that his figure rather assisted him, which was, in fact, the very title-page to a joke. He had neither the pride nor malignity of authorship: he felt the independency of his own talents, and was satisfied with them without degrading others. His friendships were of the same cast;

constant and sincere, overlooking some faults, and seeking out greater virtues."

Grose, to a stranger, says Mr. Noble, might have been supposed not a surname, but one selected as significant of his figure, which was more of the form of Sancho Pança than Falstaff; but he partook of the properties of both. He was as low, squat, and rotund as the former, and not less a sloven; equalled him, too, in his love of sleep, and nearly so in his proverbs. In his wit he was a Falstaff. He was the but for other men to shoot at, but it always rebounded with a double force. He could eat with Sancho, and drink with the knight. In simplicity, probity, and a compassionate heart, he was wholly of the Pança breed; his jocularity could have pleased a prince. In the "St. James's Evening Post," the following was proposed as an epitaph for him:—

> "Here lies FRANCIS GROSE.
> On Thursday, May 12, 1791,
> Death put an end to his
> *Views* and *prospects*."

At Hooper's, the bookseller, in High Holborn, who was publisher of Captain Grose's Works, a room was set apart, where a *conversatióne* was held between the literary characters of that period. It is asserted that the Captain was a most prominent feature in those meetings, and that the company were delighted with the peculiar felicity with which he related his various facetious stories and interesting anecdotes. Captain Grose was also a great observer of men and manners, and possessed a fine and accurate taste for painting. Dr. Griffiths, Arthur Murphy, Mr. Quick, the celebrated comedian, &c. &c. were among the persons who frequently visited the Captain a Hooper's, where they discussed the literary topics of the day.

The Captain had a funny fellow, of the name of *Tom Cocking*, one after his own heart, as an amanuensis, and who was also a draughtsman of considerable merit. He was of great service to the Captain in his Tour through England, Ireland, and Scotland. In the latter place, Captain Grose became intimately acquainted with Robert Burns, the poet, who thus describes the Antiquarian:—

If in your bounds ye chance to light
Upon a fine, fat, fodgel wight
O' stature short, but genius bright,
That's he, mark weel—
And wow! he has an unco slight
O' cauk and keel.

It's tauld he was a sodger bred,
And ane wad rather fa'n than fled:
But now he's quat the spurtle-blade,
And dog-skin wallet,
And taen the——*Antiquarian trade*,
I think they call it.

But wad ye see him in his glee,
For mekle glee and fun has he,
Then set him down, and twa or three
Gude fellows wi' him;
And *port, O port!* shine thou a wee,
And then ye'll see him!

Now, by the Pow'rs o' Verse and Prose!
Thou art a dainty chield, O Grose!—
Whae'er o' thee shall ill suppose,
They sair misca' thee;
I'd tak the rascal by the nose,
Wad say, Shame fa' thee.

EPIGRAM ON CAPTAIN FRANCIS GROSE,

THE CELEBRATED ANTIQUARIAN.

The following Epigram, written in a moment of festivity by Burns, was so much relished by Grose, that he made it serve as an excuse for prolonging the convivial occasion that gave it birth to a very late hour.

The Devil got notice that Grose was a dying,
So whip! at the summons, old Satan came flying:
But when he approach'd where poor Francis lay moaning,
And saw each bed-post with its burden a groaning
Astonished! confounded! cry'd Satan, by G-d,
I'll want 'im, ere I take such a d———ble load.

The Captain, it seems, was extremely fond of taking his porter of an evening at the King's Arms,* in Holborn, nearly opposite Newton-Street, a house distinguished for the company of wits, men of talent, and the most respectable tradesmen in the neighbourhood of Bloomsbury-Square. Mr. Quick was also a constant visiter at the King's Arms. Here the Captain was the hero of the tale; and often in turn shook his fat sides with laughter, at the number of "good things," in the shape of *bon mots*, repartees, &c. which nightly passed between the company at one table or the other.

The Captain had a man of the name of *Batch*, who was a sort of companion and servant united in the same per-

* It is worthy of remark, that the King's Arms has, for upwards of the last forty years, been a tavern of the same description: and at the present period (1823), under the management of Mr. Dawson, it still retains its *character* in being the resort of men of literature: persons connected with the press; artists; distinguished performers belonging to the Theatres Royal; men of talent in general; and merchants and tradesmen of the highest respectability in society, where, after the fatigues of their various vocations are over for the day, they *unbend*, with that playfulness of disposition, and liberality of mind, which makes the remembrance of worthy and upright companions vibrate on the heart with magical effect. The late much-lamented and celebrated comedian, Mr. John Emery, till a short time before his decease, was a constant visiter: here his enlivening conversation, choice anecdotes, and humourous songs, never failed to "set the table in a roar." The King's Arms is also distinguished for an harmonic society of the most select description, denominated the HYGEIAN CLUB.

son. *Batch* and his master used frequently to start at midnight from the King's Arms, in search of adventures. The *Back Slums* of St. Giles's were explored again and again; and the Captain and *Batch* made themselves as affable and jolly as the rest of the motley crew among the beggars, cadgers, thieves, &c. who at that time infested the *Holy Land!** The *Scout-Kens*, too, were often visited by them, on the "*look-out*" for a bit of fun; and the dirty "smoke-pipes" in Turnmill-Street did not *spoil* the Captain's *taste* in his search after *character!*

* A note cannot be deemed superfluous here, otherwise the sentence might remain a perfect paradox—the *Holy Land*, infested with thieves, &c. It most certainly is not the "*Land of Promise*;" neither can I vouch for the accuracy of the derivation, which states the meaning to be, that the inhabitants of the *Holy Land* (St. Giles's) are more *hole-ly* in their garments than *righteous* in their conduct.—*Sacer*, in Latin, and *Sacre*, in French, are used in the double sense of *holy* or *cursed!*

Neither were the rough squad at St. Kitts, and "the sailor-boys cap'ring a-shore" at Saltpetre-Bank, forgotten in their nightly strolls by *Batch* and his master.

In short, wherever a "bit of life" could be seen to advantage, or the "*knowledge-box*" of the Captain obtain any thing like a "*new light*" respecting mankind, he felt himself happy, and did not think his time misapplied. It was from these nocturnal sallies, and the *slang* expressions which continually assailed his ears, that Captain Grose was first induced to compile a CLASSICAL DICTIONARY OF THE VULGAR TONGUE, intended for the amusement, if not for the benefit, of the public.

Batch, at the request of his master, was directed one evening to dress himself in the Captain's regimentals, in order to personate Mr. Grose on a particular occasion; but, like the character of FALSTAFF, he was obliged to be "*stuffed*" with pillows, &c. before he could play the part; the regimentals of the captain being big enough to contain *two* such fellows as *Batch*. But somewhat different from the old axiom of "like master, like man," poor *Batch* was scarcely dressed for the character, when attempting in the street to ascend the steps of a hackney-coach to join the party in which he was destined to represent the Captain, his foot slipped, and he was nearly rolling into the kennel. *Batch* felt so encumbered with the *stuffing* that he could not get upon his legs, and loudly solicited the assistance of *Coaches* once more to enable him to obtain his equilibrium. On Jervy's lifting him up, one of his hands *sunk in*, and appeared to be lost in the belly of the Captain; when he exclaimed with the greatest surprise, "By G—, I never felt any person in all my life half so *soft*; what the devil is the *gemman* made of?"—while Mr. Grose, in his private clothes, stood, at Hooper's door, laughing at the ludicrous scene, and enjoying it beyond description.

Tom Cocking likewise used to relate many droll circumstances which befel the Captain in his travels: it being *Tom's* province, at night, to put two straps over his master, for the purpose of keeping the bed-clothes on him, Captain Grose being so bulky and uncomfortable to himself.

Captain Grose delighted much in punning upon his own figure, of which we shall mention an instance, as a proof of his familiarity and good nature. In a culinary tête-à-tête with his housekeeper, she thus expostulated with him:—Sir, as you are *inclinable* to be FAT, you should not eat food of a nourishing kind; you should —" —"You jade, (replied he,) I am not *inclinable* to be *fat*; that I am *fat* is totally *against* my *inclination*; I consider it a misfortune to be *fat*. For the future, therefore, remember that I am *disinclined* to be FAT!"

The following anecdote is recorded of Mr. Grose: "When he went to Ireland, his curiosity led him to see every thing in the capital worthy of notice: in the course of his perambulations, he one evening strolled into the principal meat-market of Dublin, when the butchers, as usual, set up their cry of "what do you buy? what do you buy, master?" Grose parried this for some time, by saying "he wanted nothing;" as last, a butcher starts from his stall, and, eyeing Grose's figure from top to bottom, which was something like Doctor Slop's in Tristram Shandy, exclaimed, "Well, sir, though you don't want any thing at present, only say you buy your meat of me; and by G— you'll make my fortune."

The works of Mr. Grose are not only numerous, but, also, connected with the highest ranks in literature; yet this learned gentleman did not think his time mis-spent in stepping aside from subjects of a graver class to compile a "CLASSICAL DICTIONARY OF THE VULGAR TONGUE." This work was published in 1785, and has gone through several editions.

A

CLASSICAL DICTIONARY

OF THE

Vulgar Tongue.

A

ABBESS, or LADY ABBESS. The mistress of a house of ill fame.

ABBOT'S PRIORY. The King's Bench Prison; this bit of *flash* generally changes when the Lord Chief Justice of the above court retires from his situation.

ABEL-WACKETS. Blows given on the palm of the hand with a twisted handkerchief, instead of a ferula; a jocular punishment among seamen, who sometimes play at cards for wackets, the loser suffering as many strokes as he has lost games.

ABIGAIL. A lady's waiting-maid.

ABRAM. Naked. *Cant.*

ABRAM COVE. A cant word among thieves, signifying a naked or poor man; also a lusty, strong rogue.

ABRAM MEN. Pretended madmen.

ABRAM, SHAM. To pretend sickness.

ACADEMY, or PUSHING SCHOOL. A cyprian lodge. The Floating Academy; the vessels on board of which those persons are confined instead of transportation.

ACE OF SPADES. A widow.

ACCOMMODATE, or ACCOMMODATION. In the Sporting World it is to part a BET, or to let a person go halves (that is to *accommodate* him) in a bet that is likely to come off successful. It is, also, in an ironical manner, to *believe* a person when you are well assured he is uttering a lie; by observing you *believe* what he is saying, merely to *accommodate* him.

ACCOUNTS. To cast up one's accounts; to vomit.

ACORN. You will ride a horse foaled by an acorn, i.e. the

B

gallows, called also the Wooden and Three-legged Mare; you will be hanged.—*See* THREE-LEGGED MARE.

ACTEON. A cuckold, from the horns planted on the head of Acteon by Diana.

ACTIVE CITIZEN. A louse.

ADAM'S ALE. Water.

ADAM TILER. A pickpocket's associate, who receives the stolen goods and runs off with them. *Cant.*

ADDLE PATE. An inconsiderate foolish fellow.

ADDLE PLOT. A spoil-sport, a mar-all.

ADMIRAL OF THE BLUE, who carries his flag on the main-mast. A landlord or publican wearing a blue apron, as was formerly the custom among gentlemen of that vocation.

ADMIRAL OF THE NARROW SEAS. One who from drunkenness vomits into the lap of the person sitting opposite to him. *Sea phrase.*

ADRIFT. Loose, turned adrift, discharged. *Sea phrase.*

ÆGROTAT, *(Cambridge.)* A certificate from the apothecary that you are *indisposed* (i. e.) to go to chapel. He sports an Ægrotat, he is sick and unable to attend chapel or hall. It does not follow, however, but that he can *strum* a *piece*, or sport a pair of oars.

AFFIDAVIT MEN. Knights of the post, or false witnesses, said to attend Westminster-Hall, and other courts of justice, ready to swear any thing for hire.

AFTER-CLAP. A demand after the first giving in has been discharged; a charge for pretended omissions; in short, any thing disagreeable happening after all consequences of the cause have been thought at an end.

AGAINST THE GRAIN. Unwilling. It went much against the grain with him, i. e. it was much against his inclination, or against his pluck. Speaking of Bacchus, the Author of "Randall," a Fragment, says

"Wine he loves to view his altars stain,
But prime blue ruin goes against the grain."
Vide Randall's Diary.

AGOG, ALL-A-GOG. Anxious, eager, impatient; from the Italian, *agognáre*, to desire eagerly.

AGROUND. Stuck fast, stopped, at a loss, ruined; like a boat or vessel aground.

AIR AND EXERCISE. He has had air and exercise, i. e. he has been whipped at the cart's tail; or, as it is generally, though more vulgarly expressed, at the cart's a–se.

ALDERMAN. A roasted turkey garnished with sausages; the latter are supposed to represent the gold chain worn by those magistrates.

ALDERMAN LUSHINGTON. *See* LUSH.

ALDGATE. A draught on the pump at Aldgate; a bad bill of exchange drawn on persons who have no effects of the drawer.

ALE DRAPER. An ale-house keeper.

ALE POST. A may-pole.

ALL-A-MORT. Struck dumb, confounded. "What, sweet one, all-a-mort?" *Shakspeare.*

ALL HOLIDAY. It is all holiday at Peckham, or it is all holiday with him; a saying signifying that it is all over with the business or person spoken of or alluded to.

ALL HOLLOW. He was beat all hollow, i.e. he had no chance of conquering; it was all hollow, or a hollow thing, it was a decided thing from the beginning. *See* HOLLOW.

ALL MY EYE. A lame story. Fudge.

ALL NATIONS. A composition of all the different spirits sold in a dram-shop, collected in a vessel into which the drainings of the bottles and quartern pots are emptied.

ALLS. The five alls is a country sign, representing five human figures, each having a motto under him. The first is a king in his regalia; his motto, I govern all: the second, a bishop in pontificals; motto, I pray for all: third, a lawyer in his gown; motto, I plead for all: fourth, a soldier in his regimentals, fully accoutred; motto, I fight for all: fifth, a poor countryman with his scythe and rake; motto, I pay for all.

ALONG-SHORE BOYS. Landsmen. *Sea term.*

ALSATIA THE HIGHER. Whitefriars, once a place privileged from arrests for debt, as was also the Mint, but suppressed on account of the notorious abuses committed there. *Obsolete.*

ALSATIA THE LOWER. The Mint in Southwark. *Obsolete.*

ALSATIANS. The inhabitants of Whitefriars or the Mint. *Obsolete.*

ALTAMEL. A verbal or lump account, without particulars, such as is commonly produced at bawdy-houses, spunging-houses, &c. *See* DUTCH RECKONING.

ALTITUDES. The man is in his altitudes, i. e. he is drunk.

AMBASSADOR. A trick to duck some ignorant fellow or landsman, frequently played on board ships in the warm latitudes. It is thus managed: a large tub is filled with water, and two stools placed on each side of it: over the whole is thrown a tarpaulin, or old sail; this is kept tight by two persons, who are to represent the king and queen of a foreign country, and are seated on the stools. The person intended to be ducked plays the ambassador, and, after repeating a ridiculous speech dictated to him, is led in great form up to the throne, and seated between the king and queen, who rise suddenly, as soon as he is seated, he falls backwards into the tub of water.

B 2

Ambassador of Morocco. A shoemaker. *(Vide Mrs. Clarke's Examination).*

Ambidexter. A lawyer who takes fees from both plaintiff and defendant, or that goes snacks with both parties in gaming.

Amen Curler. A parish clerk.

Amen. He said Yes and Amen to every thing; he agreed to every thing.

Aminadab. A jeering name for a Quaker.

Ames Ace. Within ames ace; nearly, very near.

Ammunition Wives. Girls of the town, doxies. *Sea term.*

Amuse. To fling dust or snuff in the eyes of the person intended to be robbed; also to invent some plausible tale, to delude shop-keepers and others, thereby to put them off their guard. *Cant.*

Amusers. Rogues who carry snuff or dust in their pockets, which they throw into the eyes of any person they intend to rob, and, running away, their accomplices (pretending to assist and pity the half-blinded person) take that opportunity of plundering him.

Anabaptist. A pickpocket caught in the fact and punished with the discipline of the pump or horse-pond.

Anchor. Bring your a–se to an anchor, i. e. sit down. To let go an anchor to the windward of the law; to keep within the letter of the law. *Sea wit.*

Andrew Miller's Lugger. A king's ship or vessel. *Sea cant.*

Anglers. Pilferers, or petty thieves, who, with a stick having a hook at the end, steal goods out of shop-windows, grates, &c.; also those who draw in or entice unwary persons to prick at the belt, or such like devices.

Angling for Farthings. Begging out of a prison-window with a cap, or box, let down at the end of a long string.

Ankle. A girl who is got with child is said to have sprained her ankle.

Anodyne Necklace. A halter.

Anthony, to knock. Said of an in-kneed person, or one whose knees knock together; to cuff Jonas. See Jonas.

Ape Leader. An old maid; their punishment after death, for neglecting to increase and multiply, will be, it is said, leading apes in hell.

Apostles. To manœuvre the apostles, i. e. rob Peter to pay Paul; that is, to borrow money of one man to pay another.

Apostles. *(Cambridge.)* Men who are plucked, refused their degree.

Apothecary. To talk like an apothecary; to use hard or

gallipot words: from the assumed gravity and affectation of knowledge generally put on by the gentlemen of this profession, who are commonly as superficial in their learning as they are pedantic in their language.

APPLE-CART. Down with his apple-cart; knock or throw him down.

APPLE-DUMPLING SHOP. A woman's bosom.

APPLE-PIE BED. A bed made apple-pie fashion, like what is called a turnover apple-pie, where the sheets are so doubled as to prevent any one from getting at his length between them: a common trick played by frolicsome country lasses on their sweethearts, male relations, or visiters.

APRON-STRING-HOLD. An estate held by a man during his wife's life.

ARCH DUKE. A comical or eccentric fellow.

ARCH ROGUE, DIMBER DAMBER UPRIGHT MAN. The chief of a gang of thieves or gypsies.

ARCH DELL, or ARCH DOXY, signifies the same in rank among the female canters or gypsies.

ARD. Hot. *Cant.*

AREA SNEAK, or AREA SLUM. The practice of slipping unperceived down the areas of private houses, and robbing the lower apartments of plate or other articles.

ARMOUR. In his armour, pot valiant.

ARK. A boat or wherry. Let us take an ark and winns, let us take a sculler. *Cant.*

ARK PIRATES. Thieves who rob and plunder on navigable rivers. *Sea cant.*

ARK RUFFIANS. Rogues who, in conjunction with watermen, rob, and sometimes murder, on the water, by picking a quarrel with the passengers in a boat, boarding it, plundering, stripping, and throwing them overboard, &c. A species of badger. *Cant.*

ARM-PITS. To work under the arm-pits, is to practise only such kinds of depredation, as will amount, upon conviction, to what the law terms single, or petty larceny; the extent of punishment for which is transportation for seven years. By following this system, a thief avoids the halter, which certainly is applied *above* the arm-pits.

ARRAH NOW. An unmeaning expletive, frequently used by the vulgar Irish.

ARS MUSICA. A bum fiddle.

ARSE. To hang an arse; to hang back, to be afraid to advance. He would lend his a–se, and sh–te through his ribs; a saying of any one who lends his money inconsiderately. He would lose his a–se if it was loose; said of a careless person. A–se about; turn round.

ARSY VARSEY. To fall arsy varsey, i. e. head over heels.

Article. A wench. A prime article. A handsome girl. She's a prime article (*whip slang*), she's a develish good piece, a hell of a *goer*.

Ask, or Ax my A—se. A common reply to any question; still deemed wit at sea, and formerly at court, under the denomination of selling bargains. *See* Bargain.

Assig. An assignation.

Athanasian Wench, or Quicunque Vult. A forward girl, ready to oblige every man that shall ask her.

Aunt. Mine aunt; a bawd or procuress; a title of eminence for the senior *dells*, who serve for instructresses, midwives, &c. for the *dells*. *Cant.* *See* Dells.

Avoir du pois Lay. Stealing brass weights off the counters of shops. *Cant.*

Autem. A church.

Autem Bawler. A parson. *Cant.*

Autem Cacklers. } **Autem Prickears.** } Dissenters of every denomination. *Cant.*

Autem Cackle-Tub. A conventicle or meeting-house for dissenters. *Cant.*

Autem Dippers. Anabaptists. *Cant.*

Autem Divers. Pickpockets who practise in churches; also churchwardens and overseers of the poor. *Cant.*

Autem Mort. A married woman; also a female beggar with several children hired or borrowed to excite charity. *Cant.*

Autem Quaver-Tub. A Quaker's meeting-house. *Cant.*

Awake. An expression used on many occasions; as a thief will say to his accomplice, on perceiving the person they are about to rob is aware of their intention, and upon his guard, *stow it*, the *cove's awake*. To be awake to any scheme, deception, or design, means, generally, to see through or comprehend it.

B

Babes in the Wood. Criminals in the stocks, or pillory.

Babble. Confused, unintelligible talk, such as was used at the building of the tower of Babel.

Back Biter. One who slanders another behind his back, i. e. in his absence. His bosom friends are become his back biters, said of a lousy man.

Backed. Dead. He wishes to have the senior, or old square-toes, backed; he longs to have his father on six men's shoulders; that is, carrying to the grave.

Back Jump. A back-window.

Back Slang. To enter or come out of a house by the back-door; or, to go a circuitous or private way through the streets, in order to avoid any particular place in the direct road, is termed back-slanging it.

Back Slum. A back-room; also the back entrance to any house or premises; thus, we'll give it 'em on the back-slum, means, we'll get in at the back-door.

Back up. His back is up, i. e. he is offended or angry; an expression or idea taken from a cat; that animal, when angry, always raising its back. An allusion also sometimes used to jeer a crooked man; as, So, sir, I see somebody has offended you, for your back is up.

Bacon. He has saved his bacon; he has escaped. He has a good voice to beg bacon; a saying in ridicule of a bad voice.

Bacon-faced. Full-faced.

Bacon-fed. Fat, greasy.

Bad Bargain. One of his majesty's bad bargains; a worthless soldier, a malingeror. *See* Malingeror.

Bad Halfpenny. When a man has been upon any errand, or attempting any object which has proved unsuccessful or impracticable, he will say, on his return, It's a bad halfpenny; meaning he has returned as he went.

Badge. A term used for one burned in the hand. He has got his badge, and piked; he was burned in the hand, and is at liberty. *Cant.*

Badge-Coves. Parish pensioners. *Cant.*

Badgers. A crew of desperate villains who rob near rivers, into which they throw the bodies of those they murder. *Cant.*

Bag. He gave them the bag, i. e. left them.

Bag of Nails. He squints like a bag of nails, i. e. his eyes are directed as many ways as the points of a bag of nails. The old Bag of Nails at Pimlico; originally the Bacchanals.

Baggage. Heavy baggage; women and children. Also a familiar epithet for a woman; as, cunning baggage, wanton baggage, &c.

Baker's Dozen. Fourteen; that number of rolls being allowed to the purchasers of a dozen.

Baker-kneed. One whose knees knock together in walking, as if kneading dough.

Balderdash. Adulterated wine. Lewd conversation.

Ball of Fire. A glass of brandy. *Cant.*

Balsam. Money.

Balum Rancum. A hop or dance, where the women are all prostitutes. N.B. The company dance in their *birthday* suits.

Bam. A jocular imposition, the same as a humbug. *See* Humbug.

Bamboozle. To make a fool of any one, to humbug or impose on him.

Bandbox. My a--se on a bandbox; an answer to the offer of any thing inadequate to the purpose for which it is proffered, like offering a bandbox for a seat.

Banded. Hungry. *Cant.*

Bandog. A bailiff or his follower; also a very fierce mastiff: likewise, a bandbox. *Cant.*

Bands. To wear the bands, is to be hungry, or short of food for any length of time; a phrase chiefly used on board the hulks, or in jails.

Bandy. A sixpence. *Cant.*

Bang Up. *(Whip.)* Quite the thing. Well done. Complete. Dashing. In a handsome stile. A bang up cove; a dashing fellow who spends his money freely. To bang up prime: to bring your horses up in a dashing or fine style: as the swell's rattler and prads are bang up prime; the gentleman sports an elegant carriage and fine horses. A man, who has behaved with extraordinary spirit and resolution in any enterprise he has been engaged in, is also said to have come bang up to the mark; any article which is remarkably good or elegant, or any fashion, act, or measure which is carried to the highest pitch, is likewise illustrated by the same emphatical phrase.

Bang. To beat.

Banging. Great; a fine banging boy.

Bang Straw. A nick-name for a thresher, but applied to all the servants of a farmer.

Bankrupt Cart. A one-horse chaise, said to be so called by a Lord Chief Justice, from their being so frequently used on Sunday jaunts by extravagant shopkeepers and tradesmen.

Bankruptcy List, to be put on the, signifies, in pugilism—To be completely finished. Randall, in his poetic Farewell to the Prize Ring, says,

> " Oh sad is the heart that can say ' the deuce take her,'
> To Fame, when she's backing a blade of the fist;
> But Turner I've *clean'd out;* and Martin *the Baker,*
> I'd very near put on the *Bankruptcy list.*"
>
> *Vide Randall's Diary.*

Banks's Horse. A horse famous for playing tricks, the property of one Banks. It is mentioned in *Sir Walter Raleigh's Hist. of the World, p.* 178; also by *Sir Kenelm Digby and Ben Jonson. Obsolete.*

Bantling. A young child.

Banyan Day. A sea term for those days on which no meat

is allowed to the sailors: the term is borrowed from the Banyans in the East Indies, a cast that eat nothing that has had life.

BAPTISED, or CHRISTENED. Rum, brandy, or any other spirits, that have been lowered with water.

BARBER'S CHAIR. She is as common as a barber's chair, in which a whole parish sit to be trimmed; said of a prostitute.

BARBER'S SIGN. A standing pole and two wash-balls.

BARGAIN. To sell a bargain: a species of wit, much in vogue about the latter end of the reign of Queen Anne, and frequently alluded to by Dean Swift, who says the maids of honour often amused themselves with it. It consisted in the seller naming his or her hinder parts, in answer to the question, What? which the buyer was artfully led to ask. As a specimen, take the following instance: A lady would come into a room full of company, apparently in a fright, crying out, It is white, and follows me! On any of the company asking, What? she sold the bargain, by saying, My a–se.

BARGEES. *(Cambridge.)* Barge-men on the river.

BARKER. The shopman of a bow-wow shop, or dealer in second-hand clothes, particularly about Monmouth-street, who walks before his master's door, and deafens every passenger with his cries of—Clothes, coats or gowns;—what d'ye want, gemmen?—what d'ye buy? See BOW-WOW SHOP.

BARKSHIRE. A member or candidate for Barkshire, said of one troubled with a cough; vulgarly styled barking.

BARKING-IRONS. Pistols, from their explosion resembling the bow-wow or barking of a dog. *Irish.*

BARN. A parson's barn; never so full but there is still room for more. Bit by a barn mouse, tipsey, probably from an allusion to barley.

BARNABY. An old dance to a quick movement. See *Cotton*, in his Virgil Travesti; where, speaking of Æolus, he has these lines,

> "Bounce cry the port-holes, out they fly,
> And make the world dance Barnaby."

BARNACLE. A good job, or snack easily got: also shell-fish growing at the bottoms of ships; a bird of the goose kind; an instrument like a pair of pincers to fix on the noses of vicious horses whilst shoeing; a nick-name for spectacles, and also for the gratuity given to grooms by the buyers and sellers of horses.

BARREL FEVER. He died of the barrel fever; he killed himself by drinking.

BARROW MAN. A man under sentence of transportation;

alluding to the convicts at Woolwich, who are principally employed in wheeling barrows full of brick or dirt.

BARTHOLOMEW BABY. A person dressed up in a tawdry manner, like the dolls or babies sold at Bartholomew fair.

BASH. To bounce over any person, to blow up.

BASKET. An exclamation frequently made use of in cock-pits, at cock-fightings, where persons refusing or unable to pay their losings, are adjudged by that respectable assembly to be put into a basket suspended over the pit, there to remain during that day's diversion: on the least demur to pay a bet, Basket is vociferated *in terrorem*. He grins like a basket of chips: a saying of one who is on the broad grin.

BASKET-MAKING. The good old trade of basket-making; copulation, or making feet for children's stockings.

BASTARDLY GULLION. A bastard's bastard.

BASTE. To beat. I'll give him his bastings, I'll beat him heartily.

BASTILE. A flash term for the House of Correction, in Cold Bath Fields; so termed when under the management of Governor Aris. For shortness termed the *Steel*.

BASTING. A beating.

BASTONADING. Beating any one with a stick; from baton, a stick, formerly spelt baston.

BAT. A low whore: so called from moving out like bats in the dusk of the evening.

BATCH. We had a pretty batch of it last night; we had a hearty dose of liquor. Batch originally means the whole quantity of bread baked at one time in an oven.

BATTNER. An ox: beef being apt to batten or fatten those that eat it. The cove has hushed the battner; i. e. has killed the ox.

BATCHELOR'S FARE. Bread and cheese and kisses.

BATCHELOR'S SON. A bastard.

BATTLE ROYAL. A battle or bout at cudgels or fisty-cuffs, wherein more than two persons are engaged: perhaps from its resemblance, in that particular, to more serious engagements fought to settle royal disputes.

BAWBEE. A halfpenny. *Scotch*.

BAWBELS, or BAWBLES. Trinkets; a man's testicles.

BAWD. A female procuress.

BAWDY BASKET. The twenty-third rank of canters, who carry pins, tape, ballads, and obscene books, to sell, but live mostly by stealing. *Cant.*

BAWDY-HOUSE BOTTLE. A very small bottle; short measure being among the many means used by the keepers of those houses to gain what they call an honest livelihood: indeed this is one of the least reprehensible; as the less they give a man of their beverages for his money the kinder they behave to him.

Bay Fever. A term of ridicule applied to convicts, who sham illness, to avoid being sent to Botany Bay.

Bay of Condolence. Where we console our friends, if plucked, and left at a Nonplus. *Oxf. Univ. Cant.*

Beadle. A blue roquelaure, *to sport a Beadle, to fly a Beadle, &c. &c.* *Cant.*

Beak. A justice of peace, or magistrate. Also a judge or chairman who presides in court. I clapp'd my peepers full of tears, and so the old beak set me free; I began to weep, and the judge set me free. The late Sir John Fielding, of police memory, was known among *family people* by the title of the *blind beak*.

Bean. A guinea. **Half Bean**; half a guinea.

Bear. One who contracts to deliver a certain quantity or sum of stock in the public funds, on a future day, and at a stated price; or, in other words, sells what he has not got, like the huntsman in the fable, who sold the bear's skin before the bear was killed. As the bear sells the stock he is not possessed of, so the bull purchases what he has not money to pay for; but, in case of any alteration in the price agreed on, either party pays or receives the difference. *Stock Exchange.*

Bear-garden Jaw or Discourse. Rude, vulgar language, such as was used at the bear-gardens.

Bear Leader. A travelling tutor.

Beard Splitter. A man much given to wenching.

Bearings. I'll bring him to his bearings; I'll bring him to reason. *Sea term.*

Beast. To drink like a beast, i. e. only when thirsty.

Beast with Two Backs. A man and woman in the act of copulation. *Shakspeare in Othello.*

Beater Cases. Boots. *Cant.*

Beau-nasty. A slovenly fop; one finely dressed, but dirty.

Beau Trap. A loose stone in the pavement, under which water lodges, and on being trod upon squirts it up, to the great damage of white stockings; also a sharper neatly dressed, lying in wait for raw country squires, or ignorant fops.

Becalmed. A piece of sea wit, sported in hot weather. I am becalmed, the sail sticks to the mast; that is, my shirt sticks to my back. His prad is becalmed; his horse is knocked up.

Beck. A beadle. See **Hermanbeck**.

Bed. Put to bed with a mattock, and tucked up with a spade; said of one that is dead and buried. You will go up a ladder to bed, i. e. you will be hanged. In many country places, persons hanged are made to mount up a ladder, which is afterwards turned round or taken away; whence the term, "Turned off."

BEDFORDSHIRE. I am for Bedfordshire, i. e. for going to bed.

BEDIZENED. Dressed out, over-dressed, or awkwardly ornamented.

BED-MAKER. Women employed at Cambridge to attend on the students, sweep their rooms, &c. They will put their hands to any thing, and are generally blest with a pretty family of daughters; who unmake the beds as fast as they are made by their mothers.

BEEF. To cry beef; to give the alarm. They have cried beef on us. *Cant.* To be in a man's beef; to wound him with a sword. To be in a woman's beef; to having carnal knowledge of her. Say you bought your beef of me; a jocular request from a butcher to a fat man, implying that he credits the butcher who serves him.

BEEF EATER. A yeoman of the guards, instituted by Henry VII. Their office was to stand near the bouffet, or cupboard, thence called Bouffetiers, since corrupted to Beef Eaters. Others suppose they obtained this name from the size of their persons, and the easiness of their duty, as having scarcely more to do than to eat the king's beef.

BEES-WAX. Cheese. *Cant.*

BEETLE-BROWED. One having thick projecting eye-brows.

BEETLE-HEADED. Dull, stupid.

BEGGAR MAKER. A publican, or ale-house keeper.

BEGGAR'S BULLETS. Stones. The beggar's bullets began to fly, i. e. they began to throw stones.

BEILBY'S BALL. He will dance at Beilby's Ball, where the sheriff pays the music; he will be hanged. Who Mr. Beilby was, or why that ceremony was so called, remains, with the quadrature of the circle, the discovery of the philosopher's stone, and divers other desiderata, yet undiscovered.

BELAY. To stop. *Sea term.*

BELCH. All sorts of beer; that liquor being apt to cause eructation.

BELCHER. A yellow silk handkerchief, intermixed with white and a little black. *The kiddy flashes his Belcher;* the young fellow wears a silk handkerchief round his neck. First introduced by the celebrated Jem Belcher.

BELL, BOOK, AND CANDLE. They cursed him with bell, book, and candle; an allusion to the popish form of excommunicating and anathematizing persons who had offended the church.

BELL, TO BEAR THE. To excel or surpass all competitors, to be the principal in a body or society; an allusion to the fore horse or leader of a team, whose harness is commonly ornamented with a bell or bells. Some suppose it a term borrowed from an ancient tournament, where the victorious knight bore away the *belle* or *fair lady*. Others derive it from a horse-race, or other rural contentions, where bells were frequently given as prizes.

Bellows. The lungs.

Bellower. The town crier.

Bellowser. Transportation for life: i. e. as long.

Belly. His eye was bigger than his belly; a saying of a person at table, who takes more on his plate than he can eat.

Bellyful. A hearty beating, sufficient to make a man yield or give out. A woman with child is also said to have got her belly full.

Belly Cheat. An apron.

Belly Plea. The plea of pregnancy, generally adduced by female felons capitally convicted, which they take care to provide for previous to their trials; every gaol having, as the Beggar's Opera informs us, one or more child-getters, who qualify the ladies for that expedient to procure a respite.

Belly Timber. Food of all sorts.

Bell Swagger. A noisy bullying fellow.

Bell Wether. The chief or leader of a mob; an idea taken from a flock of sheep, where the wether has a bell about his neck.

Bender. A sixpence. *Cant.*

Bender. An ironical word used in conversation by flash people; as where one party affirms or professes any thing which the other believes to be false or insincere, the latter expresses his incredulity by exclaiming, Bender! or, if one asks another to do any act which the latter considers unreasonable or impracticable, he replies, O, yes, I'll do it—Bender; meaning, by the addition of the last word, that, in fact, he will do no such thing.

Bene. Good.—**Benar.** Better. *Cant.*

Bene Bowse. Good beer, or other strong liquor. *Cant.*

Bene Cove. A good fellow. *Cant.*

Bene Darkmans. Good night. *Cant.*

Bene Feakers. Counterfeiters of bills. *Cant.*

Bene Feakers of Gybes. Counterfeiters of passes. *Cant.*

Beneshiply. Worshipfully. *Cant.*

Ben. A fool. *Cant.*

Benish. Foolish.

Benjy. A vest. *Cant.*

Bermudas. A cant name for certain places in London, privileged against arrests, like the Mint, in Southwark. *Ben Jonson.* These privileges are abolished. *Obsolete.*

Bess, or Betty. A small instrument used by house-breakers to force open doors. Bring bess and glim; bring the instrument to force the door and the dark lanthorn. Small flasks, like those for Florence wine, are also called Betties.

BESS. See BROWN BESS.

BEST. To get your money at the best, signifies to live by dishonest or fraudulent practices, without labour or industry, according to the general acceptation of the latter word; but, certainly, no persons have more occasion to be industrious, and in a state of perpetual action than cross coves; and, experience has proved, when too late, to many of them, that honesty is the best policy; and, consequently, that the above phrase is by no means *à propos*.

BEST OF A CHARLEY. Upsetting a watchman in his box.

BETTY. A picklock; to unbetty, or betty a lock, is to open or relock it, by means of the betty, so as to avoid subsequent detection.

BETTY MARTIN. That's *my eye, Betty Martin*; an answer to any one that attempts to impose or humbug: a corruption of "*Mihi beatæ martinis.*"

BEVER. A morning's luncheon; also a fine hat; beaver's fur making the best hats.

BEVERAGE. Garnish money, or money for drink, demanded of any one having a new suit of clothes.

BIBLE. A boatswain's great axe. *Sea term.*

BIBLE OATH. Supposed by the vulgar to be more binding than an oath taken on the Testament only, as being the bigger book, and generally containing both the Old and New Testaments.

BIDDY, or CHICK-A-BIDDY. A chicken; and, figuratively, a young wench.

BIDET; commonly pronounced BIDDY. A kind of tub, contrived for ladies to wash themselves, for which purpose they bestride it like a French pony, or post-horse, called, in French, *bidets*.

BIENLY. Excellently. She wheedled so bienly; she coaxed or flattered so cleverly. *French.*

BILL AT SIGHT. To pay a bill at sight; to be ready at all times for the venereal act.

BILK. To cheat. Let us bilk the rattling cove; let us cheat the hackney coachman of his fare. *Cant.* Bilking a coachman, a box-keeper, and a poor whore, were, *formerly*, among men of the town, thought gallant actions.

BILL OF SALE. A widow's weeds. See HOUSE TO LET.

BILLINGSGATE LANGUAGE. Foul language or abuse. Billingsgate is the market where the fishwomen assemble to purchase fish; and where, in their dealings and disputes, they are somewhat apt to leave decency and good manners a little on the left hand.

Bing. To go. *Cant.* Bing avast; get you gone. Binged avast in a darkmans; stole away in the night. Bing we to Rumeville? shall we go to London?

Bingo. Brandy or other spirituous liquor. *Cant.*

Bingo Boy. A dram drinker. *Cant.*

Bingo Mort. A female dram drinker. *Cant.*

Binnacle Word. A fine or affected word, which sailors jeeringly offer to chalk up on the binnacle.

Bird and Baby. The sign of the eagle and child.

Bird-witted. Inconsiderate, thoughtless, easily imposed on.

Bird's-eye Wipe. A spotted handkerchief. *Cant.*

Birds of a Feather. Rogues of the same gang.

Birth-day Suit. He was in his birth-day suit, that is stark naked.

Bishop. A mixture of wine and water into which is put a roasted orange.

Bishopped, or To Bishop. A term used among horse-dealers for burning the mark into a horse's tooth after he has lost it by age: by bishopping, a horse is made to appear younger than he is. It is a common saying of milk that is burnt, too, that the bishop has set his foot in it. Formerly, when a bishop passed through a village, all the inhabitants ran out of their houses to solicit his blessing, even leaving their milk, &c. on the fire, to take its chance, which, when burnt, was said to be bishopped.

Bishop the Balls. A term used among printers, to water them.

Bit. Money. He grappled the cull's bit; he seized the man's money. A bit is also the smallest coin in Jamaica, equal to about sixpence sterling. To grab the bit; to seize the cash.

Bitch. A she dog or doggess; the most offensive appellation that can be given to an English woman, even more provoking than that of whore, as may be gathered from the regular Billingsgate or St. Giles's answer—"I may be a whore but can't be a bitch."

Bitch. To yield or give up an attempt through fear. To stand bitch; to make tea, or do the honours of the tea-table, performing a female part: bitch there standing for woman, species for genus.

Bitch Booby. A country wench. *Military term.*

Bit Faker. A coiner. *Cant.*

Bit of Gig. Fun. A spree, &c. *Cant.*

Bite. To over-reach or impose; also to steal. *Cant.* Biting was once esteemed a kind of wit, similar to the humbug. An instance of it is given in the Spectator:—A man, under sentence of death, having sold his body to a surgeon, rather below the market price, on receiving the money, cried A bite! I am to be hanged in chains. To bite the roger; to steal a portmanteau. To bite the wiper; to steal a handkerchief. To bite on the bridle; to be pinched, or reduced to difficulties. Hark ye, friend, whether do they bite in the collar or the cod-piece? *Water wit to anglers.*

BLAB. A tell-tale, or one incapable of keeping a secret.

BLACK AND WHITE. In writing. I have it in black and white; I have written evidence.

BLACK ART. The art of picking a lock. *Cant.*

BLACK A--SE. A copper or kettle. The pot calls the kettle black a--se. *Cant.*

BLACK BOOK. He is down in the black book; i. e. has a stain in his character. A black book is kept in most regiments, wherein the names of all persons sentenced to punishment are recorded.

BLACK BOX. A lawyer. *Cant.*

BLACK DIAMONDS. Coals. *Cant.*

BLACK EYE. We gave the bottle a black eye; i. e. drank it almost up. He cannot say black is the white of my eye; he cannot point out a blot in my character.

BLACK FLY. The greatest drawback on the farmer is the black fly, i. e. the parson who takes the tithe of the harvest.

BLACK GUARD. A shabby, mean fellow; a term said to be derived from a number of dirty, tattered, roguish boys, who attended at the Horse Guards and Parade, in St. James's Park, to black the boots and shoes of the soldiers, or to do any other dirty offices. These, from their constant attendance about the time of guard mounting, were nick-named the *black guards.*

BLACK JACK. A nick-name given to the late Recorder of London by the thieves.

BLACK JOKE. A popular tune to a song, having for the burden, "Her black joke and belly so white;" figuratively, the black joke signifies the monosyllable. *See* MONOSYLLABLE.

BLACK LEGS. A gambler or sharper on the turf or in the cock-pit; so called, perhaps, from their appearing generally in boots; or else from game-cocks, whose legs are always black.

BLACK MONDAY. The first Monday after the school-boys' holidays, or breaking up, when they are to go to school and produce or repeat the tasks set them.

BLACK PSALM. To sing the black psalm; to cry: a saying used to children.

BLACK SPICE RACKET. To rob chimney-sweepers of their soot-bag and soot.

BLACK SPY. The devil; a smith; an informer. *Cant.*

Black Strap. Bene Carlo wine; also port. A task of labour imposed on soldiers at Gibraltar, as a punishment for small offences.

Blank. To look blank; to appear disappointed or confounded.

Blanket Hornpipe. The amorous congress.

Blarney. He has licked the blarney stone; he deals in the wonderful, or tips us the traveller. The blarney stone is a triangular stone on the very top of an ancient castle of that name in the county of Cork, in Ireland, extremely difficult of access; so that to have ascended to it was considered as a proof of perseverance, courage, and agility, whereof many are supposed to claim the honour who never achieved the adventure: and to tip the blarney is, figuratively used, telling a marvellous story, or falsity; and also sometimes to express flattery. *Irish.*

Blasted Fellow, or Brimstone. An abandoned rogue or prostitute. *Cant.*

Blast. To curse.

Blater. A calf. *Cant.*

Bleached Mort. A fair-complexioned wench.

Bleaters. Those cheated by Jack in a box. *Cant.* *See* Jack in a Box.

Bleating Cheat. A sheep. *Cant.*

Bleating Rig. Sheep-stealing. *Cant.*

Bleeders. Spurs. He clapped his bleeders to his prad; he put spurs to his horse.

Bleeding Cully. One who parts easily with his money, or bleeds freely.

Blessing. A small quantity over and above the measure, usually given by huxters dealing in peas, beans, and other vegetables.

Blind. A feint, pretence, or shift.

Blind Cheeks. The breech. Buss blind cheeks; kiss mine a–se.

Blind Cupid. The backside.

Blind Excuse. A poor or insufficient excuse. A blind alehouse, lane, or alley; an obscure or little known or frequented ale-house, lane, or alley.

Blind Harpers. Beggars, counterfeiting blindness, playing on fiddles, &c.

Blindman's Holiday. Night, darkness.

Blink. A light. *Cant.*

Block-Houses. Prisons, houses of correction, &c.

Blone. A girl. *Cant.*

Blood. A riotous disorderly fellow.

Blood for Blood. A term used by tradesmen for bartering

the different commodities in which they deal. Thus a hatter furnishing a hosier with a hat, and taking payment in stockings, is said to deal blood for blood.

BLOOD MONEY. The reward given by the legislature on the conviction of highwaymen, burglars, &c.

BLOODY BACK. A jeering appellation for a soldier, alluding to his scarlet coat.

BLOODY. A favourite word used by the thieves in swearing, as *bloody* eyes, *bloody* rascal. *Irish.*

BLOODY-JEMMY. A hot baked sheep's head.

BLOSS or BLOWEN. The pretended wife of a bully or shoplifter. *Cant.*

BLOT THE SKRIP AND JAR IT. To stand engaged or bound for any one. *Cant.*

BLOW. He has bit the blow, i. e. he has stolen the goods. *Cant.*

BLOW A prostitute.

BLOWEN. A mistress or whore of a gentleman of the scamp. The blowen kidded the swell into a snoozing ken, and shook him of his dummee and thimble; the girl inveigled the gentleman into a brothel and robbed him of his pocket book and watch.

BLOWER. A pipe. How the swell funks his blower and lushes red tape; what a smoke the gentleman makes with his pipe, and drinks brandy.

BLOW A CLOUD. To smoke a pipe. *Cant.*

"Let me *blow a cloud,* or a *bender* spend
At the *Pig and Tinder-Box* nightly."
Vide Randall's Scrap Book.

"A civiller *Swell*
I'd never wish to *blow a cloud* with."
Crib's Memorial.

BLOW THE GROUNSILS. To lie with a woman on the floor. *Cant.*

BLOW THE GAB. To confess, or impeach a confederate. *Cant.*

BLOW THE GAFF. A person having any secret in his possession, or a knowledge of any thing injurious to another, when at last induced, from revenge or other motive, to tell it openly to the world and expose him publicly, is then said to have blown the gaff upon him.

BLOW-UP. A discovery, or the confusion occasioned by one.

BLOWSE, or BLOWSABELLA. A woman whose hair is dishevelled, and hanging about her face; a slattern.

BLUBBER. The mouth.—I have stopped the cull's lubber; I have stopped the fellow's mouth, meant either by gagging or murdering him.

Blubber. To cry.

Blubber, to sport. Said of a large coarse woman, who exposes her bosom.

Blubber Cheeks. Large flaccid cheeks, hanging like the fat or lubber of a whale.

Blue. To look blue; to be confounded, terrified, or disappointed. Blue as a razor; perhaps, blue as azure.

Blue Devils. Low spirits.

Blue Flag. He has hoisted the blue flag; he has commenced publican, or taken a public house; an allusion to the blue aprons worn by publicans. *See* Admiral of the Blue.

Blue Moon. In allusion to a long time before such a circumstance happens. "O yes, in a blue moon."

Blue Pigeons. Thieves who steal lead off houses and churches. *Cant.* To fly a blue pigeon; to steal lead off houses or churches.

Blue Plum. A bullet.—Surfeited with a blue plum; wounded with a bullet. A sortment of George R—'s blue plums; a volley of ball, shot from soldiers' firelocks.

Blue Ruin. Gin. *Cant.*

Blue Skin. A person begotten on a black woman by a white man. One of the blue squadron; any one having a cross of the black breed, or, as it is termed, a lick of the tar-brush.

Blue Tape, or Sky Blue. Gin.

Bluff. Fierce, surly. He looked as bluff as bull beef.

Bluffer. An inn-keeper. *Cant.*

Blunderbuss. A short gun, with a wide bore, for carrying slugs; also a stupid, blundering fellow.

Blunt. Money. *Cant.*

Blunt, post the. To tip the cash, *ex. gr.*

> "When old Jack Wiggins counts for me my score,
> I'll bid him *post the blunt* for me no more."
>
> *Vide Randall's Dairy.*

Bluster. To talk big, to hector or bully.

Board of Green Cloth. A billiard table.

Boarding School. Bridewell, Newgate, or any other prison, or house of correction.

Bob. A shoplifter's assistant, or one that receives and carries off stolen goods. All is bob; all is safe. *Cant.*

Bob. A shilling.

Bobbed. Cheated, tricked, disappointed.

Bobbish. Smart, clever, spruce, doing well.

Bob Tail. A lewd woman, or one that plays with her tail; also an impotent man, or an eunuch. Tag, rag, and bobtail; a mob of all sorts of low people. To shift one's bob; to move off, or go away. To bear a bob; to join in chorus with any singers. Also a term used by the sellers of game, for a partridge.

BODY SNATCHERS. Bum bailiffs.

BODY OF DIVINITY BOUND IN BLACK CALF. A parson.

BOG LANDER. An Irishman; Ireland being famous for its large bogs, which furnish the chief fuel in many parts of that kingdom.

BOG TROTTER. The same.

BOG HOUSE The necessary house. To go to bog; to go to stool.

BOGY. Ask bogy, i. e. ask mine a--se. *Sea-wit.*

BOH. Said to be the name of a Danish general, who so terrified his opponent Foh, that he caused him to bewray himself. Whence, when we smell a stink, it is customary to exclaim, Foh! i. e. I smell general Foh. He cannot say Boh to a goose; i. e. he is a cowardly or sheepish fellow. There is a story related of the celebrated Ben Jonson, who always dressed very plain, that, being introduced to the presence of a nobleman, the peer, struck by his homely appearance and awkward manner, exclaimed, as if in doubt, "you Ben Jonson! why you look as if you could not say Boh to a goose!" "Boh!" replied the wit. *Obsolete.*

BOLD. Bold as a miller's shirt, which every day takes a rogue by the collar.

BOLT. A blunt arrow.

BOLT UPRIGHT. As erect, or straight up, as an arrow set on its end.

BOLT. To run suddenly out of one's house, or hiding place, through fear; a term borrowed from a rabbit-warren, where the rabbits are made to bolt, by sending ferrets into their burrows: we set the house on fire, and made him bolt. To bolt, also means to swallow meat without chewing: the farmer's servants in Kent are famous for bolting large quantities of pickled pork.

BOLT-IN-TUN. A term founded on the cant word bolt, and merely a fanciful variation, very common among flash persons, there being in London a famous inn so called; it is customary when a man has run away from his lodgings, broke out of a jail, or made any other sudden movement, to say the Bolt-in-tun is concerned; or, He's gone to the Bolt-in-tun; instead of simply saying, He has bolted, &c. *See* BOLT.

BOLUS. A nick-name for an apothecary.

BONE BOX. The mouth. Shut your bone box; shut your mouth.

BONED. Seized, apprehended, taken up by a constable; *Cant.* Tell us how you was boned, signifies, tell us the story of your apprehension; a common request among fellow-prisoners in a jail, &c. which is readily complied with in general; and the various circumstances therein related afford present amusement, and also useful hints for regulating their future operations, so as to avoid the like misfortune.

BONE PICKER. A footman.

BONES. Dice.

BONE SETTER. A hard-trotting horse.

BONNET. A concealment, pretext, or pretence; an ostensible manner of accounting for what you really mean to conceal; as a man who actually lives by depredation will still outwardly follow some honest employment, as a clerk, porter, newsman, &c. By this system of policy, he is said to have a good bonnet if he happens to get boned; and, in a doubtful case, is commonly discharged on the score of having a good character. To bonnet for a person, is to corroborate any assertion he has made, or to relate facts in the most favourable light, in order to extricate him from a dilemma, or to further any object he has in view.

BOOBY, or DOG BOOBY. An awkward lout, clodhopper, or country fellow. *See* CLODHOPPER and LOUT. A bitch booby; a country wench.

BOOBY HUTCH. A one-horse chaise, noddy, buggy, or leathern bottle.

BOOKS. Cards to play with. To plant the books; to place the cards in the pack in an unfair manner.

BOOK-KEEPER. One who never returns borrowed books. Out of one's books: out of one's favour. Out of his books; out of debt.

BOOT CATCHER. The servant at an inn whose business it is to clean the boots of the guest.

BOOTS. The youngest officer of a regimental mess, whose duty it is to skink, that is, to stir the fire, snuff the candles, and ring the bell. *See* SKINK. To ride in any one's old boots; to marry or keep his cast-off mistress.

BOOTY. To play booty; cheating play, where the player purposely avoids winning.

BO-PEEP. One who sometimes hides himself, and sometimes appears publicly abroad, is said to play at bo-peep. Also one who lies perdue, or on the watch.

BORDE. A shilling. A HALF BORDE; a sixpence.

BORDELLO. A house of ill fame.

BORE. A tedious, troublesome man or woman, one who bores the ears of his hearers with an uninteresting tale; a term much in fashion about the years 1780 and 1781.

BORING. *Vide* FIBBING.

BORN UNDER A THREEPENNY HALFPENNY PLANET, NEVER TO BE WORTH A GROAT. Said of any person remarkably unsuccessful in his attempts or profession.

Bosky. In the *cant* of the Oxonians, being tipsy.

Botch. A nick-name for a tailor.

Botherred, or Both-eared. Talked to at both ears by different persons at the same time; confounded, confused. *Irish phrase.*

Bottle-headed. Void of wit.

Bottom. A polite term for the posteriors. Also, in the sporting sense, strength and spirits to support fatigue; as a bottomed horse. Among bruisers it is used to express a hardy fellow, who will bear a good beating.

Bottomless Pit. The monosyllable.

Boughs. Wide in the boughs; with large hips and posteriors.

Boughs. He is up in the boughs; he is in a passion.

Bounce. To bully, threaten, talk loud, or affect great consequence; to *bounce* a person out of any thing, is to use threatening or high words, in order to intimidate him, and attain the object you are intent upon; or to obtain goods of a tradesman, by assuming the appearance of great respectability and importance, so as to remove any suspicion he might at first entertain. A thief, detected in the commission of a robbery, has been known by this sort of finesse, aided by a genteel appearance and polite manners, to persuade his accusers of his innocence, and not only to get off with a good grace, but induce them to apologize for their supposed mistake, and the affront put upon him. This master-stroke of effrontery is called *giving it to 'em upon the bounce.*

Bounce. A person well or fashionably dressed, is said to be a rank bounce.

Bouncer. A large man or woman; also a great lie.

Bouncing Cheat. A bottle; from the explosion in drawing the cork. *Cant.*

Boung. A purse. *Cant.*

Boung Nipper. A cut purse. *Cant.* Formerly, purses were worn at the girdle, from whence they were cut.

Boose, or Bouse. Drink.

Boosey. Drunk.

Bowled Out. A man who has followed the profession of thieving for some time, when he is ultimately taken, tried, and convicted, is said to be bowled out at last. To bowl a person out, in a general sense, means to detect him in the commission of any fraud or peculation, which he has hitherto practised without discovery.

Bowman. A thief. *Cant.*

Bowsed. Tightened up, done up. *Sea term.*

Bowsing Ken. An ale-house or gin-shop.

Bowsprit. The nose, from its being the most projecting part of the human face, as the bowsprit is of a ship.

BOW-WOW MUTTON. Dog's flesh.

BOW-WOW SHOP. A salesman's shop in Monmouth-street; so called because the servant barks and the master bites. *See* BARKER.

BOX, THE. Prepare for battle. *Sea term.*

BOX THE COMPASS. To say or repeat the mariner's compass, not only backwards or forwards, but, also, to be able to answer any and all questions respecting its divisions. *Sea term.*

BOX THE JESUIT AND GET COCK ROACHES. A sea term for masturbation; a crime, it is said, much practised by the reverend fathers of that society.

BOXIANA. The name of a work, which contains the lives and battles of all the prize pugilists. A complete history of boxing, from the days of Figg and Broughton to Cribb and the *Nonpareil.*

BRACE UP, TO. To dispose of stolen goods by pledging them for the utmost you can get at a pawnbroker's, is termed bracing them up. *Cant.*

BRACE OF SNAPS. Instantly. *Sea term.*

BRACKET-FACED. Ugly, hard-featured.

BRADS. Money; but generally meant for halfpence. *Cant.*

BRAG. A money-lender. *Cant.* Fellows who advertise to relieve persons in distress, but who make them pay dearly for such accommodation; and promising, at all times, more than they intend to perform.

BRAGGET. Mead and ale sweetened with honey.

BRAGGADOCIA. A vain-glorious fellow, a boaster.

BRAINS. If you had as much brains as guts, what a clever fellow you would be! a saying to a stupid fat fellow. To have some brains in his guts; to know something.

BRAN-FACED. Freckled. He was christened by a baker, he carries the bran in his face.

BRANDY-FACED. Red-faced, as if from drinking brandy.

BRAT. A child or infant.

BRAY. A vicar of Bray; one who frequently changes his principles, always siding with the strongest party; an allusion to a vicar of Bray, in Berkshire, commemorated in a well known ballad for the pliability of his conscience.

BRAZEN-FACED. Bold-faced, shameless, impudent.

BREAD. Employment. Out of bread; out of employment. In bad bread; in a disagreeable scrape or situation.

BREAD AND BUTTER FASHION. One slice upon the other. John and his maid were caught lying bread and butter fashion. To quarrel with one's bread and butter; to act contrary to one's interest. To know on which side one's bread is buttered; to know one's interest, or what is best for one. It is no bread and butter of mine; I have no business with it;

or, rather, I won't intermeddle, because I shall get nothing by it.

Bread-Basket. The stomach; a term used by boxers. I took him a punch in his bread-basket; i.e. I gave him a blow in the stomach.

Break-teeth Words. Hard words, difficult to pronounce.

Breaking Shins. Borrowing money; perhaps from the figurative operation being, like the real one, extremely disagreeable to the patient.

Breaking up of the Spell. The nightly termination of the performances at the Theatres Royal, which is regularly attended by pickpockets of the lower order, who exercise their vocation about the doors and avenues leading thereto, until the houses are emptied and the crowd dispersed.

Breeched. Money in the pocket. The swell is well breeched, let's draw him; the gentleman has plenty of money in his pockets, let's rob him.

Breeches. To wear the breeches: a woman who governs her husband is said to wear the breeches.

Breeze. To raise a breeze; to kick up a dust, or breed a disturbance.

Bridge. To make a bridge of any one's nose; to push the bottle past him, so as to deprive him of his turn of filling his glass: to pass one over.

Bridge. To bridge a person, or throw him over the bridge, is, in a general sense, to deceive him by betraying the confidence he has reposed in you, and, instead of serving him faithfully, involve him in ruin or disgrace; or, three men being concerned alike in any transaction, two of them will form a collusion to bridge the third, and engross to themselves all the advantage that may eventually accrue. Two persons having been engaged in a long or doubtful contest or rivalship, he who, by superior art or perseverance, gains the point, is said to have thrown his opponent over the bridge. Among gamblers, it means deceiving the person who had backed you, by wilfully losing the game; the money so lost by him being shared between yourself and your confederates who had laid against you. In playing three-handed games, two of the party will play into each others' hands, so that the third must inevitably be thrown over the bridge; commonly called, *two poll one*. *See* Play across.

Brim. (Abbreviation of brimstone.) An abandoned woman: perhaps, originally, only a passionate or irascible woman, compared to brimstone for its inflammability.

Bring to. To stop. *Sea phrase.*

Bristol Milk. A Spanish wine, called Sherry, much drank at that place, particularly in the morning.

Bristol Man. The son of an Irish thief and a Welch whore.

British Champagne. Porter.

Broads. Cards. *Cant.*

Broganier. One who has a strong Irish pronunciation or accent.

Brogue. A particular kind of shoe without a heel, worn in Ireland, and figuratively used to signify the Irish accent.

Broom it. Make off, run away.

Broomsticks. *See* Queer Bail.

Brother of the
- **Blade.** A soldier.
- **Buskin.** A player.
- **Bung.** A brewer.
- **Coif.** A serjeant at law.
- **Gusset.** A pimp.
- **Quill.** An author.
- **String.** A fiddler.
- **Whip.** A coachman.

Brother Starling. One who lies with the same woman, that is, builds in the same nest.

Broughtonian. A boxer, a disciple of Broughton, who was a beef-eater, and *once* the best boxer of his day.

Brown. Doing it *Brown.* *Gammon.*

Browns and Whistlers. Bad halfpence and farthings; a term used by coiners.

Brown Bess. A soldier's firelock. To hug brown Bess; to carry a firelock, or serve as a private soldier.

Brown George. An ammunition loaf. A wig without powder; similar to the undress wig worn by his late majesty.

Brown Madam, or **Brown Miss.** The monosyllable.

Brown Study. Said of one absent, in a reverie, or thoughtful.

Bruiser. A boxer; one skilled in the art of boxing; also an inferior workman among chasers.

Brush. To run away. Let us buy a brush and lope; let us go away or off. To have a brush with a woman; to lie with her. To have a brush with a man; to fight with him. The cove cracked the peter and bought a brush; the fellow broke open the trunk and then ran away.

Brusher. A bumper, a full glass. *See* Bumper.

Bub. Strong beer.

Bubber. A drinking bowl; also a great drinker; a thief that steals plate from public-houses. *Cant.*

Bubble To Cheat.

Bar the Bubble. To except against the general rule, that he who lays the odds must always be adjudged the loser: this is restricted to bets laid for liquor.

Bubbly Jock. A turkey-cock. *Scotch.*

Bubble and Squeak. Beef and cabbage fried together. It is so called from its bubbling up and squeaking whilst over the fire.

Buck. A blind horse; also a gay debauchee.

Buck, to run a. To poll a bad vote at an election. *Irish term.*

Buck Bail. Bail given by a sharper for one of the gang.

Buck of the first Head. One who in debauchery surpasses the rest of his companions, a blood, or choice spirit. There are in London divers lodges or societies of Bucks, formed in imitation of the Free Masons; one was held at the Rose, in Monkwell-street, about the year 1705. The president is styled the Grand Buck. A buck sometimes signifies a cuckold.

Buckeen. A minor buck. *Irish.*

Bucket. To kick the bucket; to die.

Bucket. To bucket a person is synonymous with putting him in the well. *See* Well. Such treatment is said to be a bucketing concern.

Buck's Face. A cuckold.

Buck Fitch. A lecherous old fellow.

Buckinger's Boot. The monosyllable. Matthew Buckinger was born without hands and legs; notwithstanding which he drew coats of arms very neatly, and could write the Lord's Prayer within the compass of a shilling; he was married to a tall handsome woman, and traversed the country, showing himself for money.

Buckles. Fetters.

Budge, or Sneaking Budge. One that slips into houses in the dark, to steal cloaks or other clothes. Also lambs' fur formerly used for doctor's robes, whence they were called budge doctors. Standing budge; a thief's scout or spy.

Budge. To move, or quit one's station. Don't budge from hence; i. e. don't move from hence, stay here.

Budge. Drink. *Cant.*

Budge Kain. A public-house. *Scotch slang.*

Budget. A wallet. To open the budget; a term used to signify the notification of the taxes required by the minister for the expenses of the ensuing year: as, To-morrow the minister will go to the house, and open the budget.

Buff. All in buff; stript to the skin, stark naked.

Buff. To stand buff; to stand the brunt. To swear as a witness. He buffed it home, and I was served; he swore hard against me, and I was found guilty.

Buffer. A dog. Buffer's nob; a dog's head. *Cant.*

Buffer Nabber. A dog stealer. *Cant.*

Buffer. One that steals and kills horses and dogs for their skins; also an inn-keeper: it signifies also a boxer.

" And the first words the *Buffer* said,
Were,—' By the living Jingo, Ned," &c.

Vide Randall's Diary.

"And whips waved high, and fists flew out,
For Belcher leapt the ring without,
And peeled the *Buffers* dexterously."
Ibid.

"The *Buffers*, both boys of '*The Holy Ground*.'"
Crib's Memorial.

Buffer. A man who takes an oath: generally applied to Jew bail.

Buffle-headed. Confused, stupid.

Bug. A nick-name given by the Irish to Englishmen; bugs having, as it is said, been introduced into Ireland by the English.

Bug. A cant word among journeymen hatters, signifying the exchanging some of the dearest materials of which a hat is made for others of less value. Hats are composed of the furs and wool of divers animals, among which is a small portion of beavers' fur. Bugging is stealing the beaver, and substituting in lieu thereof an equal weight of some cheaper ingredient. Bailiffs who take money to postpone or refrain the serving of a writ, are said to bug the writ.

Bug-Hunter. An upholsterer.

Bugaboe. A scare-babe, or bully beggar. Sheriff's officer.

Bugaboo. A tally man: one who calls for his money weekly: the person owing the money, asks if the bugaboo has been, when he is compelled to keep out of sight from the want of cash.

Buggy. A one-horse chaise.

Bulk and File. Two pickpockets; the bulk jostles the party to be robbed, and the file does the business.

Bulker. One who lodges all night on a bulk or projection before old-fashioned shop windows.

Bulkie. A constable. *Scotch slang.*

Bull. A Stock Exchange term for one who buys stock on speculation for time, i. e. agrees with the seller, called a bear, to take a certain sum of stock at a future day, at a stated price: if at that day stock fetches more than the price agreed on, he receives the difference; if it falls or is cheaper, he either pays it, or becomes a lame duck, and waddles out of the Alley. *See* Lame Duck and Bear.

Bull. A blunder; from one Obadiah Bull, a blundering lawyer of London, who lived in the reign of Henry VII.: by a bull, is now always meant a blunder made by an Irishman. A bull was also the name of false hair formerly much worn by women. To look like bull beef, or as bluff as bull beef; to look fierce or surly. Town bull, a great whore-master.

Bull. A crown piece. Half Bull; half a crown.

Bull Beggar, or **Bully Beggar**. An imaginary being with which children are threatened by servants and nurses, like Raw Head and Bloody Bones.

Bull Calf. A great bulkey or clumsy fellow. *See* Hulkey.

Bull Chin. A fat chubby child.

Bull Dogs. Pistols.

Bull Hankers. Men who delight in the sport of bull-hauking; that is, bull-baiting, or bullock-hunting, games which afford much amusement, and, at the same time, frequent opportunities of depredation, in the confusion and alarm excited by the enraged animal.

Bull in Trouble. Meaning the bull in the pound. *Cant.*

Bull's Eye. A crown-piece.

Bull's Feather. A horn: he wears the bull's feather; he is a cuckold.

Bullock. To hector, bounce, or bully.

Bully. A cowardly fellow, who gives himself airs of great bravery. A bully huff cap; a hector. *See* Hector.

Bully Back. A bully to a bawdy-house; one who is kept in pay, to oblige the frequenters of the house to submit to the impositions of the mother abbess, or bawd; and who also sometimes pretends to be the husband of one of the ladies, and, under that pretence, extorts money from greenhorns, or ignorant young men, whom he finds with her. *See* Greenhorn.

Bully Cock. One who foments quarrels in order to rob the persons quarrelling.

Bully Trap. A brave man with a mild or effeminate appearance, by whom the bullies are frequently taken in.

Bum. The breech or backside.

Bum. To arrest a debtor. The gill bummed the swell for a thimble; the tradesman arrested the gentleman for a watch.

Bum Trap. A sheriff's officer who arrests debtors. Ware hawke! the bum traps are fly to our panny; keep a good look out, the bailiffs know where our house is situated.

Bum Bailiff, or **Trap**. A sheriff's officer, who arrests debtors; so called, perhaps, from following his prey, and being at their bums, or, as the vulgar phrase is, hard at their a—ses. Blackstone says it is a corruption of bound bailiff, from their being obliged to give bond for their good behaviour.

Bum Boat. A boat attending ships to retail greens, drams, &c. commonly rowed by a woman; a kind of floating chandler's shop.

Bum Brusher. A schoolmaster.

Bum Charter. A name given to bread steeped in hot water, by the first unfortunate inhabitants of the *English Bastile*, where this miserable fare was their daily breakfast, each man receiving, with his scanty portion of bread, a quart of boiled water from the cook's coppers.

Bum Fodder. Soft paper for the necessary house, or torchecul.

Bumfiddle. The backside, the breech. *See* Ars Musica.

Bumbo. Brandy, water, and sugar; also the negro name for the monosyllable.

Bumkin. A raw country fellow.

Bummed. Arrested.

Bumper. A full glass; in all likelihood from its convexity or bump at the top: some derive it from a full glass formerly drank to the health of the pope—*au bon père.*

Bumping. A ceremony performed on boys perambulating the bounds of a parish on Ascension-day, when they have their posteriors bumped against the stones marking the boundaries, in order to fix them in their memory.

Bun. A common name for a rabbit, also for the monosyllable. To touch bun for luck; a practice observed among sailors going on a cruize.

Bunce. Money. *Cant.*

Bunch of Fives. The fist. *Pugilistic cant.*—

> "Your powers of *handling* we saw in a trice,
> When your *bunch of five tickled his muns,* and then *ribbed him.*"
> *Lines to Painter, on his Fight with Oliver.—Vide Randall's Diary.*

Bundling. A man and woman sleeping in the same bed, he with his small-clothes, and she with her petticoats on; an expedient practised in America, on a scarcity of beds, where, on such an occasion, husbands and parents frequently permitted travellers to bundle with their wives and daughters. This custom is now abolished. *Vide* Duke of Rochefoucault's Travels in America. But it is a common practice in Wales among sweethearts.

Bung upwards. Said of a person lying on his face.

Bung your Eye. Drink a dram; strictly speaking, to drink till one's eye is bunged up or closed.

Bunt. An apron.

Bunter. A low dirty prostitute, half whore and half beggar.

Buntlings. Petticoats. *Cant.*

Burick. A prostitute. *Cant.*

Burn Crust. A jocular name for a baker.

Burn the Ken. Strollers living in an ale-house without paying their quarters are said to burn the ken. *Cant.*

Burning Shame. Having a watchman placed at the door of a bawdy-house, with a lantern on his staff, in the daytime, to deter persons from going in and out: done by parish-officers to clear the neighbourhood of such sorts of houses.

Burner. A clap. The blowen tipped the swell a burner: the girl gave the gentleman a clap.

Burner. He is no burner of navigable rivers; i. e. he is no conjurer, or man of extraordinary abilities; or, rather, he is but a simple fellow. *See* Thames.

Burnt. Poxed or clapped. He was sent out a sacrifice, and came home a burnt offering; a saying of seamen who have been "in for the plate" abroad. He has burnt his fingers; he has suffered by his meddling.

Burr. A hanger on, or dependant; an allusion to the field burrs, which are not easily got rid of. Also the Northumbrian pronunciation: the people of that country, but chiefly about Newcastle and Morpeth, are said to have a burr in their throats, particularly called the Newcastleburr.

Burster, tup-penny. A two-penny loaf. *Cant.*

Bushed. Poor, without money.

Bushel Bubby. A full breasted woman.

Bushy Park. A man who is poor is said to be at Bushy-park, or in the park.

Busk. A piece of whalebone, or ivory, formerly worn by women, to stiffen the fore part of their stays: hence the toast —both ends of the busk.

Buss Beggar. An old superannuated fumbler, whom none but beggars will suffer to kiss them.

Bus Napper. A constable. *Cant.*

Bus Napper's Kenchin. A watchman. *Cant.*

Bustle. A cant term for money.

Bustle. Any object effected very suddenly, or in a hurry, is said to be done upon the bustle. To give it to a man upon the bustle is to obtain any point, as borrowing money, &c. by some sudden story or pretence, and affecting great haste, so that he is taken by surprise and becomes duped before he has time to consider of the matter.

Busy. As busy as the devil in a high wind: as busy as a hen with one chick.

Butcher's Dog. To be like a butcher's dog; i. e. lie by the beef without touching it: a simile often applicable to married men.

Butt. A dependant, poor relation, or simpleton, on whom all kinds of practical jokes are played off; and who serves as a butt for all the shafts of wit and ridicule.

Butter and Eggs Trot. A kind of short jog trot, such as is used by women going to market, with butter and eggs. She looks as if butter would not melt in her mouth, yet I warrant you cheese would not choke her; a saying of a demure looking woman of suspected character. Don't make butter dear; a gird at the patient angler.

Buttered Bun. One lying with a woman that has just lain with another man is said to have a buttered bun.

Buttering up. Praising or flattering any person that does not deserve it. It is used in that exquisite volume, *Cribb's Memorial*, thus—

> "For, knowing how, on Moulsey's plain,
> The Champion *fibb'd* the poet's nob,
> This *buttering-up*, against the grain,
> We thought was *curr'd* genteel in Bob."
> *Vide Cribb's Memorial.*

BUTTOCK. A whore. *Cant.*

BUTTOCK-BROKER. A bawd, or match-maker. *Cant.*

BUTTOCK BALL. The amorous congress. *Cant.*

BUTTOCK AND FILE. A common whore and a pickpocket. *Cant.*

BUTTOCK AND TWANG, or DOWN BUTTOCK AND SHAM FILE. A common whore, but no pickpocket.

BUTTOCK AND TONGUE. A scolding wife.

BUTTOCKING SHOP. A brothel.

BUTTON. A bad shilling, among coiners.

BUZ. To buz a person is to pick his pocket. The *buz* is the *game* of picking pockets in general.

BUZ COVE, or BUZ GLOAK. A pickpocket: a person who is clever at this practice is said to be a good buz.

BUZZARD. A simple fellow. A blind buzzard; a pur-blind man or woman.

BYE BLOW. A bastard.

C

CAB. A brothel. Mother, how many tails have you in your cab? how many girls have you in your nanny house?

CABBAGE. Cloth, stuff, or silk, purloined by tailors from their employers, which they deposit in a place called *hell* or their *eye;* from the first, when taxed with their knavery, they equivocally swear that, if they have taken any, they wish they may find it in *hell:* or, alluding to the second, protest that what they have over and above is not more than they could put in their *eye.*

CABBAGE PLANT, or SUMMER CABBAGE. An umbrella. *Cant. See* SPREAD.

CABIN. A house. *Irish term.*

CACKLE. To blab, or discover secrets. The cull is leaky, and cackles; the rogue tells all. *Cant. See* LEAKY.

CACKLER. A hen.

CACKLER'S KEN. A hen-roost. *Cant.*

CACKLING CHEATS. Fowls. *Cant.*

CACKLING FARTS. Eggs. *Cant.*

CADDEE. A helper. An understrapper.

CADGE. To beg. Cadge the swells; beg of the gentlemen.

Cadger. A beggar, one of the lowest of the low. *Cant.*

Caffan. Cheese. *Cant.*

Cag. To be cagged, To be sulky or out of humour. The cove carries the cag; the man is vexed or sullen.

Cagg. To cagg; a military term used by the private soldiers, signifying a solemn vow or resolution not to get drunk for a certain time; or, as the term is, till their cagg is out: which vow is commonly observed with the strictest exactness. *Ex.* I have cagged myself for six months. Excuse me this time, and I will cagg myself for a year. This term is also used in the same sense among the common people of Scotland, where it is performed with divers ceremonies.

Cagg Maggs. Old Lincolnshire geese, which, having been plucked ten or twelve years, are sent up to London to feast the cockneys.

Cag Magg. Bits and scraps of provisions. Bad meat.

Cake, or Cakey. A foolish fellow.

Calf-skin Fiddle. A drum. To smack calf's skin: to kiss the book in taking an oath. It is held by the St. Giles's casuists, that, by kissing one's thumb instead of smacking calf's skin, the guilt of taking a false oath is avoided.

Calves. His calves are gone to grass; a saying of a man with slender legs without calves. Veal will be cheap, calves fall; said of a man whose calves fall away.

Calves Head Club. A club instituted by the Independents and Presbyterians, to commemorate the decapitation of King Charles I. Their chief fare was calves heads; and they drank their wine and ale out of calves skulls.

Calibogus. Rum and spruce beer, American beverage.

Calle. A cloak or gown. *Cant.*

Cambridge Fortune. A wind-mill and a water-mill, used to signify a woman without any but personal endowments.

Cambridge Oak. A willow.

Camesa. A shirt or shift. *Cant. Spanish.*

Camp Candlestick. A bottle, or soldier's bayonet.

Cam Roads. Retreat to Cambridge by way of a change. *Oxf. Univ. Cant.*

Canary Bird. A jail bird, a person used to be kept in a cage; also, in the canting sense, guineas; also a kept woman. *Cant.*

Candlesticks. Bad, small, or untunable bells. Hark! how the candlesticks rattle.

Candy. Drunk. *Irish.*

Cane. To lay Cane upon Abel; to beat any one with a cane or stick.

Canister. The head. To mill his canister; to break his head.

Cank. Dumb.

Canniken. A small can: also, in the canting sense, the plague.

Cant. A hypocrite, a double-tongued palavering fellow. *See* Palaver.

Cant. The flash language.

Cant. To cant; to toss or throw: as, cant a slug into your bread room; drink a dram. *Sea wit.*

Canterbury Story. A long roundabout tale.

Canters, or The Canting Crew. Thieves, beggars, and gypsies, or any others using the canting lingo. *See* Lingo.

Canticle. A parish clerk.

Canting. Preaching with a whining, affected tone, perhaps a corruption of chaunting; some derive it from Andrew Cant, a famous Scotch preacher, who used that whining manner of expression. Also, a kind of gibberish used by thieves and gypsies, called likewise pedlar's French, the slang, &c. &c.

Cant of Dobbin. A roll of ribbon. *Cant.*

Cap. To take one's oath. I will cap downright; I will swear home. *Cant.*

Cap. To take off one's hat or cap. To cap the quadrangle; a lesson of humility, or rather servility, taught undergraduates at the universities, where they are obliged to cross the area of the college, cap in hand, in reverence to the fellows who sometimes walk there. The same ceremony is observed on coming on quarter deck of ships of war, although no officer should be on it.

Cap. To support another's assertion or tale. To assist a man in cheating. The file kidded the joskin with sham books, and his pal capped; the deep one cheated the countryman with false cards, and his confederate assisted in the fraud.

Cap Acquaintance. Persons slightly acquainted, or only so far as mutually to salute with the hat on meeting. A woman who endeavours to attract the notice of any particular man, is said to set her cap at him.

Caper Merchant A dancing master, or hop merchant; *marchand des capriolles.—French term.* To cut capers; to leap or jump in dancing. *See* Hop Merchant.

Capon. A castrated cock, also an eunuch.

Capricornified. Cuckolded, hornified.

Capsize. To overturn or reverse. He took his broth till he capsized; he drank till he fell out of his chair. *Sea term.*

Captain Copperthorne's Crew. All officers; a saying of a company where every one strives to rule.

Captain Podd. A celebrated master of a puppet-show, in Ben Jonson's time, whose name became a common one to signify any of that fraternity. *Obsolete.*

Captain Queernabs. A shabby ill-dressed fellow.

Captain Sharp. A cheating bully, or one, in a set of gamblers, whose office is to bully any pigeon who, suspecting roguery, refuses to pay what he has lost. *Cant.*

Captain Tom. The leader of a mob; also, the mob itself.

Caravan. A large sum of money; also, a person cheated of such a sum. *Cant.*

Carbuncle Face. A red face, full of pimples.

Cardinal. A cloak in fashion about the year 1760.

Carriers. A set of rogues who are employed to look out and watch upon the roads, at inns, &c. in order to carry information to their respective gangs of a booty in prospect.

Carrion Hunter. An undertaker; called, also, a cold cook, and death hunter. See Cold Cook and Death Hunter.

Carrots. Red hair.

Carrotty-pated. Ginger-hackled, red-haired. See Ginger-hackled.

Carry the Keg. Any person who is easily vexed or put out of humour by any joke passed upon him, and cannot conceal his chagrin, is said to *carry the keg*, or is compared to a *walking distiller*.

Carry Witchet. A sort of conundrum, puzzlewit, or riddle.

Cart. To put the cart before the horse; to mention the last part of a story first. To be flogged at the cart's a-se or tail; persons guilty of petty larceny are frequently sentenced to be tied to the tail of a cart, and whipped, by the common executioner, to a certain distance: the degree of severity in the execution is left to the discretion of the executioner, who, it is said, has cats of nine tails of all prices.

Carvel's Ring. The monosyllable. Ham Carvel, a jealous old doctor, being in bed with his wife, dreamed that the Devil gave him a ring, which, so long as he had it on his finger, would prevent his being made a cuckold: waking, he found he had got his finger the L—d knows where. *See Rabelais and Prior's versification of the story.*

Carver and Gilder. A match-maker.

Cascade. To vomit.

Case. A house of ill-fame; perhaps from the Italian *casa*. In the canting lingo is meant a store or ware house, as well as a dwelling-house. Tout that case; mark or observe that house. It is all bob, now let's dub the gig of the case; now the coast is clear, let us break open the door of the house.

Case Vrow. A prostitute attached to a particular bawdy-house.

Cash, or Caffan. Cheese. *Cant.* *See* Caffan.

Castle of St. Thomas. The Penitentiary in St. Thomas's

parish, where the frail part of the Oxford belles are sent under surveillance. *Oxf. Univ. Cant.*

CASTER. A cloak. *Cant.*

CASTING UP ONE'S ACCOUNTS. Vomiting.

CASTOR. A hat. To prig a castor; to steal a hat.

> "Tom Trot
> Took his new *castor* from his head."
> *Vide Randall's Diary.*

CAT. A common prostitute. An old cat; a cross old woman.

CAT, or SHOOT THE CAT. To vomit from drunkenness.

CATAMARAN. An old scraggy woman; from a kind of float made of spars and yards lashed together, for saving shipwrecked persons.

CAT AND KITTEN RIG. Stealing of pewter quart and pint pots from public-houses. *Cant.*

CAT-CALL. A kind of whistle, chiefly used at theatres to interrupt the actors and damn a new piece. It derives its name from one of its sounds, which greatly resembles the modulation of an intriguing boar-cat.

CATCH CLUB. A member of the catch club; a bum bailiff.

CATCH FART. A footboy; so called from such servants commonly following close behind their master or mistress.

CATCHING HARVEST. A dangerous time for a robbery, when many persons are on the road, on account of a horse-race, fair, or some other public meeting.

CATCH PENNY. Any temporary contrivance to raise a contribution on the public.

CATCH POLE. A bum bailiff, or sheriff's officer.

CATER COUSINS. Good friends. He and I are not cater cousins, i. e. we are not even cousins in the fourth degree, or four times removed; that is, we have not the least friendly connexion.

CATERPILLAR. A nick name for a soldier. In the year 1745, a soldier, quartered at a house near Derby, was desired by his landlord to call upon him whenever he came that way; for, added he, soldiers are the pillars of the nation. The Rebellion being finished, it happened the same regiment was quartered in Derbyshire, when the soldier resolved to accept of his landlord's invitation, and, accordingly, obtained leave to go to him: but, on his arrival, he was greatly surprised to find a very cold reception; whereupon, expostulating with his landlord, he reminded him of his invitation, and the circumstance of his having said, soldiers were the pillars of the nation. If I did, answered the host, I meant *caterpillars*.

CATERWAULING. Going out in the night in search of intrigues, like a cat in the gutters.

Cat-harping Fashion. Drinking cross-ways, and not, as usual, over the left thumb. *Sea term.*

Cat-Heads. A woman's breasts. *Sea phrase.*

Cathedral. Old-fashioned. An old cathedral bedstead, chair, &c.

Cat in Pan. To turn cat in pan, to change sides or parties; supposed originally to have been to turn *cate* or *cake* in pan.

Cat Lap. Tea, called also scandal broth. *See* Scandal Broth.

Cat Match. When a rook or cully is engaged amongst bad bowlers.

Cat of nine Tails. A scourge composed of nine strings of whipcord, each string having nine knots.

Catoller. A noisy, prating fool: one who annoys the company with proposals for betting, and ultimately never makes a bet. Few evenings pass over at the Castle-Tavern, Holborn, without meeting with a *Catoller:* in fact, the pass word is, at this celebrated sporting house, that Tom Belcher would be in danger of losing his *licence*, if he did not often have a fool or *Catoller* exhibit himself for the amusement of his visiters.

Cat's Foot. To live under the cat's foot; to be under the dominion of a wife, hen-pecked. To live like dog and cat; spoken of married persons who live unhappily together. As many lives as a cat; cats, according to vulgar naturalists, have nine lives, that is one less than a woman. No more chance than a cat in Hell without claws; said of one who enters into a dispute or quarrel with another greatly above his match.

Cat's Meat. A slang phrase for the lungs: applied when any person is touched with a consumption; i. e. his *Cat's meat* is bad.

Cat's Paw. To be made a cat's paw of; to be made a tool or instrument to accomplish the purpose of another; an allusion to the story of the monkey, who made use of a cat's paw to scratch a roasted chestnut out of the fire.

Cat's Sleep. Counterfeit sleep; cats often counterfeiting sleep, to decoy their prey near them, and then suddenly spring on them.

Cat whipping, or Whipping the Cat. A trick often practised on ignorant country fellows, vain of their strength, by laying a wager with them that they may be pulled through a pond by a cat. The bet being made, a rope is fixed round the waist of the party to be catted, and the end thrown across the pond, to which the cat is also fastened by a packthread, and three or four sturdy fellows are appointed to lead and whip the cat; these, on a signal given, seize the end of the cord and, pretending to whip the cat, haul the astonished booby through the water.—To whip the cat, is, also, a term among tailors for working jobs at private houses, as practised in the country.

CATTLE. Sad cattle: whores or gypsies. Black cattle, bugs. *Cant.*

CAUDGE-PAWED. Left-handed.

CAULIFLOWER. A large white wig, such as is commonly worn by the dignified clergy, and was formerly by physicians. Also, the private parts of a woman; the reason for which appellation is given in the following story: A woman, who was giving evidence in a cause, wherein it was necessary to express those parts, made use of the term cauliflower; for which the judge on the bench, a peevish old fellow, reproved her, saying she might as well call it artichoke. Not so, my lord, replied she, for an artichoke has a bottom, but a cunt and a cauliflower have none.

CAUTIONS. The four cautions: I. Beware of a woman before.—II. Beware of a horse behind.—III. Beware of a cart sideways.—IV. Beware of a priest every way.

CAVAULTING SCHOOL. A bawdy-house.

CAVE OF ANTIQUITY. Depôt of old authors. *Oxf. Univ. Cant.*

CAW-HANDED, or CAW-PAWED. Awkward, not dexterous, ready, or nimble.

CAXON. An old weather-beaten wig.

CAZ. Cheese: *As good as caz,* is a phrase signifying that any projected fraud or robbery may be easily and certainly accomplished; any person who is the object of such attempt, and is known to be an easy dupe, is declared to be *as good as caz,* meaning that success is certain.

CENT PER CENT. An usurer.

CHAFED. Well beaten; from *chauffé,* warmed.

CHAFF-CUTTER. A knowing person, one whose tongue is of great use to him, in order to silence an antagonist, whether right or wrong. *Cant.*

CHAFFING. To blow up; to talk aloud. *Cant.*

CHANCERY. Getting your head "*in chancery,*" among pugilists, is when your *nob* is completely at the mercy of your opponent; or, in other words, you cannot protect it. Receiving blow after blow. RANDALL, termed the NONPAREIL of the Prize Ring, was distinguished for this peculiar trait among the boxers.

CHANT. A person's name, address, or designation; thus, a thief, who assumes a feigned name on his apprehension to avoid being known, or a swindler who gives a false address to a tradesman, is said to *tip them a queer chant.*

CHANT. A cipher, initials, or mark of any kind, on a piece of plate, linen, or other article; any thing so marked is said to be *chanted.*

CHANT. An advertisement in a newspaper or hand-bill; also a paragraph in the newspaper describing any robbery or other recent event; any lost or stolen property, for the recovery of which, or a thief, &c., for whose apprehension a reward is held out by advertisement, are said to be *chanted*.

CHAP. A fellow. An odd chap; a strange fellow.

CHAPERON. The cicisbeo, or gentleman usher to a lady; from the French.

CHAPT. Dry or thirsty.

CHARACTERED, or LETTERED. Burnt in the hand. They have palmed the character upon him; they have burned him in the hand. *Cant.—See* LETTERED.

CHARING. A flash term for any thing that is wrong; i. e. on the cross: derived from Charing Cross.

CHARLEY. A watchman.

CHARLEY-KEN. A watch-box.

CHARM. A picklock. *Cant.*

CHARREN. The smoke of Charren. His eyes water from the smoke of Charren; a man of that place coming out of his house weeping, because his wife had beat him, told his neighbours the smoke had made his eyes water.

CHATES. The gallows. *Cant.*

CHATTER BOX. One whose tongue runs twelve score to the dozen; a chattering man or woman.

CHATTER BROTH. Tea. *See* CAT LAP and SCANDAL BROTH.

CHATTERERS. The teeth. *Cant.*

CHATTERING. A blow given on the mouth. Set all his teeth a chattering. *A flash phrase.*

CHATTERY. Cotton or linen goods.

CHATTS. Seals.

CHATTS. Lice: perhaps an abbreviation of chattels, lice being the chief live stock or chattels of beggars, gypsies, and the rest of the canting crew. *Cant.* Also, according to the canting academy, the gallows.

CHAUNT. A song.

CHAUNT. To sing. To publish an account in the newspapers. The kiddey was chaunted for a toby; his examination concerning a highway robbery was published in the papers.

CHAUNTED. Advertised. *Cant.*

CHAUNTER CULLS. Grub-street writers, who compose songs, carrols, &c. for ballad-singers. *Cant.*

CHAUNTING COVES. Horse-dealers. A certain class of these fellows impose on the public by specious and imposing advertisements; who set forth qualities their horses never possessed: in short, a dead take in. Such advertisements are to be met with daily in the London newspapers.

CHAW BACON. A countryman. A stupid fellow.

CHEAPSIDE. He came at it by way of Cheapside; he gave little or nothing for it, he bought it cheap.

CHEATS. Sham sleeves to put over a dirty shift or shirt. *See* SHAMS.

CHEEK BY JOWL. Side by side; hand to fist.

CHEEKS. Ask cheeks near cunnyborough; the repartee of a St. Giles's fair one, who bids you ask her backside, *anglicè* her a–se. A like answer is current in France: any one asking the road or distance to Macon, a city near Lyons, would be answered by a French lady of easy virtue, 'Mettez votre nez dans mon cul, et vous serrez dans les Faux-bourgs.'

CHEESE IT. Be silent, be quiet, don't do it. Cheese it, the coves are fly; be silent, the people understand our discourse.

CHEESE-TOASTER. A sword.

CHELSEA. A village near London, famous for the military hospital. To get Chelsea; to obtain the benefit of this hospital. "Dead Chelsea, by G–d!" an exclamation uttered by a grenadier at Fontenoy, on having his leg carried away by a cannon-ball.

CHERRY-COLOURED CAT. A black cat, their being black cherries as well as red.

CHERUBIM. Peevish children, because cherubim and seraphim continually do cry.

CHESHIRE CAT. He grins like a Cheshire cat; said of any one who shows his teeth and gums in laughing.

CHEST OF TOOLS. Implements for house-breaking.

CHICK-AM-A-TRICK. A vulgar phrase used by the Jews, meaning, "of no good," "It's all *chice*."

CHICK-A-BIDDY. A chicken, so called to and by little children.

CHICKEN-BREASTED. Said of a woman with scarce any breasts.

CHICKEN-BUTCHER. A poulterer.

CHICKEN-HAMMED. Persons whose legs and thighs are bent or arched outwards.

CHICKEN-HAZARD. A table at which persons play for low stakes.

CHICKEN-HEARTED. Fearful, cowardly.

CHICKEN NABOB. One returned from the East Indies with but a moderate fortune of fifty or sixty thousand pounds; a diminutive nabob: a term borrowed from the chicken turtle.

CHILD. To eat a child; to partake of a treat given to the parish-officers, in part of commutation for a bastard child: the common price was formerly ten pounds and a greasy chin. *See* GREASY CHIN.

CHIMNEY CHOPS. An abusive appellation for a negro.

CHINA-STREET. Bow-street, Covent Garden, where the head police office is situated. *Cant.*

CHINK. Money.

CHIP. A child. A chip of the old block; a child who, either in person or sentiments, resembles its father or mother.

CHIP. A brother chip; a person of the same trade or calling.

CHIPS. A nick name for a carpenter.

CHIRPING MERRY. Exhilirated with liquor. Chirping glass, a cheerful glass, that makes the company chirp like birds in spring.

CHIT. An infant or baby.

CHITTERLINS. The bowels. There is a rumpus among my bowels, i. e. I have the colick. The frill of a shirt.

CHITTY-FACED. Baby-faced; said of one who has a childish look.

CHIVE, or CHIFF. A knife, file, or saw. To chive the darbies; to file off the irons or fetters. To chive the boungs of the frows; to cut off a woman's pockets.

CHIVEY. I gave him a good chivey; I gave him a hearty scolding.

CHIVING LAY. Cutting the braces of coaches behind, on which, the coachman quitting the box, an accomplice robs the boot; also, formerly, cutting the back of the coach to steal the fine large wigs then worn.

CHOAK. Choak away, the churchyard's near; a jocular saying to a person taken with a violent fit of coughing, or who has swallowed any thing, as it is called, the wrong way. Choak, chicken, more are hatching; a like consolation.

CHOAKING PYE, or COLD PYE. A punishment inflicted on any person sleeping in company; it consists in wrapping up cotton in a case or tube of paper, setting it on fire, and directing the smoke up the nostrils of the sleeper. *See* HOWELL'S COTGRAVE.

CHOAK OFF. A person who is impudent in company; or a man that might do another some mischief by giving evidence before a magistrate, or on his trial, against him; it is said, he must be *choaked* off;—at all events, he must be got rid of.

CHOAK PEAR. Figuratively, an unanswerable objection; also a machine formerly used in Holland by robbers: it was of iron, shaped like a pear; this they forced into the mouths of persons from whom they intended to extort money, and on turning a key, certain interior springs thrust forth a number of points, in all directions, which so enlarged it, that it could not be taken out of the mouth; and the iron, being case-hardened, could not be filed: the only methods of getting rid of it were, either by cutting the mouth, or advertizing a reward for the key. These pears were also called pears of agony.

CHOCOLATE. To give chocolate without sugar; to reprove. *Military term.*

CHOICE SPIRIT. A gay, thoughtless, laughing, singing, merry, fellow.

CHOPPER. In bruising, is a blow struck on the face with the back of the hand. Mendoza claims the honour of its invention, but unjustly; he certainly revived, and considerably improved it. It was practised long before our time—Broughton occasionally used it: and Slack, it also appears, struck the *chopper* in giving the return in many of his battles.

CHOP AND CHANGE. To exchange backwards and forwards. To chop, in the canting sense, means making despatch, or hurrying over any business: ex. The *autem bawler* will soon quit the *hums*, for he *chops up* the *whiners;* the parson will soon quit the pulpit, for he hurries over the prayers. *See* AUTEM BAWLER, HUMS, and WHINERS.

CHOP CHURCHES. Simoniacal dealers in livings, or other ecclesiastical preferments.

CHOPPING. Lusty. A chopping boy or girl; a lusty child.

CHOPS. The mouth. I gave him a wherrit, or a souse, across the chops: I gave him a blow over the mouth. *See* WHERRIT.

CHOP-STICK. A fork.

CHOUDER. A sea-dish, composed of fresh fish, salt pork, herbs, and sea-biscuits, laid in different layers, and stewed together.

CHOUSE. To cheat or trick: he choused me out of it. Chouse is, also, the term for a game like chuck-farthing.

CHRIST-CROSS ROW. The alphabet in a horn-book: called Christ-cross Row, for having, as an Irishman observed, Christ's cross *prefixed* before and *after* the twenty-four letters.

CHRISTENING. Erasing the name of the true maker from a stolen watch, and engraving a fictitious one in its place.

CHRISTIAN PONY. A chairman.

CHRISTIAN. A tradesman who has faith, i. e. will give credit.

CHRISTMAS COMPLIMENTS. A cough, kibed heels, and a snotty nose.

CHUB. He is a young chub, or a mere chub; i. e. a foolish fellow, easily imposed on: an allusion to a fish of that name, easily taken.

CHUBBY. Round-faced, plump.

CHUCK. My chuck; a term of endearment.

CHUCK. To show a propensity for a man. The mort chucks; the wench wants to be doing.

CHUCK FARTHING. A parish clerk.

CHUCKLE-HEADED. Stupid, thick-headed.

CHUFFY. Round-faced, chubby, jolly, merry.

CHUM. A chamber-fellow, particularly at the universities and in prisons.

CHUMMAGE. Money paid by the richer sort of prisoners in the Fleet and King's Bench, to the poorer, for their share of a room. When prisons are very full, which is too often the case, particularly on the eve of an insolvent act, two or three persons are obliged to sleep in a room. A prisoner who can pay for being alone, chuses two poor chums, who, for a stipulated price, called chummage, give up their share of the room, and sleep on the stairs, or, as the term is, ruff it.

CHURCH WARDEN. A Sussex name for a shag, or cormorant, probably from its voracity.

CHURCH WORK. Said of any work that advances slowly.

CHURCHYARD COUGH. A cough that is likely to terminate in death.

CHURK. The udder.

CHURL. Originally, a labourer or husbandman: figuratively, a rude, surly, boorish fellow. To put a churl upon a gentleman; to drink malt liquor immediately after having drunk wine.

CHURY. A knife. *Cant.*

CINDER GARBLER. A servant maid, from her business of sifting the ashes from the cinders. *Custom-house wit.*

CIRCUMBENDIBUS. A roundabout way, or story. He took such a circumbendibus; he took such a circuit.

CIT. A citizen of London.

CITY COLLEGE. Newgate.

CIVILITY MONEY. A reward claimed by bailiffs for executing their office with civility.

CIVIL RECEPTION. A house of civil reception; a bawdy-house or nanny-house. *See* NANNY-HOUSE.

CLACK. A tongue, chiefly applied to women; a simile drawn from the clack of a water-mill.

CLACK-LOFT. A pulpit, so called by orator Henley.

CLAN. A family's tribe or brotherhood; a word much used in Scotland. The head of the clan; the chief. An allusion to a story of a Scotchman, who, when a very large louse crept down his arm, put him back again, saying he was the head of the clan, and that, if injured, all the rest would resent it.

Clank. A silver tankard. *Cant.*

Clank Napper. A silver tankard stealer. *See* Rum Bubber.

Clanker. A great lie.

Clap. A delicate taint. He went out by Had'em, and came round by Clapham home; i. e. he went out a wenching and got a clap.

Clap on the Shoulder. An arrest for debt; whence a bum bailiff is called a shoulder-clapper.

Clapper. The tongue of a bell, and, figuratively, of a man or woman.

Clapper Claw. To scold, to abuse, or claw off with the tongue.

Clapperdogeon. A beggar born. *Cant.*

Claret. French red wine; figuratively, blood. I tapped his claret; I broke his head, and made the blood run. Claret-faced; red-faced.

Clawed off. Severely beaten or whipped; also, smartly poxed or clapped.

Clean. Expert; clever. Amongst the knuckling coves he is reckoned very clean; he is considered very expert as a pickpocket.

Cleaned out. A sporting phrase, in alluding to any person who has lost all his money in betting. *To clean out* also signifies the same as *to dish*, or sew up. *ex. gr.*

> "For Turner I've *clean'd out* and Martin the baker,
> I'd very near put on the bankruptcy list."
>
> *Randall's Farewell to the Ring. Vide Randall's Diary.*

Clear. Very drunk. The cull is clear, let's bite him; the fellow is very drunk, let's cheat him. *Cant.*

Clearing out at Custom-house. Eased of an incumbrance. *See term.*

Cleaver. One that will cleave; said of a forward or wanton woman.

Clerked. Soothed, funned, imposed on. The cull will not be clerked; *i. e.* the fellow will not be imposed on by fair words.

Clew. To hold fast. *See term.*

Cleymes. Artificial sores, made by beggars to excite charity.

Click. A blow. A click in the muns; a blow or knock in the face. *Cant.*

Click. To snatch. To click a nab; to snatch a hat. *Cant.*

Clicker. A salesman's servant; also, one who proportions out the different shares of the booty among thieves.

Clicket. Copulation of foxes; and thence used, in a canting sense, for that of men and women: as, The cull and the mort are at clicket in the dyke; the man and woman are copulating in the ditch.

CLIMB. To climb the three trees with a ladder; to ascend the gallows.

CLINCH. A pun or quibble. To clinch, or to clinch the nail: to confirm an improbable story by another: as, A man swore he drove a tenpenny nail through the moon; a by-stander said it was true, for he was on the other side and clinched it.

CLINK. A place in the Borough of Southwark, formerly privileged from arrests; and inhabited by lawless vagabonds of every denomination, called, from the place of their residence, clinkers. Also a gaol, from the clinking of the prisoners' chains or fetters: he is gone to clink.

CLINKERS. A kind of small Dutch bricks; also, irons worn by prisoners; crafty fellows.

CLIP. To hug or embrace; to clip and cling. To clip the coin; to diminish the current coin. To clip the king's English; to be unable to speak plain through drunkenness.

CLOAK TWITCHERS. Rogues who lurk about the entrances into dark alleys, and bye-lanes, to snatch cloaks from the shoulders of passengers.

CLOD HOPPER. A country farmer, or ploughman.

CLOD PATE. A dull, heavy booby.

CLOD POLE. The same.

CLOSE-FISTED. Covetous or stingy.

CLOSE YOUR DEAD-LIGHTS. Bung up your eyes. *Sea term.*

CLOSH. A general name given by the mobility to Dutch seamen, being a corruption of *Claus*, the abbreviation of Nicholas, a name very common among the men of that nation.

CLOTH MARKET. He is just come from the cloth market, i. e. from between the sheets, he is just risen from bed.

CLOUD. Tobacco. Under a cloud; in adversity.

CLOUT. A handkerchief of any kind.

CLOUT. A blow. I'll give you a clout on your jolly nob; I'll give you a blow on your head. It also means a handkerchief. *Cant.* Any pocket-handkerchief except a silk one.

CLOUTED SHOON. Shoes tipped with iron.

CLOUTING. The practice of picking pockets exclusively of handkerchiefs.

CLOUTING LAY. Picking pockets of handkerchiefs.

CLOVEN, CLEAVE, or CLEFT. A term used for a woman who passes for a maid, but is not one.

CLOVEN FOOT. To spy the cloven foot in any business; to discover some roguery or something bad in it: a saying that alludes to a piece of vulgar superstition, which is that, let the Devil transform himself into what shape he will, he cannot hide his cloven foot.

CLOVER. To be, or live, in clover; to live luxuriously. Clover is the most desirable food for cattle.

CLOWES. Rogues.

CLOY. To steal. To cloy the clout; to steel the handkerchief. To cloy the lour; to steal money. *Cant.*

CLOYES. Thieves, robbers, &c.

CLUB. A meeting or association, where each man is to spend an equal and stated sum, called his club.

CLUB LAW. Argumentum baculinum, in which an oaken stick is a better plea than an act of parliament.

CLUMP. A lump. Clumpish; lumpish, stupid.

CLUNCH. An awkward clownish fellow.

CLUNCH THE FIST. To clench or shut the hand. Clunchfisted; covetous, stingy. *See* CLOSE-FISTED.

CLUTCHES. Hands, gripe, power.

CLUTTER. A stir, noise, or racket: what a confounded clutter here is!

CLY. Money; also, a pocket. He has filed the cly; he has picked a pocket. *Cant.*

CLY-FAKER. A pickpocket. *Cant.*

CLY THE JERK. To be whipped. *Cant.*

CLYSTER PIPE. A nick name for an apothecary.

COACH WHEEL. A half-crown piece is a fore coach wheel, and a crown piece a hind coach wheel; the fore wheels of a coach being less than the hind ones.

COAX. To fondle, or wheedle. To coax a pair of stockings; to pull down the part soiled into the shoes, so as to give a dirty pair of stockings the appearance of clean ones. Coaxing is also used, instead of darning, to hide the holes about the ancles.

COB. A Spanish dollar.

COB, or COBBING. A punishment used by the seamen for petty offences or irregularities among themselves: it consists in bastonading the offender on the posteriors with a cobbing stick, or pike staff; the number usually inflicted is a dozen. At the first stroke the executioner repeats the word *watch*, on which all persons present are to take off their hats, on pain of like punishment: the last stroke is always given as hard as possible, and is called *the purse*. Ashore, among soldiers, where this punishment is sometimes adopted, *watch* and *the purse* are not included in the number, but given over and above, or, in the vulgar phrase, free gratis for nothing. This piece of discipline is also inflicted in Ireland, by the school-boys, on persons coming into the school without taking off their hats; it is there called school butter.

COBBLE. To mend, or patch; likewise to do a thing in a bungling manner.

COBBLE COLTER. A turkey.

COBBLER. A mender of shoes, an improver of the understanding of his customers; a translator.

COBBLER'S PUNCH. Treacle, vinegar, gin, and water.

COCK, or CHIEF COCK OF THE WALK. The leading man in any society or body; the best boxer in a village or district.

COCK AND A BULL STORY. A roundabout story, without head or tail, i. e. beginning or ending.

COCK AND HEN CLUB. These sort of clubs are always held upon the *sly:* in consequence of their appearing, in the eyes of the police, *disorderly*. The chairs (or chairman and chairwoman) are occupied by an *out-and-out* COVE and a *flash woman:* it is a horrid scene of depravity, drunkenness, and obscenity: a visit from the police-officers puts all to the rout in an instant, but those that are *boned* are locked up for the night, and have to give an account of themselves before the *Beak* the next morning.

COCK-A-WHOOP. Elevated, in high spirits, transported with joy.

COCK BAWD. A male keeper of a bawdy-house.

COCKER. One fond of the diversion of cock-fighting.

COCK HOIST. A cross buttock.

COCKISH. Wanton, forward. A cockish wench; a forward, coming girl.

COCKLES. To cry cockles; to be hanged: perhaps, from the noise made while strangling. *Cant.* This will rejoice the cockles of one's heart; a saying in praise of wine, ale, or spirituous liquors.

COCKNEY. A nickname given to the citizens of London, or persons born within the sound of Bow bell, derived from the following story:—A citizen of London being in the country, and hearing a horse neigh, exclaimed, Lord! how that horse laughs! A bystander informed him that that noise was called *neighing*. The next morning, when the cock crowed, the citizen, to show he had not forgotten what was told him, cried out, Do you hear how the *cock neighs?* The king of the cockneys is mentioned among the regulations for the sports and shows formerly held, in the Middle Temple, on Childermas Day, where he had his officers, a marshal, constable, butler, &c. *See* DUGDALE'S ORIGIN. JURIDICIALES, p. 247. Ray says the interpretation of the word cockney is, a young person, coaxed or conquered, made wanton; or a nestle cock delicately bred and brought up, so as, when arrived at man's estate, to be unable to bear the least hardship. Whatever may be the origin of this appellation, we learn from the following verses, attributed to Hugh Bigot, Earl of Norfolk, that it was in use in the time of King Henry II.

> "Was I in my castle at Bungey,
> Fast by the river Waveney,
> I would not care for the King of Cockney:"

i. e. the King of London.

COCK OF THE COMPANY. A weak man, who, from the desire of being the head of the company, associates with low people, and pays all the reckoning.

COCK PIMP. The supposed husband of a bawd.

COCK ROBIN. A soft, easy fellow.

COCKSHUT TIME. The evening, when fowls go to roost.

COCK-SURE. Certain. A metaphor borrowed from the cock of a firelock, as being much more certain to fire than the match.

COCK YOUR EYE. Shut one eye: thus translated into apothecaries' Latin,—*Gallus tuus ego*,

COD. A cod of money, a good sum of money.

CODDERS. Persons employed by the gardeners to gather peas.

CODGER. An old codger, an old fellow.

COD PIECE. The fore-flap of a man's breeches. Do they bite, master? where, in the cod piece or collar? A jocular attack on a patient angler by watermen, &c.

CODRINGTON'S MANORS, MOSTYN'S HUNTING DISTRICT, AND SOMERSET RANGE. The three packs of hounds contiguous to Oxford. *Univ. Cant.*

COD'S HEAD A stupid fellow.

COG. The money, or whatsoever the sweeteners drop to draw in a bubble.

COG. A tooth. A queer cog, a rotten tooth. How the cull flashes his queer cogs, how the fool shows his rotten teeth.

COG. To cheat with dice; also, to wheedle or coax. To cog a die, to conceal or secure a die. To cog a dinner, to wheedle one out of a dinner.

COGUE. A glass of gin. *Cant.*

COKER. A lie.

COLCANNON. Potatos and cabbage pounded together in a mortar, and then stewed with butter: an Irish dish.

COLD. You will catch cold at that; a vulgar threat or advice to desist from an attempt. He caught cold by lying in bed barefoot: a saying of any one extremely tender or careful of himself.

COLD COOK. An undertaker of funerals, or carrion hunter. *See* CARRION HUNTER.

COLD IRON. A sword or any other weapon for cutting or stabbing. I gave him two inches of cold iron into his beef.

COLD MEAT. A dead wife is the best cold meat in a man's house.

COLD PIG. To give cold pig is a punishment inflicted on sluggards who lie too long in bed: it consists in pulling off all the bed-clothes from them, and throwing cold water upon them.

COLD PUDDING. This is said to settle one's love.

COLE. Money. Post the cole: pay down the money.

COLIANDER, or CORIANDER SEEDS. Money.

COLLAR DAY. Execution day.

COLLECTOR. A highwayman.

COLLEGE. Newgate or any other prison. New College, the Royal Exchange. King's College, the King's Bench prison. He has been educated at the steel, and has taken his last degree at College; he has received his education at the house of correction, and was hanged at Newgate.

COLLEGE COVE. The college cove has numbered him, and, if he is knocked down, he'll be twisted; the turnkey of Newgate has told the judge how many times the prisoner has been tried before, and, therefore, if he is found guilty, he certainly will be hanged. It is said to be the custom of the Old Bailey for one of the turnkeys of Newgate to give information to the judge how many times an old offender has been tried, by holding up as many fingers as the number of times the prisoner has been before arraigned at that bar.

COLLEGIATES. Prisoners of the one, and shopkeepers of the other of those places.

COLLOGUE. To wheedle or coax.

COLLYWOBBLES. The gripes.

COOK RUFFIAN, who roasted the devil in his feathers. A bad cook.

COOL CRAPE. A shroud.

COOLER. A woman.

COOL LADY. A female follower of the camp who sells brandy.

COOL NANTS. Brandy.

COOL TANKARD. Wine and water, with lemon, sugar, and burrage.

COLQUARRON. A man's neck. His colquarron is just about to be twisted, he is just going to be hanged. *Cant.*

COLT. One who lets horses to highwaymen: also, a boy newly initiated into roguery: a grand or petty juryman on his first assize. *Cant.*

COLTAGE. A fine or beverage paid by colts on their first entering into their offices.

COLT BOWL. Laid short of the jack by a colt bowler, i. e. a person raw or inexperienced in the art of bowling.

Colt's Tooth. An old fellow, who marries or keeps a young girl, is said to have a colt's tooth in his head.

Colt Veal. Coarse red veal, more like the flesh of a colt than that of a calf.

Comb. To comb one's head, to clapperclaw or scold any one: a woman who lectures her husband is said to comb his head. She combed his head with a joint-stool, she threw a stool at him.

Come. To come, to lend. Has he come it? has he lent it? To come over any one, to cheat or over-reach him. Coming wench, a forward wench; also, a breeding woman.

Come. A thief, observing any article in a shop, or other situation, which he conceives may be easily purloined, will say to his accomplice, I think there is so and so *to come.*

Come it. To divulge a secret; to tell any thing of one party to another. They say of a thief, who has turned evidence against his accomplices, that he is *coming* all he knows, or that he *comes it as strong as a horse.*

Come to the Heath. A phrase signifying to pay or give money, and synonymous with *tipping,* from which word it takes its rise, there being a place called Tiptree-heath, in the county of Essex.

Come to the Mark. To abide strictly by any contract previously made: to perform your part manfully in any exploit or enterprise you engage in; or to offer what is considered a fair price for any article in question.

Comfortable Importance. A wife.

Coming! so is Christmas. Said of a person who has long been called, and at length answers, Coming!

Commission. A shirt. *Cant.*

Commode. A woman's head-dress.

Commodity. A woman's commodity, the monosyllable of a modest woman, and the public parts of a prostitute.

Commoner. A novice. *Cant.*

Commons. The house of commons, the necessary house.

Company. To see company, to enter into a course of prostitution.

Compliment. *See* Christmas.

Comus's Court. A social meeting formerly held at the Half-Moon-tavern, Cheapside.

Confect. Counterfeited.

Conger. To conger; the agreement of a set or knot of booksellers of London, that whosoever of them shall buy a good copy, the rest shall take off a particular number, in quires, at a stated price: also, booksellers joining to buy either a considerable or dangerous copy. *Obsolete.*

Congou. Will you lap your congou with me? will you drink tea with me?

Coniah Cove. A gentleman. *Scotch Cant.*

Conk. The nose.

Conk. A thief who impeaches his accomplices, a spy, informer, or tell-tale. *See* Nose, and Wear it.

Conny Wabble. Eggs and brandy beat up together. *Irish.*

Conscience Keeper. A superior, who, by his influence, makes his dependents act as he pleases.

Content. The cull's content, the man is past complaining: a saying of a person murdered for resisting robbers. *Cant.*

Content. A thick liquor, in imitation of chocolate, made of milk and gingerbread.

Contra Dance. A dance where the dancers of the different sexes stand opposite each other, instead of side by side, as in the minuet, rigadoon, louvre, &c. and now corruptly called a country dance.

Conundrums. Enigmatical conceits.

Convenient. A mistress. *Cant.*

Conveniency. A necessary. A leathern conveniency, a coach.

Convocation Castle. Where the twenty-five heads of colleges and the masters meet to transact and investigate university affairs. *Oxford Cant.*

Cooped up. Imprisoned, confined like a fowl in a coop.

Coored. Whipped. *Scotch Cant.*

Coquet. A jilt.

Corinth. A bawdy-house.

Corinthians. The highest order of *swells.* *Cant.*

> "If this *Corinthian* were the sun,
> And we could not well do without him,
> Why then, &c."
>
> *Vide Randall's Diary.*

> "'Twas diverting to see, as one *ogled* around,
> How *Corinthians* and *commoners* mix'd on the ground."
>
> *Vide Crib's Memorial.*

> "Brave Tom, the Champion, with an air
> Almost *Corinthian*, took the chair."
>
> *Ibid.*

Cork-brained. Light-headed, foolish.

Corned. Drunk.

Cornish Hug. A particular lock in wrestling, peculiar to the people of the county of Cornwall.

Corny-faced. A very red pimpled face.

Corporal. To mount a corporal and four, to be guilty of onanism; the thumb is the corporal, the four fingers the privates.

Corporation. A large belly. He has a glorious corporation, he has a very prominent belly.

Corporation. The magistrates, &c. of a corporate town, *corpus sine ratione.* Freemen of a corporation's work, neither strong nor handsome.

Cosset. A foundling. Cosset colt or lamb, a colt or lamb brought up by hand.

Costard. The head. I'll smite your costard, I'll give you a knock on the head.

Costard Monger. A dealer in fruit, particularly apples.

Cot, or Quot. A man who meddles with women's household business, particularly in the kitchen. The punishment, commonly inflicted on a quot, is pinning a greasy dishclout to the skirts of his coat.

Couch a Hogshead. To lie down to sleep. *Cant.*

Counterfeit Crank. A general cheat, assuming all sorts of characters; counterfeiting the falling sickness.

Country Harry. A waggoner. *Cant.*

Country Put. An ignorant country fellow.

Country Work. Said of any work that advances slowly.

Court Card. A gay fluttering coxcomb.

Courtezan. A prostitute.

Court Holy Water. } Fair speeches and promises, without
Court Promises. } performance.

Court of Assistants. A court often applied to by young women who marry old men.

Cove. The master of a house or shop is called *the cove.* On other occasions, when joined to particular words, as a *cross-cove*, a *flash-cove*, a *leary-cove*, &c. it simply implies a man of those several decriptions: sometimes, in speaking of any third person, whose name you are either ignorant of, or don't wish to mention, the word *cove* is adopted by way of emphasis, as may be seen under the word Awake.

Cove of the Ken. The master of the house. *Cant.*

Covess. The mistress of a house or shop, and used, on other occasions, in the same manner as *cove*, when applied to a man.

Covent, or Convent Garden, vulgarly called Common Garden. Anciently, the garden belonging to a dissolved monastery; now famous for being the chief market in London for fruit, flowers, and herbs. The theatres are situated near it. In its environs are many brothels, and, not long ago, the lodgings of the second order of ladies of easy virtue were either there, or in the purlieus of Drury-lane.

Covent Garden Abbess. A bawd.

Covent Garden Ague. The ladybird disease. He broke his shins against Covent Garden rails, he caught the disorder.

Covent Garden Nun. A lady of easy virtue.

Coventry. To send one to Coventry; a punishment inflicted by officers of the army on such of their brethren as are testy, or have been guilty of improper behaviour, not worthy the cognizance of a court-martial. The person sent to Coventry is considered as absent; no one must speak to or answer any question he asks, except relative to duty, under penalty of being also sent to the same place. On a proper submission, the penitent is recalled and welcomed by the mess, as just returned from a journey to Coventry.

Cover. To cover, in betting, is to put down the money: if a person is a stranger upon the turf, or is considered *doubtful*, he is called upon to *cover* by his opponent. Among the *family people*, it is to stand in such a situation as to obscure your *pal*, who is committing a robbery, from the view of the by-standers or persons passing, it is called *covering him*. Any person belonging to the gang, whose dress or stature renders him particularly eligible for this purpose, is termed a *good coverer*.

Covey. A collection of whores. What a fine covey here is, if the Devil would but throw his net!

Cow Juice. Milk.

Cow's Baby. A calf.

Cow's Courant. Gallop and sh—e.

Cow-handed. Awkward.

Cow-hearted. Fearful.

Cow Itch. The product of a sort of bean, which excites an insufferable itching, used chiefly for playing tricks.

Cow's Spouse. A bull.

Cow's Thumb. Done to a cow's thumb; done exactly.

Coxcomb. Anciently, a fool. Fools, in great families, wore a cap with bells, on the top of which was a piece of red cloth, in the shape of a cock's comb. At present, coxcomb signifies a fop, or vain self-conceited fellow.

Crab. To catch a crab; to fall backwards by missing one's stroke in rowing.

Crab. To prevent the perfection or execution of any intended matter of business, by saying any thing offensive or unpleasant, is called *crabbing it*, or *throwing a crab;* to *crab* a person, is to use such offensive language or behaviour as will highly displease, or put him in an ill humour.

Crabbed. Sour, ill-tempered, difficult.

Crab Louse. A species of louse peculiar to the human body; the male is denominated a cock, the female a hen.

Crab Shells. Shoes. *Irish.*

Crabs. A losing throw to the main at hazard.

Crack. A whore.

Crack. To boast or brag; also to break. I cracked his napper; I broke his head.

Crack. To break open; *the crack* is the *game* of house-breaking; *a crack* is the breaking any house or building for the purpose of plunder.

Crack, the, or All the Crack. The fashionable theme, the go. The Crack Lay is used, of late, in the cant language, to signify the art and mystery of house-breaking.

Cracker. Crust, sea biscuit, or ammunition loaf; also the backside. Farting crackers; breeches.

Cracking Tools. Implements of house-breaking, such as a crow, a centre-bit, false keys, &c.

Crackish. Whorish.

Crackmans. Hedges. The cull thought to have loped by breaking through the crackmans, but we fetched him back by a nope on the costard, which stopped his jaw; the man thought to have escaped by breaking through the hedge, but we brought him back by a great blow on the head, which laid him speechless.

Cracksman. A house-breaker. The kiddy is a clever cracksman; the young fellow is a very expert house-breaker.

Crag. The neck.

Cramp Rings. Bolts, shackles, or fetters. *Cant.*

Cramp Words. Sentence of death passed on a criminal by a judge. He has just undergone the cramp word; sentence has just been passed on him. *Cant.*

Crank. Gin and water; also, brisk, pert.

Crank. The falling sickness. *Cant.*

Crap. The gallows. *Cant.*

Crapped. Hanged. *Cant.*

Crash. To kill. Crash that cull; kill that fellow. *Cant.*

Crashing Cheats. Teeth.

Craw Thumpers. Roman Catholics, so called from their beating their breasts in the confession of their sins.

Cream-pot Love. Such as young fellows pretend to dairy-maids, to get cream and other good things from them.

Creeme. To slip or slide any thing into the hand of another. *Cant.*

Creepers. Gentlemen's companions, lice.

Crew. A knot or gang; also a boat or ship's company. The canting crew are thus divided into twenty-three orders, which see under the different words:—

MEN.

1 Rufflers	4 Rogues
2 Upright Men	5 Wild Rogues
3 Hookers or Anglers	6 Priggers of Prancers

7 Palliardes	11 Drummerers
8 Fraters	12 Drunken Tinkers
9 Jarkmen, or Patricoes	13 Swaddlers, or Pedlars
10 Fresh Water Mariners, or Whip Jackets	14 Abrams.

WOMEN.

1 Demanders for Glimmer or Fire	5 Walking Morts
2 Bawdy Baskets	6 Doxies
3 Morts	7 Delles
4 Autem Morts	8 Kinching Morts
	9 Kinching Coes.

CRIB. A house. To crack a crib: to break open a house. Sometimes applied to shops, as, a *thimble-crib*, a watch-maker's shop; a *stocking-crib*, a hosier's, &c.

CRIB. To purloin, or appropriate to one's own use, part of any thing intrusted to one's care.

CRIBBAGE-FACED. Marked with the small pox, the pits bearing a kind of resemblance to the holes in a cribbage-board.

CRIBBEYS, or CRIBBY ISLANDS. Blind alleys, courts, or bye-ways; perhaps from the houses built there being cribbed out of the common way or passage; and islands, from the similarity of sound to the Caribbee Islands.

CRIMP. A broker or factor, as a coal crimp, who disposes of the cargoes of the Newcastle coal ships; also persons employed to trapan or kidnap recruits for the East India and African Companies. To crimp, or play crimp; to play foul or booty: also, a cruel manner of cutting up fish alive, practised by the London fishmongers, in order to make it eat firm; cod, and other crimped fish, being a favourite dish among voluptuaries and epicures.

CRIPPLE. A crooked or bent sixpence.

CRISPIN. A shoemaker; from a romance, wherein a prince of that name is said to have exercised the art and mystery of a shoemaker, thence called the gentle craft: or, rather, from the saints Crispinus and Crispianus, who, according to the legend, were brethren born at Rome, from whence they travelled to Soissons, in France, about the year 303, to propagate the Christian religion; but, because they would not be chargeable to others for their maintenance, they exercised the trade of shoemakers: the governor of the town, discovering them to be Christians, ordered them to be beheaded, about the same year; from which time they have been the tutelar saints of the shoemakers.

CRISPIN'S HOLIDAY. Every Monday throughout the year, but most particularly the 25th of October, being the anniversary of Crispinus and Crispianus.

Crispin's Lance. An awl.

Croak. To die. *Cant.*

Croaked. Hanged. A flash term among keepers of prisons, who, speaking of a thief that was executed, observe, "He was *croaked*."

Croaker. One who is always foretelling some accident or misfortune: an allusion to the croaking of a raven, supposed ominous.

Croakumshire. Northumberland; from the particular croaking in the pronunciation of the people of that county, especially about Newcastle and Morpeth, where they are said to be born with a burr in their throats, which prevents their pronouncing the letter *r*.

Croakers. Forestallers, called also Kidders and Tranters.

Crocodiles' Tears. The tears of a hypocrite. Crocodiles are fabulously reported to shed tears over their prey before they devour it.

Croker. A groat, or four-pence.

Crone. An old ewe whose teeth are worn out; figuratively, a toothless old beldam.

Crony. An intimate companion, a comrade; also, a confederate in a robbery.

Crook. Sixpence.

Crook Back. Sixpence; for the reason of this name, *see* Cripple.

Crook Shanks. A nick name for a man with bandy legs. He buys his boots in Crooked-lane, and his stockings in Bandy-legged Walk; his legs grew in the night, therefore they could not see to grow straight: jeering sayings of men with crooked legs.

Crook your Elbow. To crook one's elbow, and wish it may never come straight, if the fact then affirmed is not true; according to the casuists of Bow-street and St. Giles's, it adds great weight and efficacy to an oath.

Crop. A nick name for a Presbyterian: from their cropping their hair, which they trimmed close to a bowl-dish, placed as a guide on their heads; whence they were likewise called roundheads. *See* Roundheads.

Crop. To be knocked down for a crop; to be condemned to be hanged. Cropped, hanged.

Croppen. The tail. The croppen of the rotan; the tail of the cart. Croppen ken: the necessary house. *Cant.*

Cropping Drums. Drummers of the foot guards, or Chelsea-hospital, who find out weddings, and beat a point of war to serenade the new married couple, and thereby obtain money.

Cropsick. Sickness in the stomach, arising from drunkenness.

Cross. To come home by Weeping-cross; to repent at the conclusion.

Cross. To cheat. To throw a match over, either in horse-racing, or in a prize battle, or any article which has been improperly obtained, is said to have been got upon the *cross*. *Cant.*

Cross Bite. One who combines with a sharper to draw in a friend; also, to counteract or disappoint. *Cant.* This is peculiarly used to signify entrapping a man so as to obtain *crim. con.* money, in which the wife, real or supposed, conspires with the husband.

Cross Buttock. A particular lock or fall in the Broughtonian art, which, as Mr. Fielding observed, conveyed more pleasant sensations to the spectators than the patient.

Cross-cove, or Cross-molisher. A man and woman who live upon the cross. *Cant.*

Cross-crib. A house kept by *family people*. *Cant.*

Cross-fam. To pick a pocket, by crossing your arms in a particular position. *Cant.*

Cross Patch. A peevish boy or girl, or rather an unsocial ill-tempered man or woman.

Crow. To brag, boats, or triumph. To crow over any one; to keep him in subjection: an image drawn from a cock, who crows over a vanquished enemy. To pluck a crow; to reprove any one for a fault committed, to settle a dispute. To strut like a crow in a gutter; to walk proudly, or with an air of consequence.

Crowd. A fiddle: probably from *crooth*, the Welch name for that instrument.

Crowdero. A fiddler.

Crowdy. Oatmeal and water, or milk; a mess much eaten in the north.

Crow Fair. A visitation of the clergy. *See* Review of the Black Cuirassiers.

Crown Office. The head. I fired into her keel upwards; my eyes and limbs, Jack, the crown office was full; a woman with her head downwards. *Sea-phrase.*

Cruisers. Beggars, or highway spies, who traverse the road to give intelligence of a booty; also, rogues ready to snap up any booty that may offer, like privateers or pirates on a cruise.

Crummy. Fat, fleshy. A fine crummy dame; a fat woman. He has picked up his crumbs finely of late; he has grown very fat, or rich, of late.

Crump. One who helps solicitors to affidavit men, or false witnesses. 'I wish you had, Mrs. Crump;' a Gloucestershire saying, in answer to a wish for any thing; implying, you must not expect any assistance from the speaker. It is said to have originated from the following incident: One Mrs. Crump, the wife of a substantial farmer, dining with the old Lady Coventry, who was extremely deaf, said to one of the footmen, waiting at table, 'I wish I had a draught of small beer,' her modesty not permitting her to desire so fine a gentleman to bring it: the fellow, conscious that his mistress could not hear either the request or answer, replied, without moving, 'I wish you had, Mrs. Crump.' These wishes being again repeated by both parties, Mrs. Crump got up from the table to fetch it herself; and being asked by my lady where she was going, related what had passed. The story being told abroad, the expression became proverbial.

CRUSTY BEAU. One that uses paint and cosmetics, to obtain a fine complexion.

CRUSTY FELLOW. A surly fellow.

CUB. An unlicked cub; an unformed, ill-educated, young man; a young nobleman or gentleman on his travels: an allusion to the story of the bear, said to bring its cub into form by licking. Also, a new gamester.

CUCKOLD. The husband of an incontinent wife: cuckolds, however, are Christians, as we learn by the following story: An old woman hearing a man call his dog Cuckold, reproved him sharply, saying, 'Sirrah, are not you ashamed to call a dog by a Christian's name?' To cuckold the parson; to go to bed with one's wife before she has been churched.

CUCUMBERS. Tailors, who are jocularly said to subsist, during the summer, chiefly on cucumbers.

CUDDIE. A Jack-ass. *Sea cant.*

CUFF. An old cuff; an old man. To cuff Jonas; said of one who is knocked-kneed, or who beats his sides to keep himself warm in frosty weather; called, also, Beating the Booby.

CUFFIN. A man.

CULL. A man, honest or otherwise. A bob cull; a good-natured, quiet fellow. *Cant.*

CULLABILITY. A disposition liable to be cheated, an unsuspecting nature, open to imposition.

CULLY. A fop or fool: also, a dupe to women: from the Italian word *coglione*, a blockhead.

CULP. A kick or blow: from the words *mea culpa*, being that part of the popish liturgy at which the people beat their breasts; or, as the vulgar term is, thump their craws.

CUNNING MAN. A cheat, who pretends by his skill in astrology to assist persons in recovering stolen goods; and, also, to tell them their fortunes, and when, how often, and to whom, they shall be married; likewise answers all lawful questions, both by sea and land. This profession is frequently occupied by ladies.

CUNNING SHAVER. A sharp fellow, one that trims close, i. e. cheats ingeniously.

CUNNY-THUMBED. To double one's fist with the thumb inwards, like a woman.

CUPBOARD LOVE. Pretended love to the cook, or any other person, for the sake of a meal. My guts cry cupboard; i. e. I am hungry.

CUPID, BLIND CUPID. A jeering name for an ugly blind man: Cupid, the god of love, being frequently painted blind. *See* BLIND CUPID.

CUP OF THE CREATURE. A cup of good liquor.

CUP-SHOT. Drunk.

CUR. A cut or curtailed dog. According to the forest-laws, a man who had no right to the privilege of the chase, was obliged to cut or law his dog: among other modes of disabling him from disturbing the game, one was by depriving him of his tail: a dog so cut was called a cut or curtailed dog, and by contraction a cur. A cur is figuratively used to signify a surly fellow.

CURBING LAW. The act of hooking goods out of windows: the curber is the thief, the curb the hook. *Cant.*

CURLE. Clippings of money, which curls up in the operation. *Cant.*

CURMUDGEON. A covetous old fellow, derived, according to some, from the French term *cœur mechant.*

CURRY. To curry favour; to obtain the favour of a person by coaxing or servility. To curry any one's hide; to beat him.

CURSE OF SCOTLAND. The nine of diamonds. Diamonds, it is said, imply royalty, being ornaments to the imperial crown; and every ninth king of Scotland has been observed, for many ages, to be a tyrant and a curse to that country. Others say it is from its similarity to the arms of Argyle; the Duke of Argyle having been very instrumental in bringing about the union, which, by some Scotch patriots, has been considered as detrimental to their country.

CURSE OF GOD. A cockade.

CURSITORS. Broken petty-fogging attornies, or Newgate solicitors. *Cant.*

CURTAILS. Thieves who cut off pieces of stuff hanging out of shop windows, the tails of women's gowns, &c.; also, thieves wearing short jackets.

CURTAIN LECTURE. A woman who scolds her husband when in bed, is said to read him a curtain lecture.

CUSHION. He has deserved the cushion; a saying of one

whose wife is brought to bed of a boy: implying, that, having done his business effectually, he may now indulge or repose himself.

CUSTOM-HOUSE GOODS. The stock in trade of a prostitute, because fairly entered.

CUT. Drunk. A little cut over the head; slightly intoxicated. To cut; to leave a person or company. To cut up well; to die rich.

CUT. (*Cambridge.*) To renounce acquaintance with any one is to *cut* him. There are several species of the CUT. Such as the cut direct, the cut indirect, the cut sublime, the cut infernal, &c. The cut direct is to start across the street, at the approach of the obnoxious person, in order to avoid him. The cut indirect is to look another way, and pass without appearing to observe him. The cut sublime is to admire the top of King's College Chapel, or the beauty of the passing clouds, till he is out of sight. The cut infernal is to analyze the arrangement of your shoe-strings, for the same purpose.

CUT BENE. To speak gently. To cut bene whiddes; to give good words. To cut queer whiddes; to give foul language. To cut a bosh, or a flash; to make a figure. *Cant.*

CUT ONE'S STICK. To be off. *Cant.*

CUTTING GLOAK. A man famous for drawing a knife, and cutting any person he quarrels with.

CUTTY-EYED. To look out of the corners of one's eyes, to leer, to look askance. The cull cutty-eyed at us; the fellow looked suspicious at us.

D

DAB. An adept; a dab at any feat or exercise. Dab, quoth Dawkins, when he hit his wife on the a--se with a pound of butter. It also signifies a bed.

DAB IT UP. To *dab it up* with a woman, is to agree to cohabit with her; also, to run a score at a public-house.

DACE, or DUCE. Two pence. Tip me a dace; lend me two pence. *Cant.*

DADDLES. Hands. Tip us your daddle; give me your hand. *Cant.*

DADDY. Father. Old daddy; a familiar address to an old man. To beat daddy mammy; the first rudiments of drum beating, being the elements of the roll.

DAD'S WILL. Parental authority. *Oxf. Univ. Cant.*

DAFFY. Vulgarly called GIN: but it has numerous other names. For instance, the *squeamish* fair one, who takes it on the *sly*, merely to cure the *vapours*, politely names it to her friends, as "*white wine.*" The *swell* chaffs it as "*blue ruin*" to elevate his notions. The *laundress* loves dearly a *drain* of "*Ould Tom,*" from its strength to *comfort* her inside. The *drag fiddler* can toss off a quartern of "*max*" without making a *wry* mug. The *coster monger* illumines his ideas with a "*flash of lightning!*" The *hoarse Cyprian* owes her existence to copious draughts of "*Jackey.*" The *link boy*, and *mud lark*, in joining their *browns* together, are for some "*stark naked.*" And the *out and outers*, by the addition of *bitters* to it, in order to sharpen up a dissipated and damaged *victualling office*, cannot take any thing but "*Fuller's earth!*" *Picture of the Fancy.*

DAFFY CLUB. This original Society was founded by Mr. JAMES SOARES, at the Castle-tavern, Holborn, and who is the perpetual president of it. The sporting world is its *hobby;* and, respecting original anecdotes of the turf; the incidents of the prize-ring, and promoting scientific pugilism; the merits of the swift pedestrians of the day; a knowledge of the first-rate TROTTERS; an acquaintance with the best *shots;* good cockers; great cricketers; distinguished anglers; and thorough bred cattle, dogs, &c. most of the members of the club can prize themselves not deficient riders, whenever necessity requires them to mount. It is also conspicuous for its *accommodation* to *story* tellers. The spirituous liquor drank by the club is DAFFY, (i. e. *gin,*) but in small quantities: as, the *third* of a quartern is the allowance for each member, at one time. It has obtained much notoriety from its good *chaunting*, every Friday night, during the season. *Ibid.*

DAGGERS. They are at daggers drawing; i. e. at enmity, ready to fight.

DAIRY. A woman's breasts, particularly one who gives suck. She sported her dairy; she pulled out her breast.

DAISY CUTTER. A jockey term for a horse that does not lift up his legs sufficiently, or goes too near the ground, and is therefore apt to stumble.

DAISY. A sea term applied to dock-mates.

DAM. A small Indian coin, mentioned in the Gentoo code of laws: hence etymologists may, if they please, derive the common expression, I do not care a dam, i. e. I do not care half a farthing for it.

DAMBER. A rascal. *See* DIMBER.

DAMNED SOUL. A clerk in a counting-house, whose sole business it is to clear or swear off merchandize at the custom-house; and who, it is said, guards against the crime of perjury, by taking a previous oath, never to swear truly on those occasions.

DAMPER. A luncheon, or snap before dinner; so called

from its damping, or allaying, the appetite; eating and drinking being, as the proverb wisely observes, apt to take away the appetite.

DANCE UPON NOTHING. To be hanged.

DANCERS. Stairs.

DANDY. That's the dandy; i. e. the ton, the clever thing; an expression of similar import to "That's the barber."

DANDY. In 1820, a fashionable non-descript. Men who wore *stays* to give them a fine shape, and were more than ridiculous in their apparel.

> Now a DANDY's a thing, describe him who can?
> That is very much made in the shape of a man;
> But if for but once could the fashion prevail,
> He'd be more like an APE if he had but a tail.
>
> I'm sure with the DANDIES we well may dispense,
> As neither possessing wit, learning, nor sense;
> And if in such follies they still will persist,
> Throw them all in the *Thames*, and they'll never be miss'd.

DANDY GREY RUSSET. A dirty brown. His coat's dandy grey russet, the colour of the devil's nutting-bag.

DANDY PRAT. An insignificant or trifling fellow.

DANGLE. To follow a woman without asking the question. Also, to be hanged: I shall see you dangle in the sheriff's picture-frame; I shall see you hanging on the gallows.

DANGLER. One who follows women in general, without any particular attachment.

DANNA. Human, or other excrement. *Cant.*

DAPPER FELLOW. A smart, well-made, little man.

DARBIES. Fetters. *Cant.*

DARBY. Ready money. *Cant.*

DARK CULLY. A married man that keeps a mistress, whom he visits only at night, for fear of discovery.

DARKEE. A dark lanthorn used by housebreakers. Stow the darkee, and bolt, the cove of the crib is fly; hide the dark lanthorn, and run away, the master of the house knows that we are here.

DARKMANS. The night. *Cant.*

DARKMAN'S BUDGE. One that slides into a house in the dark of the evening, and hides himself, in order to let some of the gang in at night to rob it.

DART. A straight-armed blow in boxing.

DASH. A tavern drawer. To cut a dash: to make a figure.

DAVID JONES. The Devil, the spirit of the sea: called Neckon in the north countries, such as Norway, Denmark, and Sweden.

DAVID JONES'S LOCKER. The sea.

DAVID'S SOW. As drunk as David's sow; a common saying, which took its rise from the following circumstance: One David Lloyd, a Welchman, who kept an alehouse at Hereford, had a living sow with six legs, which was greatly resorted to by the curious; he had also a wife much addicted to drunkenness, for which he used sometimes to give her due correction. One day, David's wife having taken a cup too much, and being fearful of the consequences, turned out the sow, and lay down to sleep herself sober in the stye. A company coming in to see the sow, David ushered them into the stye, exclaiming, 'there is a sow for you! did any of you ever see such another?' all the while supposing the sow had really been there; to which some of the company, seeing the state the woman was in, replied, it was the drunkenest sow they had ever beheld; whence the woman was ever after called David's sow.

DAVY. I'll take my davy of it; vulgar abbreviation of affidavit.

DAWB. To bribe. The cull was scragged because he could not dawb; the rogue was hanged because he could not bribe. All bedawbed with lace; all over lace.

DAY LIGHTS. Eyes. To darken his day-lights, or sow up his sees; to close up a man's eyes in boxing.

DEAD CARGO. A term used by thieves, when they are disappointed in the value of their booty.

DEAD HORSE. To work for the dead horse; to work for wages already paid.

DEAD-LOUSE. Vulgar pronunciation of the Dedalus ship of war.

DEAD MEN. A cant word among journeyman bakers, for loaves falsely charged to their masters' customers; also, empty bottles. To be found, also, in that classic volume, Crib's Memorial.

DEADLY NEVERGREEN, that bears fruit all the year round. The gallows, or three-legged mare. *See* THREE-LEGGED MARE.

DEADY. One of the multitudinous epithets applied to gin; used by the poets of the *Holy Land* in many instances, as

> "Grows your hand more firm and steady,
> In handing out the cheering *Deady*?"
>
> *Epistle to Randall, vide Randall's Diary.*

> "Taught by thee, we've quaff'd the *Deady's* stream
> At Belcher's or at Randall's seat of strife."
>
> *Lines to Caleb Baldwin, Ibid.*

Speaking of pleasure, the bard says,

> "I've sought her face on *Moulsey's* ground,
> Her aërial form in *Deady's gin*."
>
> *Vide Randall's Scrap Book.*

DEATH HUNTER. An undertaker; one who furnishes the necessary articles for funerals. See CARRION HUNTER.

DEATH'S HEAD UPON A MOP-STICK. A poor, miserable, emaciated fellow; one quite an otomy. See OTOMY. He looked as pleasant as the pains of death.

DECKER. A thief kept in pay by a trap. *Scotch cant.*

DEEP-ONE. A thorough-paced rogue, a sly designing fellow: in opposition to a shallow or foolish one.

DEGEN, or DAGEN. A sword. Nim the degen; steal the sword. Degen is Dutch for a sword. *Cant.*

DELLS. Young buxom wenches ripe for enjoyment, but who have not lost their virginity, which the *upright man* claims by virtue of his prerogative; after which they become free for any of the fraternity. Also, a common strumpet. *Cant.*

DEMAND THE BOX. Call for a bottle. *Sea term*

DEMURE. As demure as an old whore at a christening.

DEMY-REP. An abbreviation of demy-reputation; a woman of doubtful character.

DERBY. To come down with the derbies; to pay the money.

DERRICK. The name of the finisher of the law, or hangman, about the year 1608.—'For he rides his circuit with the Devil, and Derrick must be his host, and Tiburne the inne at which he will lighte.' *Vide* Bellman of London, in art. PRIGGIN LAW.—'At the gallows, where I leave them, as to the haven at which they must all cast anchor, if Derrick's cables do but hold.' *Ibid.*

DEVIL. A printer's errand-boy. Also, a small thread in the king's ropes and cables, whereby they may be distinguished from all others. The Devil himself; a small streak of blue thread in the king's sails. The Devil may dance in his pocket; i.e. he has no money; the cross on our ancient coins being jocularly supposed to prevent him from visiting that place, for fear, as it is said, of breaking his shins against it. To hold a candle to the Devil; to be civil to any one out of fear: in allusion to the story of the old woman who set a wax taper before the image of St. Michael, and another before the Devil, whom that saint is commonly represented as trampling under his feet: being reproved for paying such honour to Satan, she answered, as it was uncertain which place she should go to, heaven or hell, she chose to secure a friend in both places. That will be when the Devil is blind, and he has not got sore eyes yet; said of any thing unlikely to happen. It rains while the sun shines; the Devil is beating his wife with a shoulder of mutton: this phenomenon is also said to denote that cuckolds are going to heaven; on being informed of this, a loving wife cried out, with great vehemence, 'Run, husband, run!'

> The Devil was sick, the Devil a monk would be;
> The Devil was well, the Devil a monk was be;

a proverb signifying that we are apt to forget promises made in time of distress. To pull the Devil by the tail; to be reduced to one's shifts. The Devil go with you and sixpence, and then you will have both money and company.

DEVIL. The gizzard of a turkey or fowl, scored, peppered, salted, and broiled: it derives its appellation from being hot in the mouth.

DEVIL CATCHER, or DEVIL DRIVER. A parson. *See* SNUB DEVIL.

DEVIL DRAWER. A miserable painter.

DEVILISH. Very: an epithet which, in the English vulgar language, is made to agree with every quality or thing; as, devilish bad, devilish good; devilish sick, devilish well; devilish sweet, devilish sour; devilish hot, devilish cold; &c. &c.

DEVIL'S BOOKS. Cards.

DEVIL'S DAUGHTER. It is said of one who has a termagant for his wife, that he has married the Devil's daughter, and lives with the old folks.

DEVIL'S DAUGHTER'S PORTION:

> Deal, Dover, and Harwich,
> The Devil gave with his daughter in marriage;
> And, by a codicil to his will,
> He added Helvoet and the Brill.

a saying occasioned by the shameful impositions practised by the inhabitants of those places on sailors and travellers.

DEVIL'S DUNG. Asafœtida.

DEVIL'S GUTS. A surveyor's chain: so called by farmers, who do not like their land should be measured by their landlords.

DEW BEATERS. Feet. *Cant.*

> "Long may you stand on your *dew-beaters* well."
> *Vide Randall's Scrap Book.*

DEWS WINS, or DEUX WINS. Two pence. *Cant.*

DIAL PLATE. The face. To alter his dial plate; to disfigure his face.

DICE. The names of false dice:
A bale of bard cinque deuces.
A bale of flat cinque deuces.
A bale of flat sice aces.
A bale of bard cater traes.

A bale of flat cater traas.
A bale of fulhams.
A bale of light graniers.
A bale of langrets contrary to the ventage.
A bale of gordes, with as many highmen as lowmen, for passage.
A bale of demies.
A bale of long dice for even and odd.
A bale of bristles.
A bale of direct contraries.

DICK. That happened in the reign of queen Dick, i. e. never: said of any absurd old story. I am as queer as Dick's hatband; that is, out of spirits, or don't know what ails me.

DICKED IN THE NOB. Silly. Crazed.

DICKEY. A sham shirt.

DICKEY. An ass. Roll your dickey; drive your ass. Also, a seat for servants to sit in behind a carriage, when their masters drive.

DICKY. A woman's under petticoat. It's all Dicky with him; i. e. it's all over with him.

DIDDEYS. A woman's breasts or bubbies.

DIDDLE. To cheat. To defraud. The cull diddled me out of my dearee; the fellow robbed me of my sweetheart.

DIDDLE. Gin.

DIDDLER. A fellow who lives by his impudence and address; a character that knows how to *gammon* the flats; and even to puzzle the *knowing ones*.

DIE HARD, or GAME. To die hard, is to show no signs of fear or contrition at the gallows; not to whiddle or squeak. This advice is frequently given to felons going to suffer the law, by their old comrades, anxious for the honour of the gang.

DIGGERS. Spurs. *Cant.*

DIGS. Hard blows. *Cant.*

DILDO. [From the Italian *diletto*, q. d. a woman's delight; or from our word, *dally*, q. d. a thing to play withal.] Penissuccadaneus, called, in Lombardy, Passo Tempo. *Bailey.*

DILIGENT. Double diligent; like the Devil's apothecary; said of one affectedly diligent.

DILLY. [An abbreviation of the word *diligence*.] A public voiture or stage, commonly a post-chaise, carrying three persons; the name is taken from the public stage vehicles in France and Flanders. The dillies first began to run in England about the year 1779.

DIMBER. Pretty. A dimber cove; a pretty fellow. Dimber mort; a pretty wench. *Cant.*

F

Dimber Damber. A top man, or prince, among the canting crew; also, the chief rogue of the gang, or the completest cheat. *Cant.*

Dimmock. Money. *Cant.*

Ding. To knock down. To ding it in one's ears; to reproach or tell one something one is not desirous of hearing: also, to throw away: particularly any article you have stolen, either because it is worthless, or that there is danger of immediate apprehension. To *ding* a person, is to drop his acquaintance totally; also, to quit his company, or leave him for the time present; to *ding* to your *pal*, is to convey to him, privately, the property you have just stolen; and he who receives it is said to *take ding*, or to *knap the ding*.

Dingable. Any thing considered worthless, or which you can well spare, having no further occasion for it, is declared to be *dingable*. This phrase is often applied by *sharps* to a *flat* whom they have *cleaned out*; and by abandoned women to a keeper, who, having spent his all upon them, must be discarded, or *dinged* as soon as possible.

Ding Boy. A rogue, a hector, a bully, or sharper. *Cant.*

Ding Dong. Helter skelter, in a hasty, disorderly, manner.

Dingey Christian. A mulatto; or any one who has, as the West-Indian term is, a lick of the tar-brush, that is, some negro blood in him.

Dining-Room-Post. A mode of stealing in houses that let lodgings, by rogues pretending to be postmen, who send up sham letters to the lodgers, and, whilst waiting in the entry for the postage, go into the first room they see open, and rob it.

Dip. To dip for a wig. Formerly, in Middle-row, Holborn, wigs of different sorts were, it is said, put into a close-stool box, into which, for three-pence, any one might dip, or thrust in his hand, and take out the first wig he laid hold of; if he was dissatisfied with his prize, he might, on paying three halfpence, return it and dip again. A punning name for a tallow-chandler.

Dippers. Anabaptists.

Dipt. Pawned or mortgaged.

Dishclout. A dirty greasy woman. He has made a napkin of his dishclout; a saying of one who has married his cook-maid. To pin a dishclout to a man's tail; a punishment often threatened by the female servants in a kitchen, to a man who pries too minutely into the secrets of that place.

Dished up. He is completely dished up; he is totally ruined. To throw a thing in one's dish; to reproach or twit one with any particular matter.

DISMAL DITTY. The psalm sung by the felons at the gallows, just before they are turned off.

DISPATCHERS. False dice used by gamblers, so contrived as always to throw a *nick*.

DISPATCHES. A mittimus, or justice of the peace's warrant, for the commitment of a rogue.

DISTRACTED DIVISION. Husband and wife fighting.

DISTRESSED. In boxing, when a man is *distressed*, he is *out*

DITTO. A suit of ditto; coat, waistcoat, and breeches, all of one colour.

of wind, and nearly exhausted from his exertions. It, also, shows bad condition.

DIVE. To dive; to pick a pocket. To dive for a dinner; to go down into a cellar to dinner. A dive, is a thief who stands ready to receive goods thrown out to him by a little boy put in at a window. *Cant.*

DIVER. A pickpocket: also, one who lives in a cellar.

DIVIDE. To divide the house with one's wife; to give her the outside, and to keep all the inside to one's self, i. e. to turn her into the street.

DO. To do any one; to rob and cheat him. I have done him; I have robbed him. It is a term used by *smashers; to do a queer half-quid*, or *a queer screen*, is to utter a counterfeit half-guinea, or a forged bank-note: also, to overcome in a boxing-match: witness those laconic lines written on the field of battle, by Humphries to his patron.—' *Sir, I have done the Jew.*' It is absolutely criminal to omit any thing so exquisite as this in the Elegant Epistles.

DOBIN RIG. Stealing ribands from haberdashers early in the morning or late at night; generally practised by women in the disguise of maid servants.

DOCK. To lie with a woman. The cull docked the dell all the darkmans; the fellow laid with the wench all night. Docked smack smooth; one who has suffered an amputation of his penis from a venereal complaint. He must go into dock; a sea phrase, signifying that the person spoken of must undergo a salivation. Docking is also a punishment inflicted by sailors on the prostitutes who have infected them with the venereal disease; it consists in cutting off all their clothes, petticoats, shift and all, close to their stays, and then turning them into the street.

DOCK-SHANKERS. Dock-mates. *Sea term.*

DOCTOR. Milk and water, with a little rum, and some nutmeg; also, the name of a composition used by distillers, to make spirits appear stronger than they really are, or, in their phrase, better proof.

DOCTORS. Loaded dice, that will run but two or three

chances. They put the doctors upon him; they cheated him with loaded dice.

DOBSEY. A woman: perhaps a corruption of Doxey. *Cant.*

DOG. An old dog at it; expert or accustomed to any thing. Dog in a manger; one who would prevent another from enjoying what he himself does not want: an allusion to the well-known fable. The dogs have not dined; a common saying to any one whose shirt hangs out behind. To dog, or dodge; to follow at a distance. To blush like a blue dog, i. e. not at all. To walk the black dog on any one; a punishment inflicted in the night on a fresh prisoner, by his comrades, in case of his refusal to pay the usual footing or garnish.

DOG BUFFERS. Dog stealers, who kill those dogs not advertised for, sell their skins, and feed the remaining dogs with their flesh.

DOGGED. Surly.

DOGGESS, DOG'S WIFE or LADY, PUPPY'S MAMMA. Jocular ways of calling a woman a bitch.

DOG IN A DOUBLET. A daring, resolute fellow. In Germany and Flanders the boldest dogs used to hunt the boar, having a kind of buff doublet buttoned on their bodies. Rubens has represented several so equipped, so has Sneyders.

DOG LATIN. Barbarous Latin, such as was formerly used by the lawyers in their pleadings.

DOG'S PORTION. A lick and a smell. He comes in for only a dog's portion; a saying of one who is a distant admirer or dangler after women. *See* DANGLER.

DOG'S RIG. To copulate till you are tired, and then turn tail to it.

DOG'S SOUP. Rain water.

DOG VANE. A cockade. *Sea term.*

DO IT AWAY. To *fence* or dispose of a stolen article beyond the reach of probable detection.

DO IT UP. To accomplish any object you have in view; to obtain any thing you are in quest of, is called *doing it up for* such a thing; a person who contrives by *nob-work*, or ingenuity, to live an easy life, and appears to improve daily in circumstances, is said *to do it up in good twig.*

DOLL. Bartholomew doll; a tawdry, over-drest woman, like one of the *children's* dolls at Bartholomew-fair. To mill doll; to beat hemp at Bridewell, or any other house of correction.

DOLLOP. *A dollop* is a large quantity of any thing; *the whole dollop* means the total quantity.

DOLLY. A Yorkshire dolly; a contrivance for washing, by

means of a kind of wheel fixed in a tub, which, being turned about, agitates and cleanses the linen put into it, with soap and water.

Domine do little. An impotent old fellow.

Dominee. A parson. *Cant.*

Domineer. To reprove or command in an insolent or haughty manner. Don't think as how you shall domineer here.

Domino Box (To open the). To open the mouth. *Cant.*

Done, or Done over. Robbed: also, convicted or hanged. *Cant.* As, he was *done for a crack;* he was convicted of house-breaking.

Don Peninsula. The range of all who bear long hanging sleeves, and the name of Domini. *Oxf. Univ. Cant.*

Done up. Ruined by gaming and extravagance. *Modern term.*

Donkey, Donkey Dick. A he, or jack-ass: called donkey, perhaps, from the Spanish or don-like gravity of that animal: entitled, also, the king of Spain's trumpeter.

Doodle. A silly fellow, or noodle. *See* Noodle. Also, a child's penis. Doodle doo, or, Cock a doodle doo, a childish appellation for a cock, in imitation of its note when crowing.

Doodle Sack. A bagpipe. *Dutch.*

Do over. Carries the same meaning as Do, but is not so briefly expressed; the former having received the polish of the present times.

Dopey. A beggar's trull.

Dorse. A snoozing ken: to dorse with a woman, signifies to sleep with her. *Cant.*

Dot. A ribbon. *Sea cant.*

Dot and go one. To waddle: generally applied to persons who have one leg shorter than the other; and who, as the sea phrase is, go upon an uneven keel: also, a jeering appellation for an inferior writing-master, or teacher of arithmetic.

Dot-drag. A watch-ribbon. *Sea cant.*

Do the trick. To accomplish any robbery, or other business successfully; a thief who has been fortunate enough to acquire an independence, and prudent enough to *tie it up* in time, is said by his former associates to have *done the trick;* on the other hand, a man who has imprudently involved himself in some great misfortune, from which there is little hope of extrication, is declared by his friends, with an air of commiseration, to have *done the trick* for himself; that is, his ruin or downfall is nearly certain.

Double. To tip any one the double; to run away in his or her debt.

Double. To *double* a person, or *tip* him the *Dublin packet,* signifies either to run away from him openly, and elude his attempts to overtake you, or to give him the slip in the streets, or elsewhere, unperceived, commonly done to escape from an officer who has you in custody, or to *turn up a flat* of any kind, whom you have a wish to get rid of.

DOUBLE JUGG. A man's backside. *Cotton's Virgil.*

DOUBLE SLANGS. Double irons. *Cant.*

DOUGLAS. Roby Douglas, with one eye and a stinking breath; the breech. *Sea wit.*

DOVE-TAIL. A species of regular answer, which fits into the subject, like the contrivance whence it takes its name: *ex.* Who owns this? The dove-tail is, Not you by your asking.

DOWDY. A coarse, vulgar-looking woman.

DOWN. Aware of a thing. Knowing it. There is *no down.* A cant phrase used by house-breakers to signify that the persons belonging to any house are not on their guard, or that they are fast asleep, and have not heard any noise to alarm them.

DOWN. Sometimes synonymous with *awake*, as, when the party you are about to rob sees or suspects your intention, it is then said that *the cove is down.* A *down* is a suspicion, alarm, or discovery, which, taking place, obliges yourself and *palls* to give up or desist from the business or depredation you were engaged in; to *put a down upon* a man, is to give information of any robbery or fraud he is about to perpetrate, so as to cause his failure or detection; to *drop down to* a person is to discover or be aware of his character or designs; to *put* a person *down to* any thing, is to apprise him of, elucidate, or explain, it to him; to *put a swell down*, signifies to alarm or put a gentleman on his guard when in the attempt to pick his pocket, you fail to effect it at once, and, by having touched him a little too roughly, you cause him to suspect your design, and to use precautions accordingly; or, perhaps, in the act of *sounding* him, by being too precipitate or incautious, his suspicions may have been excited, and it is then said that you have *put* him *down*, *put* him *fly*, or *spoiled* him. *See* SPOIL IT. To *drop down upon yourself*, is to become melancholy, or feel symptoms of remorse or compunction, on being committed to jail, cast for death, &c. To sink under misfortunes of any kind. A man who gives way to this weakness, is said to be *down upon himself.*

DOWN AS A HAMMER, DOWN AS A TRIPPET. These are merely emphatical phrases, used *out of flash*, to signify being *down*, *leary*, *fly*, or *awake*, *to* any matter, meaning, or design.

DOWN HILLS. Dice that run low.

DOWSE. To take down: as, Dowse the pendant. Dowse

your dog vane; take the cockade out of your hat. Dowse the glim; put out the candle.

DOWSE ON THE CHOPS. A blow in the face.

DOWSER. Vulgar pronunciation of *douceur*.

DOXIES. She beggars, wenches, whores.

DRAG. A cart. *The drag* is the *game* of robbing carts, waggons, or carriages, either in town or country, of trunks, bale-goods, or any other property. *Done* for *a drag*, signifies convicted for a robbery of the before-mentioned nature.

DRAG-COVE. The driver of a cart.

DRAGGLETAIL, or DAGGLETAIL. One whose garments are bespattered with dag or dew: generally applied to the female sex, to signify a slattern.

DRAG LAY. Waiting in the streets to rob carts or waggons.

DRAGSMAN. A thief who follows the *game* of *dragging*.

DRAIN. Gin: so called from the diuretic qualities imputed to that liquor.

DRAKED. A thief forced into a pond by a mob, as a summary mode of punishment, is termed being *draked*, or *ducked*. *Cant*.

DRAM. A glass or small measure of any spirituous liquors, which, being originally sold by apothecaries, were estimated by drams, ounces, &c. Dog's dram; to spit in his mouth, and clap his back.

DRAM-A-TICK. A dram served upon credit.

DRAP. A nasty sluttish whore.

DRAPER. An ale draper; an alehouse keeper.

DRAUGHT, or BILL, ON THE PUMP AT ALDGATE. A bad or false bill of exchange. *See* ALDGATE.

DRAW. Stealing from any person his pocket-book, or handkerchief, is termed, among the flash coves, *drawing him* of his *reader*, &c. also, to obtain money or goods of a man by a plausible story, is called *drawing him* of it.

DRAWERS. Stockings. *Cant*.

DRAWING THE CORK. To give a man a bloody nose: i.e. I have drawn his *cork*. *Pugilistic cant*.

DRAWING THE KING'S PICTURE. Coining. *Cant*.

DRAW LATCHES. Robbers of houses, the doors of which are only fastened with latches.

DRESS. To beat. I'll dress his hide neatly; I'll beat him soundly.

DRIBBLE. A method of pouring out, as it were, the dice from the box, gently, by which an old practitioner is enabled to cog one of them with his fore-finger.

DRIPPER. A gleet.

DRIZ. A card of lace, belonging to haberdashers. *Cant*.

DROMEDARY. A heavy, bungling thief or rogue. A purple dromedary; a bungler in the art and mystery of thieving. *Cant*.

DROMMERARS. See DOMMERER.

DROP. The new drop; a contrivance for executing felons at Newgate, by means of a platform, which drops from under them: this is, also, called the last drop. See LEAF and MORNING DROP.

DROP. The *game* of ring-dropping is called *the drop*.

DROP. To give or present a person with money; as, he *dropped* me a *quid*, he gave me a guinea. A *kid* who delivers his bundle to a sharper without hesitation, or a shopkeeper who is easily duped of his goods by means of a forged order or false pretence, is said to *drop the swag in good twig*, meaning, to part with it freely.

DROP A COG. To let fall, with design, a piece of gold or silver, in order to draw in and cheat the person who sees it picked up; the piece so dropped is called a dropt cog.

DROP A WHID. To let fall a word, either inadvertently or designedly.

DROP COVES. Persons who practise the fraud of dropping a ring or other article, and picking it up before the person intended to be defrauded, they pretend that the thing is very valuable to induce their gull to lend them money, or to purchase the article. See FAWNY RIG and MONEY DROPPERS.

DROP DOWN. To be dispirited. This expression is used by thieves to signify that their companion did not die game; as, the kiddy dropped down when he went to be twisted; the young fellow was very low spirited when he walked out to be hanged.

DROP IN THE EYE. Almost drunk.

DROP ONE'S LEAF. To die; very poetic, obviously allusive to the falling of the leaves in autumn.

DRUB. To beat any one with a stick, or rope's end: perhaps a contraction of *dry rub*. It is also used to signify a good beating with any instrument.

DRUMMER. A jockey term for a horse that throws about his fore-legs irregularly: the idea is taken from a kettle drummer, who, in beating, makes many flourishes with his drumsticks.

DRUMMOND. Any scheme or project considered to be infallible, or any event which is deemed inevitably certain, is declared to be a *Drummond;* meaning, it is as sure as the credit of that respectable banking-house, Drummond and Co.

DRUNK. Drunk as a wheel-barrow. Drunk as David's sow. See DAVID'S SOW.

DRURY-LANE AGUE. The venereal disorder.

DRURY-LANE VESTAL. A woman of the town, or prostitute; Drury-lane and its environs being the residence of many of those ladies.

Dry Bob. A smart repartee: also, copulation without emission; in law Latin, *siccus robertulus.*

Dry Boots. A sly humorous fellow.

Dub. A picklock, or master-key. *Cant.*

Dub at a Knapping-jigger. A turnpike-man. *Cant.*

Dubber. A picker of locks. *Cant.*

Dub Cove. A turnkey. *Cant.*

Dub Lay. Robbing houses by picking the locks.

Dub o' th' Hick. A lick on the head.

Dub the Jigger. Open the door. *Cant.*

Duce. Two-pence.

Duchess. A woman enjoyed with her pattens on, or by a man in boots, is said to be made a duchess.

Duck. A lame duck; an Exchange-alley phrase for a stock-jobber, who either cannot or will not pay his losses, or differences, in which case he is said to *waddle out of the Alley,* as he cannot appear there again till his debts are settled and paid; should he attempt it, he would be hustled out by the fraternity.

Duck Legs. Short legs.

Ducks and Drakes. To make ducks and drakes; a school-boy's amusement, practised with pieces of tile, oyster-shells, or flattish stones, which, being skimmed along the surface of a pond, or still river, rebound many times. To make ducks and drakes of one's money; to throw it idly away.

Dundering Rake. A thundering rake; a buck of the first head, one extremely lewd.

Dudders, or Whispering Dudders. Cheats who travel the country, pretending to sell smuggled goods: they accost their intended dupes in a whisper. The goods they have for sale are old shop-keepers, or damaged; purchased by them of large manufacturers. *See* **Duffer.**

Dudgeon. Anger.

Duds. Clothes.

Dues. This term is sometimes used to express money, where any certain sum or payment is spoken of; a man asking for money due to him for any service done, or a *blowen* requiring her previous compliment from a *family-man,* would say, Come, *tip us the dues.* So a thief, requiring his share of booty from his *palls,* will desire them to *bring the dues to light.*

Dues. This word is often introduced by the lovers of *flash* on many occasions, but merely *out of fancy,* and can only be understood from the context of their discourse; like many other cant terms, it is not easily explained on paper; for example, speaking of a man likely to go to jail, one will say, there will be *quodding dues concerned;* of a man likely to be executed, there will be *topping dues;* if any thing is alluded to that will require a fee or bribe, there must be *tipping dues*, or *palming dues concerned*, &c.

DUFFERS. Cheats who ply in different parts of the town, and pretend to deal in smuggled goods, stopping all country people, or such as they think they can impose on; which they frequently do, by selling them Spital-fields goods at double their current price.

DUGS. A woman's breasts.

DUKE HUMPHREY. To dine with Duke Humphrey; to fast. In old St. Paul's church was an aisle called Duke Humphrey's walk, (from a tomb vulgarly called his, but in reality belonging to John of Gaunt,) and persons who walked there, while others were at dinner, were said to dine with Duke Humphrey.

DUKE OF LIMBS. A tall, awkward, ill-made, fellow.

DUKE, or RUM DUKE. A queer unaccountable fellow.

DULL SWIFT. A stupid sluggish fellow, one long going on an errand.

DUMB ARM. A lame arm.

DUMB-FOUNDED. Silenced: also, soundly beaten.

DUMB GLUTTON. The monosyllable.

DUMB WATCH. A bubo in the groin.

DUMMEE. A pocket-book. A dummee-hunter; a pick-pocket, who lurks about to steal pocket-books out of gentlemen's pockets. Frisk the dummee of the screens; take all the bank-notes out of the pocket-book: ding the dummee, and bolt, they sing out beef; throw away the pocket-book, and run off, as they call out "stop thief."

DUMMIE. A wooden man. A fool.

DUMPLIN. A short thick man or woman. Norfolk dumplin; a jeering appellation of a Norfolk man, dumplins being a favourite kind of food in that county.

DUMPS. Down in the dumps; low-spirited, melancholy: jocularly said to be derived from Dumpos, a king of Egypt, who died of melancholy. Dumps are also small pieces of lead, cast by schoolboys in the shape of money.

DUN. An importunate creditor. Dunny, in the provincial dialect of several counties, signifies *deaf;* to dun, then, perhaps, may mean to deafen with importunate demands: some derive it from the word *donnez*, which signifies *give*. But the true original meaning of the word owes its birth to one Joe Dun, a famous bailiff of the town of Lincoln, so extremely active, and so dexterous in his business, that it became a proverb, when a man refused to pay, Why do not you *Dun* him? that is, Why do not you set Dun to arrest him? Hence it became a cant word, and is now as old as since the days of Henry VII. Dun was also the general name for the hangman, before that of Jack Ketch.

> "And presently a helter get,
> Made of the best strong hempen teer,
> And, ere a cat could lick her ear,
> Had tied it up with as much art
> As DUN himself could do for's heart."
>
> *Cotton's Virgil Trav. book iv.*

DUNAGAN. A privy. *Cant.*

DUNAGAN DRAG. A nightman's cart. *Cant.*

DUNAKER. A stealer of cows and calves.

DUNEGAN. A privy, a water-closet.

DUNGHILL. A coward: a cockpit phrase, all but gamecocks being stiled dunghills. To die dunghill; to repent or show any signs of contrition at the gallows. Moving dunghill; a dirty, filthy man or woman. Dung, an abbreviation of dunghill, also means a journeyman tailor who submits to the law for regulating journeymen tailors' wages, therefore deemed, by the flints, a coward. *See* FLINTS.

DUNNOCK. A cow. *Cant.*

DUN TERRITORY. Circle of creditory to be had. *Oxf. Univ. cant.*

DUP. To open a door, a contraction of *do ope* or *open*. *See* DUB.

DURHAM MAN. Knocker kneed, he grinds mustard with his knees: Durham is famous for its mustard.

DUST. Money. Down with your dust; deposit the money. To raise or kick up a dust, to make a disturbance or riot. *See* BREEZE. Dust it away; drink about.

DUSTMAN. To let the dustman get hold of you; to fall asleep. *Cant.*

DUTCH COMFORT. Thank God it is no worse.

DUTCH CONCERT. Where every one plays or sings a different tune.

DUTCH FEAST. Where the entertainer gets drunk before his guest.

DUTCH RECKONING, or ALLE-MAL. A verbal or lump account, without particulars, as brought at spunging-houses or Cyprian lodgings.

DYNASTY OF VENUS. Indiscriminate love and misguided affection. *Oxf. Univ. cant.*

E

EARNEST. A deposit, in part of payment, to bind a bargain.

EARTH BATH. A grave.

EAR-WIGGING. A snake in the grass; a fellow fond of telling tales about those persons he may be employed with. A whisperer.

Easy. Make the cull easy or quiet; gag or kill him. As easy as pissing the bed.

Easy Virtue. A lady of easy virtue, an impure, or prostitute.

Eat. To eat like a beggar man, and wag his under jaw; a jocular reproach to a proud man. To eat one's words; to retract what one has said.

Edge. To excite, stimulate, or provoke, or, as it is vulgarly called, to egg a man on. Fall back, fall edge, i. e. let what will happen. Some derive to egg on from the Latin word *age, age.*

Eight Eyes. I will knock out two of your eight eyes; a common Billingsgate threat from one fish nymph to another: every woman, according to the naturalists of that society, having eight eyes:—viz. two seeing eyes, two bub-eyes, a bell-eye, two pope's eyes, and a * * *-eye. He has fallen down; and trod upon his eye; said of one who has a black eye.

Elbow Grease. Labour. Elbow grease will make an oak table shine.

Elbow Room. Sufficient space to act in. Out at elbows; said of an estate that is mortgaged.

Elbow Scraper. A fiddler. *Sea term.*

Elbow Shaker. A gamester; one who rattles Saint Hugh's bones, i. e. the dice.

Elephant and Castle. In the slang language, this sign is denominated the Pig and Tinder-box.

Emperor. Drunk as an emperor; i. e. ten times as drunk as a lord.

Ensign Bearer. A drunken man, who looks red in the face, or hoists his colours in his drink.

Equipt. Rich; also, having new clothes. Well equipt; full of money, or well dressed. The cull equipped me with a brace of meggs; the gentleman furnished me with a couple of guineas.

Essex Lion. A calf, Essex being famous for calves, and chiefly supplying the London markets.

Essex Stile. A ditch. A great part of Essex is low marshy ground, in which there are more ditches than stiles.

Eternity Box. A coffin.

Eves. Hen-roosts.

Eve's Custom House, where Adam made his *first entry.* The monosyllable.

Eves Dropper. One that lurks about to rob hen-roosts; also, a listener at doors and windows, to hear private conversation.

Evil. A halter. *Cant.* Also, a wife, an admirable synonyme.

Ewe. A white ewe; a beautiful woman. An old ewe drest lamb fashion; an old woman drest like a young girl.

EXECUTION DAY. Washing day.

EXPENDED. Killed: alluding to the gunner's accounts, wherein the articles consumed are charged under the title of expended. *See phrase.*

EYE. It's all my eye and Betty Martin; it's all nonsense, all mere stuff.

EYE-SORE. A disagreeable object. It will be an eye-sore as long as she lives, said by a man whose wife was cut for a fistula in ano.

EYE-WATER. Gin. *Cant.*

F.

FACE-MAKING. Begetting children. To face it out; to persist in a falsity. No face but his own; a saying of one who has no money in his pocket, or no court-cards in his hand.

FACER. A bumper; a glass filled so full as to leave no room for the lip: also, a violent blow on the face.

FADGE. It won't fadge; it won't do. A farthing.

FAG. To beat. Fag the bloss; beat the wench. *Cant.* A fag also means a boy of an inferior form, or class, who acts as a servant to one of a superior, who is said to fag him; he is my fag:—whence, perhaps, fagged out, for jaded or tired. To stand a good fag; not to be soon tired.

FAGGER. A little boy put in at a window to rob a house.

FAGGOT. A man hired at a muster to appear as a soldier. To faggot, in the canting sense, means to bind: an allusion to the faggots made up by the woodmen, which are all bound. Faggot the culls; bind the men.

FAIR. A set of subterraneous rooms in the Fleet prison.

FAITHFUL. One of the faithful; a tailor who gives long credit. His faith hath made him unwhole; i. e. trusting too much broke him.

FAKE. A word so variously used, that we can only illustrate it by a few examples. To *fake* any person or place may signify to rob them; to *fake* a person may also imply to shoot, wound, or cut; to *fake* a man *out and out* is to kill him; a man who inflicts wounds upon, or otherwise disfigures, himself, for any sinister purpose, is said to have *faked himself*; if a man's shoe happens to pinch or gall his foot, from its being overtight, he will complain that his shoe *fakes* his foot sadly: it also describes the doing any act, or the fabricating any thing, as, to *fake* your *slangs* is to cut your irons in order to escape from custody; to *fake* your *pinnis* to create a sore leg, as if accidentally, with an axe, &c. in hopes to obtain a discharge from the army or navy, to get into the doctor's list, &c.; to *fake* a *screeve* is to write any letter or other paper; to *fake* a *screw* is to shape out a skeleton, or false key, for the purpose of *screwing* a particular place; to *fake* a *cly* is to pick a pocket, &c. &c. &c.

FAKE AWAY, THERE'S NO DOWN. An intimation from a thief to his *pall*, during the commission of a robbery or other act; meaning, go on with your operations, there is no sign of any alarm or detection.

FAKEMAN-CHARLEY, FAKEMENT. As *to fake* signifies to do any act, or make any thing, so *the fakement* means the act or thing alluded to, and on which your discourse turns; consequently, any stranger, unacquainted with your subject, will not comprehend what is meant by *the fakement:* for instance, having recently been concerned with another in some robbery, and immediately separated, the latter taking the booty with him, on your next meeting, you will inquire, what he has done with *the fakement?* meaning the article stolen, whether it was a pocket-book, piece of linen, or what not. Speaking of any stolen property, which has a private mark, one will say, there is a *fakeman-charley* on it; a forgery, which is well executed, is said to be a *prime fakement;* in a word, any thing is liable to be termed a *fakement*, or a *fakeman-charley*, provided the person you address knows to what you allude.

FAKEMENT. A counterfeit signature. A forgery. Tell the macers to mind their fakements; desire the swindlers to be careful not to forge another's signature.

FALLALLS. Ornaments, chiefly women's, such as ribands, necklaces, &c.

FAMGRASP. To shake hands: figuratively, to agree or make up a difference. Famgrasp the cove: shake hands with the fellow. *Cant.*

FAMILY. Thieves, and others who live upon *the cross*, are denominated "*the family*."

FAMILY MAN or WOMAN. Belonging to the family; i. e. he or she are *family people*.

FAMILY OF LOVE. Lewd women; also, a religious sect.

FAM LAY. Going into a goldsmith's shop, under pretence of buying a wedding-ring, and palming one or two, by daubing the hand with some viscous matter.

FAMS, or FAMBLES. Hands. Famble-cheats; rings or gloves. *Cant.*

FAN. To beat any one. I fanned him sweetly; I beat him heartily.

FANCIFUL FORMS OF BETTING. Various. *Ex. gr.* Chelsea

College to a sentry-box: Rhodes's farm to a milk-walk: Burlington-arcade to a smock-shop: Pompey's pillar to a stick of sealing-wax: Waterloo-bridge to a deal plank, &c.

FANCY. One of the FANCY means a sporting character, that is either attached to pigeons, dog-fighting, boxing, &c. also, any article universally admired for its beauty, or which the owner sets particular store by, is termed a *fancy article*. As a *fancy clout* is a favourite handkerchief, &c.; so, a woman, who is the particular favourite of any man, is termed his *fancy woman*, and *vice versâ*.

FANCY MAN. Or, in other words, a petticoat pensioner; a fellow kept by a prostitute. *Cant.*

FANCY PIECES. Women of pleasure, doxies, &c.

FANTASTICALLY DRESSED, with more rags than ribands.

FART. He has let a brewer's fart, grains and all, said of one who has bewrayed his breeches.

> "Piss and fart,
> Sound at heart.
> *Mingere cum bumbis,*
> *Res saluberrima est lumbis.*"

I dare not trust my a–se with a fart, said by a person troubled with a looseness.

FART CATCHER. A valet or footman, from his walking behind his master or mistress.

FARTING CRACKERS. Breeches.

FASTNER. A warrant.

FASTNESSES. Bogs.

FAT. All the fat is in the fire, that is, it is all over with us; a saying used in case of any miscarriage or disappointment in an undertaking: an allusion to overturning the frying-pan into the fire. Fat, among printers, means void spaces, a good job. A *fat* work, little to do and well paid for it.

FAT AS A HEN IN THE FOREHEAD. A saying of a meagre person.

FAT CULL. A rich fellow.

FAT HEADED. Stupid.

FAULKNER. A tumbler, juggler, or shower of tricks; perhaps, because they lure the people, as a falconer does his hawks. *Cant.*

FAWNEY. A ring.

FAWNEY RIG. A common fraud, thus practised:—a fellow drops a brass ring, double gilt, which he picks up before the party meant to be cheated, and to whom he disposes of it for less than its supposed, and ten times more than its real, value. *See* MONEY DROPPER.

FAYTORS, or FATORS. Fortune-tellers.

FEAGUE. To feague a horse; to put ginger up a horse's fundament, and, formerly, as it is said, a live eel, to make him lively, and carry his tail well. It is said, a forfeit is incurred by any horse-dealer's servant, who shall show a horse without first feaguing him. Feague is used, figuratively, for encouraging or spiriting one up.

FEAK. The fundament.

FEATHER-BED LANE. A rough or stony lane.

FEATHER ONE'S NEST. To enrich one's self.

FEEDER. A spoon. To nab the feeder; to steal a spoon.

FEET. To make feet for children's stockings, to beget children. An officer of feet; a jocular title for an officer of infantry.

FEINT. A sham attack on one part, when a real one is meant at another.

FELLOW COMMONER. An empty bottle; so called at the university of Cambridge, where fellow commoners are not, in general, considered as over full of learning. At Oxford, an empty bottle is called a gentleman commoner for the same reason. They pay at Cambridge £250 a year for the privilege of wearing a gold or silver tassel to their caps. The younger branches of the nobility have the privilege of wearing a hat, and from thence are denominated HAT FELLOW COMMONERS.

FEN. A bawd, or common prostitute. *Cant.*

FENCE. To pawn or sell to a receiver of stolen goods. The kiddey fenced his thimble for three quids; the young fellow pawned his watch for three guineas. To fence invariably means to pawn or sell goods to a receiver.

FENCING KEN. The magazine or warehouse where stolen goods are secreted.

FERME. A hole. *Cant.*

FERMERDY BEGGARS. All those who have not the sham sores, or clymes.

FERRARA. Andrea Ferrara, the name of a famous sword-cutler; most of the Highland broad-swords are marked with his name: whence an Andrea Ferrara has become the common name for the glaymore, or Highland broad-sword. *See* GLAYMORE.

FERRET. A tradesman who sells goods to young unthrift heirs, at excessive rates, and then continually duns them for the debt. To ferret, to search out or expel any one from his hiding-place, as a ferret drives out rabbits; also, to cheat. Ferret-eyed, red-eyed: ferrets have red eyes.

FETCH. A trick, wheedle, or invention to deceive.

FEUTERER. A dog-keeper; from the French *vautrier*, or *vaultrier*, one that leads a lime hound for the chase.

FIB. To beat. Fib the cove's quarron in the rumpad, for the lour in his bung; beat the fellow in the highway, for the money in his purse. *Cant.* A fib is also a tiny lie.

FIBBING. In bruising, signifies the getting an adversary's head under the arm and punching it. RANDALL is more celebrated for the dexterity with which he administers a *fibbing* than any in the prize-ring, either hand being equally effective, as in the case of West Country Dick, whom, after having *fibbed*, till he was tired, with the right hand, he flung on the right arm, holding him all the time *with his feet off the ground*, and rendered him, in a few seconds, a perfect spectacle. Indeed, whoever the opponent is that is unfortunate enough to have a fibbing administered by *the Nonpareil*, he speedily realizes the poet's lines:

> "Heads, though *thick*, were made
> But to be *punch'd* or *broken*."
>
> *Vide Randall's Scrap Book.*

FIBBING GLOAK. A pugilist. *Cant.*

FICE, or FOYSE. A small windy escape backwards, more obvious to the nose than ears, frequently, by old ladies, charged on their lap-dogs. *See* FIZZLE.

FID OF TOBACCO. A quid, from the small pieces of tow with which the vent or touch-hole of a cannon is stopped. *Sea term.*

FIDDLE FADDLE. Trifling discourse, nonsense. A mere fiddle faddle fellow; a trifler.

FIDDLERS MONEY. All sixpences; sixpence being the usual sum paid by each couple for music at country wakes and hops. Fiddlers fare; meat, drink, and money. Fiddlers pay; thanks and wine.

FIDDLESTICK. A spring saw. *Scotch cant.*

FIDDLESTICK'S END. Nothing; the end of the ancient fiddlesticks ending in a point: hence metaphorically used to express a thing terminating in nothing.

FIDGETS. He has got the fidgets; said of one that cannot sit long in a place.

FIDLAM BEN. General thieves; called also St. Peter's sons, having every finger a fish-hook. *Cant.*

FIELD LANE DUCK. A baked sheep's head.

FIELDS OF TEMPTATION. The attractions held out to young men at the university. *Oxf. cant.*

FIERI FACIAS. A red-faced man is said to have been served with a writ of fieri facias.

FIGDEAN. To kill.

FIGGER. A little boy put in at a window to hand out goods to the diver. *See* DIVER.

FIGGING LAW. The art of picking pockets. *Cant.*

FIGURE. A bit of flash for "What's to pay?" i. e. "What's the figure?"

FIGURE DANCER. One who alters figures on bank-notes, converting tens to hundreds.

FILCH, or FILEL. A beggar's staff, with an iron hook at the end, to pluck clothes from a hedge, or any thing out of a casement. Filcher, the same as angler. Filching cove; a man thief. Filching mort; a woman thief.

FILE, FILE CLOY, or BUNGNIPPER. A pickpocket. To file; to rob or cheat. The file, or bungnipper, goes generally in company with two assistants, the Adam Tiler and another, called the bulk or bulker, whose business it is to jostle the person they intend to rob, and push him against the wall, while the file picks his pocket, and gives the booty to the Adam Tiler, who scours off with it. *Cant.* It also signifies a person who has had a long course of experience in the arts of fraud, so as to have become an adept, is termed *an old file upon the town;* so it is usual to say of a man who is extremely cunning, and not to be overreached, that he is a *deep file.*

FIN. An arm. A one-finned man, a fellow who has lost an arm. *Sea phrase.*

FINE. Fine as five-pence. Fine as a cow-t—d stuck with primroses.

FINE. A man imprisoned for any offence. A fine of eighty-four months; a transportation for seven years.

FINGER IN EYE. To put finger in eye, to weep; commonly applied to women. The more you cry the less you'll p-ss, a consolatory speech used by sailors to their doxies. It is as great a pity to see a woman cry as to see a goose walk barefoot, another of the same kind.

FINGER-POST. A parson; so called, because he points out a way to others which he never goes himself. Like the finger-post, he points out a way he has never been, and, probably, will never go, i. e. the way to heaven.

FINGER-SMITHS. Thieves, Midwives. *Cant.*

FINISH. The finish, a small coffee-house (in great repute to see a bit of life, in 1796) in Covent Garden market, opposite Russell-street, opened very early in the morning, and therefore resorted to by debauchees shut out of every other house.

FIPENNY. A clasp-knife. *Cant.*

FIRE A SLUG. To drink a dram.

FIRE PRIGGERS. Villains who rob at fires, under pretence of assisting in removing the goods.

FIRE SHIP. A wench who has the venereal disease.

FIRE SHOVEL. He or she, when young, was fed with a fire-shovel; a saying of persons with wide mouths.

FIRING A GUN. Introducing a story by head and shoulders. A man, wanting to tell a particular story, said to the company, "Hark; did you not hear a gun?—but now we are talking of a gun, I will tell you the story of one."

FISH. A seaman. A scaly fish; a rough, blunt tar. To have other fish to fry; to have other matters to mind, something else to do.

FIT. Suitable. It won't fit; it will not suit or do.

FIVES-COURT. A place distinguished (in addition to the game of *fives*) for sparring matches between the pugilists. The combatants belonging to the prize-ring exhibit the art of self-defence at the Fives-Court with the gloves; and it is frequently at this Court where public challenges are given and accepted by the boxers. The most refined and fastidious person may attend these exhibitions of sparring with pleasure; as they are conducted with all the neatness, elegance, and science, of FENCING. Admission, 3s. each person. It is situated in St. Martin's Street, Leicester-fields.

FIVE SHILLINGS. The sign of five shillings; i. e. the crown. Fifteen shillings; the sign of the three crowns.

FIZZLE. An escape backward.

FLABAGASTED. Confounded.

FLABBY. Relaxed, flaccid; not firm or solid.

FLAG. A groat. *Cant.* The flag of defiance, or bloody flag, is out, signifying, the man is drunk, and alluding to the redness of his face. *Sea phrase.*

FLAM. A lie or sham story: also, a single stroke on a drum. To flam; to hum, to amuse, to deceive. Flim flams; idle stories.

FLAP DRAGON. A clap or pox.

FLARE. To blaze, shine, or glare.

FLASH. Knowing. Understanding another's meaning. The swell was flash, so I could not draw his fogle; the gentleman saw what I was about, and therefore I could not pick his pocket of his silk handkerchief. To patter flash; to speak the slang language. *See* PATTER.

FLASH. A periwig. Rum flash; a fine long wig. Queer flash; a miserable, weather-beaten caxon.

FLASH. To show ostentatiously. To flash one's ivory; to laugh and show one's teeth. Don't flash your ivory, but shut your potato-trap, and keep your guts warm; the devil loves hot tripes.

> "Bill ran a hundred to ten,
> The Adonis would ne'er *flash his ivory* again."
>
> *Vide Crib's Memorial.*

To cut a dash; to appear a knowing person: to be *fly*, *down*, or *awake*; one not to be had.

Flash Cove or Covess. The master or mistress of the house. *Cant.*

Flash Chaunt. A song interlarded with flash.

Flash Ken. A house that harbours thieves.

Flash Lingo. The canting or slang language.

Flash Man. A favourite or *fancy man*; but this term is generally applied to those dissolute characters upon the town, who subsist upon the liberality of unfortunate women, and who, in return, are generally at hand, during their nocturnal perambulations, to protect them should any brawl occur, or should they be detected in robbing those whom they may have *picked up*.

Flash Mollisher. A Cyprian. *Cant.*

Flash of Lightning. A glass of gin.

> "No more let him swipe *Deady's* flashes of lightning."
>
> *Vide Randall's Scrap Book.*

Flash Panneys. Houses to which thieves and prostitutes resort.

> "Next for his favourite *mot*[1] the *kiddey*[2] looks about,
> And if she's in a *flash panney*,[3] he swears he'll have her out;
> So he *fences*[4] all his *togs*[5] to buy her *duds*,[6] and then
> He *frisks*[7] his master's *lob*[8] to take her from the *ken*.[9]"
>
> *Flash Song.*

Flash the Hash. To vomit. *Cant.*

Flat. In a general sense, any honest man, or *square cove*, in opposition to a *sharp* or *cross cove*; when used particularly, it means the person you have a design to rob or defraud, who is termed the *flat*, or the *flatty gory*. A man who does any foolish or imprudent act is called *a flat*; any person, who is found to be an easy dupe to the designs of *the family*, is said to be a *prime flat*. *It's a good flat that's never down*, is a proverb among *flash* people, meaning, that though a man may be repeatedly duped or taken in, he must, in the end, have his eyes opened to his folly.

Flat-catching. Simple persons, who are easily imposed upon, who believe any story that is told to them. *Cant.*

Flat-move. Want of judgement. *Cant.*

Flatts. Cards. *Cant.*

Flawd. Drunk.

Flaybottomist. A bum-brusher, or schoolmaster.

Flay, or Flea, the Fox. To vomit.

Flea Bite. A trifling injury. To send any one away with a flea in his ear; to give any one a hearty scolding.

[1] Girl. [2] Youth. [3] Brothel. [4] Pawns. [5] Clothes.
[6] Wearing apparel. [7] Robs. [8] Till. [9] House.

Fleece. To rob, cheat, or plunder.
Flemish Account. A losing or bad account.
Flesh Broker. A match-maker, a bawd.
Flicker. A drinking glass. *Cant.*
Flickering. Grinning, or laughing in a man's face.
Flicking. Cutting. Flick me some panam and caffan; cut me some bread and cheese. Flick the peter; cut off the cloak-bag, or portmanteau.
Flimseys. Bank-notes. *Cant.*
Fling. To trick or cheat. He flung me fairly out of it; he cheated me out of it.
Flints. Journeyman tailors, who refuse to work for the wages settled by law: those who submit are, by the mutineers, styled dungs, i. e. dunghills.
Flip. Small beer, brandy, and sugar; this mixture, with the addition of a lemon, was, by sailors, formerly called Sir Cloudsly, in memory of Sir Cloudsly Shovel, who used frequently to regale himself with it.
Flip. To shoot. *Cant.*
Flipper. The hand. *Sea term.*
Floating Academy. *See* Campbell's Academy.
Floating Hell. The hulks.
Flog. To whip.
Flogger. A horsewhip. *Cant.*
Flogging Cully. A debilitated lecher, commonly an old one. — See 1st or 2nd edition
Flogging Cove. The beadle or whipper in Bridewell.
Flogging Stake. The whipping-post.
Floor. To knock down. Floor the pig; knock down the officer.
Floored. Knocked down. *Pugilistic cant.* Also, a person drunk is said to be *floored.*
Flourish. To take a flourish; to enjoy a woman in a hasty manner, to take a flyer. *See* Flyer.
Flout. To jeer, ridicule.
Flue Faker. A chimney-sweep. *Cant.*
Flummery. Oatmeal and water boiled to a jelly; also, compliments, neither of which are over-nourishing.
Flush in the Pocket. Full of money. The cull is flush in the fob; the fellow is full of money.
Flustered. Drunk.
Flute. The recorder of a corporation: a recorder was an ancient musical instrument.
Flux. To cheat, cozen, or over-reach: also, to salivate. To flux a wig; to put it up in curl, and bake it.
Fly. Knowing. Acquainted with another's meaning or proceeding. The rattling cove is fly; the coachman knows what we are about: also, vigilant, suspicious, cunning, not easily robbed or duped; a shop-keeper or person of this

description is called a *fly cove*, or a *leary cove*; on other occasions *fly* is synonymous with *flash* or *leary*, as I'm *fly* to you, I was *put flash* to him, &c.

FLY. A waggon. *Cant.*

FLY BY NIGHT. You old fly by night; an ancient term of reproach to an old woman, signifying that she was a witch, and alluding to the nocturnal excursions attributed to witches who were supposed to fly abroad to their meetings, mounted on brooms.

FLYER. To take a flyer; to enjoy a woman with her clothes on, or without going to bed.

FLYERS. Shoes.

FLY-FLAPPED. Whipped in the stocks, or at the cart's tail.

FLYING CAMPS. Beggars plying in a body at a funeral.

FLYING GIGGERS. Turnpike gates.

FLYING HORSE. A lock in wrestling, by which he who uses it throws his adversary over his head.

FLYING PASTY. Sirreverence wrapt in paper and thrown over a neighbour's wall.

FLYING STATIONERS. Ballad-singers and hawkers of penny histories.

FLYMSEY. A bank-note.

FLY THE MAGS. Tossing up halfpence. *Cant.*

FOB. A cheat, trick, or contrivance. I will not be fobbed off so; I will not be thus deceived with false pretences. The fob is also a small breeches pocket for holding a watch.

FOGEY. Old Fogey. A nick-name for an invalid soldier; derived from the French word *fougeux*, fierce or fiery.

FOGLE. A handkerchief. *Cant.* A blue handkerchief with white diamond spots, commonly called a *blue bird's eye*. *Ex. gr.*

> "My handkerchiefs, of *bird's eye blue*,
> Bear them to Belcher when I'm gone."
>
> "The *bird's eye fogle* round his neck."
>
> *Vide Randall's Scrap Book.*

FOGLE HUNTER. A pickpocket. *Cant.*

FOGRAM. An old fogram; a fusty old fellow.

FOGUS. Tobacco. Tip me a gage of fogus; give me a pipe of tobacco. *Cant.*

FOOL. A fool at the end of a stick; a fool at one end and a maggot at the other; gibes on an angler.

FOOLISH. An expression among impures, signifying the cully who pays: in opposition to a flash man. Is he foolish or flash?

FOOT PADS, or LOW PADS. Rogues who rob on foot.

FOOT WABBLER. A contemptuous appellation for a foot-soldier, commonly used by the cavalry.

FOOTMAN'S MAWND. An artificial sore, made with un-slaked lime, soap, and the rust of old iron, on the back of a beggar's hand, as if hurt by the bite or kick of a horse.

FOOTY DESPICABLE. A footy fellow; a despicable fellow; from the French word *foutié*.

FORE FOOT, or PAW. Give us your fore foot; give us your hand.

FOREMAN OF THE JURY. One who engrosses all the talk to himself, or speaks for the rest of the company.

FOREST OF DEBT. Payment of debts. *Oxf. Univ. cant.*

FORK. A pickpocket. Let us fork him; let us pick his pocket. "The newest and most dexterous way, which is to thrust the fingers strait, stiff, open, and very quick, into the pocket, and so closing them, hook what can be held between them." *N.B.* This was taken from a book written many years ago; doubtless, the art of picking pockets, like all others, must have been much improved since that time.

FORKS. The two fore-fingers of the hand; to *put your forks down* is to pick a pocket.

FORLORN HOPE. A gamester's last stake.

FORTUNE HUNTERS. Indigent men seeking to enrich themselves by marrying women of fortune.

FORTUNE TELLER, or CUNNING MAN. A judge who tells every prisoner his fortune, lot, or doom. To go before the fortune-teller, lambskin man, or conjuror; to be tried at an assize. See LAMBSKIN MEN.

FOSS, or PHOSS. A phosphorus bottle used by *cracksmen* to obtain a light.

FOUL. To foul a plate with a man; to take dinner with him.

FOUL-MOUTHED. Abusive.

FOUNDLING. A child dropped in the street, and found and educated at the parish expense.

FOUR BELLS AT NIGHT. Ten o'clock. *Sea term*

FOUSIL. The name of a public house where the Eccentrics assemble, in May's Buildings, St. Martin's Lane.

FOX. A sharp cunning fellow: also, an old term for a sword, probably a rusty one, or else from its being stained with blood; some say this name alluded to certain swords of remarkable good temper, or metal, marked with the figure of a fox, probably the sign, or rebus, of the maker.

FOX'S PAW. The vulgar pronunciation of the French words *faux pas*. He made a confounded fox's paw.

FOXED. Intoxicated.

FOXEY. Rank, stinking.

FOXING A BOOT. Mending the boot by capping it.

FOYST. A pick-pocket, cheat, or rogue. See WOTTON'S GANG.

Foyst. To pick a pocket.

Foysted in. Words or passages surreptitiously interpolated or inserted into a book or writing.

Fraters. Vagabonds who beg with sham patents, or briefs, for hospitals, fires, innundations, &c.

Free. Free of fumbler's hall; a saying of one who cannot get his wife with child.

Free and Easy. Singing clubs in London are denominated *free and easy;* i. e. where persons sing any songs they think proper, without any control from the chairman; and, also, where every individual is welcome, from the duke to the chimney-sweeper, so that he contributes to the plate: an introduction is not required.

Free and Easy Johns. A society which meet at the Hole-in-the-Wall, Fleet-street, to tipple porter and sing bawdry.

Free Booters. Lawless robbers and plunderers; originally, soldiers who served without pay, for the privilege of plundering the enemy.

Freeholder. He whose wife accompanies him to the ale-house.

Freeman's Quay. Free of expense. To lush at freeman's quay; to drink at another's cost.

French Cream. Brandy; so called by the old tabbies and dowagers when drank in their tea.

French Disease. The delicate disease, said to have been imported from France. French gout; the same. He suffered by a blow over the snout with a French faggot-stick; i. e. he lost his nose by the pox.

French Leave. To take French leave; to go off without taking leave of the company: a saying frequently applied to persons who have ran away from their creditors.

Freshman. One just entered a member of the university.

Fresh Milk. Cambridge new comers to the university.

Freshwater Bay. Alludes to freshmen; a name conferred on novices in the university. *Oxf. cant.*

Fribble. An effiminate fop; a name borrowed from a celebrated character of that kind, in the farce of "Miss in her Teens," written by Mr. Garrick.

Friday-face. A dismal countenance. Before, and even long after the Reformation, Friday was a day of abstinence, or *jour maigre.* Immediately after the restoration of king Charles II. a proclamation was issued, prohibiting all publicans from dressing any suppers on a Friday.

Frig Pig. A trifling, fiddle-faddle fellow.

Frigate. A well-rigged frigate; a well dressed wench.

Frisk. To dance the paddington-frisk; to be hanged.

Frisk. Used by thieves to signify searching a person whom they have robbed. B—t his eyes! frisk him. To frisk a cly; to pick a pocket. *Cant.*

Froe, or Vroe. A woman, wife, or mistress. Brush to your froe, or bloss, and wheedle her for crop; run to your mistress, and sooth and coax her for some money. *Dutch.*

Froglander. A Dutchman.

Frog's Wine. Gin.

Frosty Face. One pitted with the small pox.

Frummagemmed. Choaked, strangled, suffocated, or hanged. *Cant.*

Fubsey. Plump. A fubsey wench; a plump, healthy wench.

Fuddle. Drunk. This is rum fuddle; this is excellent tipple or drink. Fuddle; drunk. Fuddle cap; a drunkard.

Fudge. Nonsense.

Fulhams. Loaded dice are called high and low men, or high and low fulhams, by Ben Jonson and other writers of his time; either because they were made at Fulham, or from that place being the resort of sharpers.

Fuller's Earth. Gin and bitters, a favourite liquor of the celebrated George Head, in whom this slang term originated.

Full of Emptiness. Jocular term for empty.

Full March. The Scotch greys are in full march by the crown-office; the lice are crawling down his head.

Fumbler. An old or impotent man. To fumble, also, means to go awkwardly about any work or manual operation.

Fun. A cheat or trick. Do you think to fun me out of it? Do you think to cheat me? also, the breech, from being the abbreviation of fundament; I'll kick your fun. *Cant.*

Funk. To use an unfair motion of the hand in plumping at taw. *Schoolboy's term.*

Funk. To smoke; figuratively, to smoke or stink through fear. I was in a cursed funk.

> " Up he rose in a *funk*, lapp'd a toothful of brandy,
> And to it again," &c.
>
> *Vide Crib's Memorial.*

To funk the cobbler; a schoolboy's trick, performed with asafœtida and cotton, which are stuffed into a pipe: the cotton being lighted, and the bowl of the pipe covered with a coarse handkerchief, the smoke is blown out, at the small end, through the crannies of a cobbler's stall.

Furmen. Aldermen.

Furmity, or Fromenty. Wheat boiled up to a jelly. To simper like a furmity kettle; to smile or look merry about the gills.

Fuss. A confusion, a hurry, an unnecessary to do about trifles.

Fussock. A lazy fat woman. An old fussock; a frowsy old woman.

FUSTIAN. Bombast language. Red fustian; port wine.
FUSTY LUGGS. A beastly sluttish woman.
FUZZ. To shuffle cards minutely; also, to change the pack.

G

GAB, or GOB. The mouth. Gift of the gab; a facility of speech, nimble-tongued eloquence. To blow the gab; to confess or peach.
GAB, or GOB, STRING. A bridle.
GABEY. A foolish fellow.
GAFF. A fair. The drop coves maced the joskins at the gaff; the ring droppers cheated the countrymen at the fair.
GAFF. To game by tossing up halfpence.
GAG. An instrument, used chiefly by housebreakers and thieves, for propping open the mouth of a person robbed, thereby to prevent his calling out for assistance.
GAGE, or FOGUS. A pipe of tobacco.
GAGGERS. Players. *Cant.*
GAGGERS. High and low. Cheats who, by sham pretences, and wonderful stories of their sufferings, impose on the credulity of well meaning people. *See* RUM GAGGER.
GALANEY. A fowl. *Cant.*
GALIMAUFREY. A hodge-podge made up of the remains and scraps of the larder.
GALL. His gall is not yet broken; a saying used in prisons of a man just brought in, who appears dejected.
GALLEY. Building the galley; a game formerly used at sea, in order to put a trick upon a landsman or fresh-water sailor. It being agreed to play at that game, one sailor personates the builder, and another the merchant or contractor: the builder first begins by laying the keel, which consists of a number of men laid all along on their backs, one after another, that is, head to foot; he next puts in the ribs or knees, by making a number of men sit feet to feet, at right angles to, and on each side of, the keel; he now, fixing on the person intended to be the object of the joke, observes he is a fierce-looking fellow, and fit for the lion; he, accordingly, places him at the head, his arms being held or locked in by the two persons next to him, representing the ribs. After several other dispositions, the builder delivers over the galley to the contractor, as complete; but he, among other faults and objections, observes the lion is not gilt, on which the builder, or one of his assistants, runs to the head, and dipping a mop in excrement, thrusts it into the face of the lion.

GALLIED. Hurried, vexed, over-fatigued, perhaps, like a galley-slave.

GALLIGASKINS. Breeches.

GALLIPOT. A nickname for an apothecary.

GALLOOT. A soldier. *Cant.*

GALLOPER. A blood-horse, a hunter. The toby gill clapped his bleeders to his galloper, and tipped the traps the double; the highwayman spurred his horse, and got away from the officers.

GALLORE, or GOLORE. Plenty.

GALLOWS BIRD. A thief, or pickpocket; also, one that associates with them.

GAMBADOES. Leathern cases of stiff leather, used in Devonshire instead of boots: they are fastened to the saddle, and admit the leg, shoe, and all: the name was at first jocularly given.

GAMBLER. A sharper, or tricking gamester.

GAMBS. Thin, ill-shaped legs. A corruption of the French word *jambes*. Farcy gambs, sore or swelled legs.

GAME. Any mode of robbing. The toby is now a queer game; to rob on the highway is now a bad mode of acting. This observation is frequently made by thieves; the roads being now so well guarded by the horse-patrole, and gentlemen travel with little cash in their pockets.

GAME. Bubbles or pigeons drawn in to be cheated: also, at Cyprian temples, lewd women. Mother, have you any game? mother, have you any girls? To die game; to suffer at the gallows without showing any signs of fear or repentance. Game pullet, a young whore, or forward girl in the way of becoming one.

GAME. Among pugilists, courage of the highest order. He is a *game* man; he will not give up the contest, until nature forsakes him. He will not say, NO!

GAMMON. To humbug, to deceive, to tell lies. What rum gammon the old file pitched to the flat; how finely the knowing old fellow humbugged the fool. Any assertion which is not strictly true, or professions believed to be insincere; as, I believe you're *gammoning*, or, that's all *gammon*, meaning, you are no doubt jesting with me, or, that's all a farce. To *gammon* a person, is to amuse him with false assurances, to praise, or flatter him, in order to obtain some particular end: to *gammon* a man *to* any act, is to persuade him to it by artful language or pretence: to *gammon* a shopkeeper, &c. is to engage his attention to your discourse, while your accomplice is executing some preconcerted plan of depredation upon his property: a thief detected in a house, which he has entered, *upon the sneak*, for the purpose of robbing it, will endeavour, by some *gammoning* story, to account for his intrusion, and to get off with a good grace: a man, who is ready at invention, and has always a flow of plausible language on these occasions, is said to be a *prime gammoner:* to *gammon lushy* or *queer*, is to pretend drunkenness or sickness, for some private end.

GAMMON AND PATTER. Commonplace talk of any profession; as, the gammon and patter of a horse-dealer, sailor, &c.

GAMMON THE TWELVE. A man, who has been tried by a criminal court, and, by a plausible defence, has induced the jury to acquit him, or to banish the capital part of the charge, and so save his life, is said, by his associates, to have *gammoned the twelve in prime twig*, alluding to the number of jurymen.

GAN. The mouth or lips. *Cant.*

GANDER MONTH. That month in which a man's wife lies in: wherefore, during that time, husbands plead a sort of indulgence in matters of gallantry.

GANG. A company of men, a body of sailors, a knot of thieves, pickpockets, &c. A gang of sheep-trotters; the four feet of a sheep.

GAOLER'S COACH. A hurdle: traitors being usually conveyed from the gaol to the place of execution on a hurdle or sledge.

GAPESEED. Sights, any thing to feed the eye. I am come abroad for a little gapeseed.

GAPSTOPPER. A whoremaster.

GARDEN. To *put* a person *in the garden, in the hole, in the bucket*, or *in the well*, are synonymous phrases, signifying to defraud him of his due share of the booty by embezzling a part of the property, or the money it is *fenced* for; this phrase also applies generally to defrauding any one, with whom you are confidentially connected, of what is justly his due.

GARNISH. An entrance-fee demanded by the old prisoners of one just committed to gaol.

GARRET, or UPPER STORY. The head. His garret, or upper story is empty, or unfurnished; i. e. he has no brains, he is a fool: it also signifies the *fob pocket*.

GARRET ELECTION. A ludicrous ceremony, practised every new parliament: it consists of a mock election of two members to represent the borough of Garret (a few straggling cottages, near Wandsworth, in Surrey). The qualification of a voter is, having enjoyed a woman, in the open air, within that district: the candidates are commonly fellows of low humour, who dress themselves up in a ridiculous manner. As this brings a prodigious concourse of people to Wandsworth, the publicans of that place jointly contribute to the expense, which is sometimes considerable.

GAWKEY. A tall, thin, awkward young man or woman.

GEACH. A thief. *Cant.*

GEE. It won't gee; it won't hit or do, it does not suit or fit.

GELDING. An eunuch.

GELT. Money. *German.* Also, castrated.

GENTLE CRAFT. The art of shoemaking. One of the gentle craft; a shoemaker: so called because once practised by St. Crispin.

GENTLEMAN COMMONER. An empty bottle. An university joke; gentlemen commoners not being deemed over full of learning.

GENTLEMAN'S COMPANION. A louse.

GENTLEMAN'S MASTER. A highway robber; because he makes a gentleman obey his commands, i. e. stand and deliver.

GENTLEMAN OF THREE INS. In debt, in gaol, and in danger of remaining there for life: or, in gaol, indicted, and in danger of being hanged in chains.

GENTLEMAN OF THREE OUTS. That is, without money, without wit, and without manners; some add another out; i. e. without credit.

GENTRY COVE. A gentleman. *Cant.*

GENTRY COVE KEN. A gentleman's house. *Cant.*

GENTRY MORT. A gentlewoman.

GEORGE. Yellow George; a guinea. Brown George; an ammunition loaf.

GERMAN DUCK. Half a sheep's head boiled with onions.

GET. One of his get; one of his offspring or begetting.

GIB. A face. *Sea term.*

GIBBERISH. The cant language of thieves and gypsies, called Pedlars' French, and St. Giles's Greek. *See* ST. GILES'S GREEK. Also, the mystic language of Geber, used by chymists. Gibberish likewise means a sort of disguised language, formed by inserting any consonant between each syllable of an English word; in which case, it is called the gibberish of the letter inserted: if F, it is the F gibberish; if G, the G gibberish; as in the sentence, How do you do? Howg dog youg dog?

GIBBE. A horse that shrinks from the collar, and will not draw.

GIB CAT. A northern name for a he-cat, there commonly called Gilbert. As melancholy as a gib cat; as melancholy as a he-cat who has been caterwauling, whence they always return scratched, hungry, and out of spirits.

Aristotle says, *Omne animal post coitum est triste;* to which an anonymous author has given the following exception, *preter gallum gallinaceum, et sacerdotem gratis fornicantem.*

GIBLETS. To join giblets; said of a man and woman who cohabit as husband and wife without being married: also, to copulate.

GIFTS. Small white specks under the finger nails, said to portend gifts or presents. A stingy man is said to be as full of gifts as a brazen horse of his farts.

GIFT OF THE GAB. A facility of speech.

GIGG. A nose. Snitchel his gigg; fillip his nose. Grunter's gigg; a hog's snout. Gigg is also a high one-horse chaise. To gigg a Smithfield hank; to hamstring an over-drove ox, vulgarly called a mad bullock.

GIGGER. A latch, or door. Dub the gigger; open the door. Gigger dubber; the turnkey of a gaol.

GIGGLE. To suppress a laugh. Gigglers; wanton women.

GILES'S, or ST. GILES'S BREED. Fat, ragged, and saucy. Newton and Dyot streets, the grand head-quarters of most of the thieves and pickpockets about London, are in St. Giles's parish. St. Giles's Greek, the cant language, called also Slang, Pedlars' French, and Flash.

GILFLURT. A proud minx, a vain, capricious woman.

GILL. The abbreviation of Gillian, figuratively used for woman. Every jack has his gill, i. e. every jack has his gillian, or female mate. It is also a word used by way of variation, similar to *cove*, *gloak*, or *gory;* but generally coupled to some other descriptive term, as a *flash-gill*, *toby-gill*, &c.

GILLS. The cheeks. To look rosy about the gills; to have a fresh complexion. To look merry about the gills; to appear cheerful.

GILT, or RUM DUBBER. A thief who picks locks, so called from the gilt or picklock key; many of them are so expert, that, from the lock of a church door to that of the smallest cabinet, they will find means to open it: these go into reputable public-houses, where, pretending business, they contrive to get into private rooms, up stairs, where they open any bureaus or trunks they happen to find there.

GIMBLET-EYED. Squinting, either in man or woman.

GIMCRACK, or JIMCRACK. A spruce wench: a gimcrack also means a person who has a turn for mechanical contrivances.

GINGAMBOBS. Toys, bawbles. *See* THINGAMBOBS.

GINGERBREAD. A cake made of treacle, flour, and grated ginger: also, money. He has the gingerbread; he is rich.

Gingerbread Work. Gilding and carving; these terms are particularly applied, by seamen on board Newcastle colliers, to the decorations of the sterns and quarters of West-Indiamen, which they have the greatest pleasure in defacing.

Gingerly. Softly, gently, tenderly. To go gingerly to work; to attempt a thing gently or cautiously.

Ginger-pated, or Ginger-hackled. Red-haired: a term borrowed from the cockpit, where red cocks are called gingers.

Ginny. An instrument to lift up a grate, in order to steal what is in the window. *Cant.*

Gin Spinner. A distiller.

Gip. From γυψ, a *wolf*. A servant at college.

Give it to. To rob or defraud any place or person; as, I *gave it to* him *for* his *reader*, I robbed him of his pocket-book. What *suit* did you *give it* them *upon?* In what manner, or by what means, did you effect your purpose? also, to impose upon a person's credulity by telling him a string of falsehoods; or to take any unfair advantage of another's inadvertence or unsuspecting temper, on any occasion; in either case, the party at last *dropping down*, that is, detecting your imposition, will say, I believe you have been *giving it to* me nicely all this while.

Give lip to. To chatter, blow up. *Sea term.*

Giver. A good boxer. *Pugilistic phrase.*

Gizzard. To grumble in the gizzard; to be secretly displeased.

Glass Eyes. A nick name for one wearing spectacles.

Glaymore. A Highland broad-sword; from the Erse *glay*, or *glaive*, a sword; and *more*, great.

Glaze. A window.

Glazier. One who breaks windows and show-glasses, to steal goods exposed for sale. Glaziers; eyes. *Cant.* Is your father a glazier; a question asked of a lad or young man, who stands between the speaker and the candle, or fire. If it is answered in the negative, the rejoinder is—I wish he was, that he might make a window through your body, to enable me to see the fire or light.

Glib. Smooth, slippery. Glib tongued; talkative.

Glim. A candle, or dark lantern, used in housebreaking: also, fire. To glim; to burn in the hand: also, signifies sight or eye. *Cant.*

> "His *glims* I've made look like a couple of rainbows."
>
> *Vide Randall's Scrap Book.*

Glimfenders. Andirons. *Cant.*

Glimflashy. Angry, or in a passion. *Cant.*

Glimjack. A link-boy. *Cant.*

Glimmer. Fire. *Cant.*

Glimmerers. Persons begging with sham licences, pretending losses by fire.

Glimms. Eyes.

Glimstick. A candlestick. *Cant.*

Glistner. A sovereign. *Cant.*

Gloach. A man. *Scotch cant.*

Gloves. Used by pugilists to communicate the art of self-defence to their pupils.

Gloves. To give any one a pair of gloves; to make them a present or bribe. To win a pair of gloves; to kiss a man whilst he sleeps: for this a pair of gloves is due to any lady who will thus earn them.

Gluepot. A parson: from joining men and women together in matrimony.

Glum. Sullen.

Glutton. A term used by bruisers to signify a man who will bear a great deal of beating.

Glybe. A writing. *Cant.*

Gnarler. A little dog that, by his barking, alarms the family when any person is breaking into the house.

Go. The dash. The mode. He is quite the go, he is quite varment, he is prime, he is bang up, are synonymous expressions.

Goads. Those who wheedle in chapmen for horse-dealers.

Go-alonger. A simple easy person, who suffers himself to be made a tool of, and is readily persuaded to any act or undertaking by his associates, who inwardly laugh at his folly, and ridicule him behind his back.

Goat. A lascivious person. Goats jigg; making the beast with two backs, copulation.

Gob. The mouth; also, a bit or morsel; whence gobbets. Gift of the gob; wide-mouthed, or one who speaks fluently, or sings well. In Randall, an heroic fragment, may be found the following invocation:—

> "Shade of Jem Belcher hover round his *nob*,
> Protect his *lugs*, his *chatterers*, and *gob*."
>
> *Vide Randall's Dairy.*

> "And when we well had *sluic'd our gobs*,
> And all were in *prime twig for chatter*," &c.
>
> *Crib's Memorial.*

Gobbler. A turkey cock.

Go Between. A pimp or bawd.

Gob String. A bridle.

Go by the Ground. A little short person, man or woman.

Godfather. He who pays the reckoning, or answers for the rest of the company; as, Will you stand godfather? and we will take care of the brat; i. e. repay you another time. Jurymen are also called godfathers, because they name the crime the prisoner before them has been guilty of, whether felony, petit larceny, &c.

Gog. All-a-gog; impatient, anxious, or desirous of a thing.

Gog and Magog. Two giants, whose effigies stand on each side of the clock in Guildhall, London; of whom there is a tradition, that, when they hear the clock strike one, on the first of April, they will walk down from their places.

Goggles. Eyes. *See* Ogles. Goggle eyes; large prominent eyes. To goggle; to stare.

Going upon the Dub. Going out to break open, or pick the locks of, houses.

Gold Droppers. Sharpers, who drop a piece of gold, which they pick up in the presence of some inexperienced person, for whom the trap is laid; this they pretend to have found, and, as he saw them pick it up, they invite him to a public-house to partake of it; when there, two or three of their comrades drop in, as if by accident, and propose cards, or some other game, when they seldom fail of stripping their prey.

Goldfinch. One who has commonly a purse full of gold. Goldfinches; guineas.

Gold Finder. One whose employment is to empty necessary houses; called also a tom-t—d-man, and nightman; the latter, from that business being always performed in the night.

Golgotha, or the Place of Sculls. Part of the Theatre at Oxford, where the heads of houses sit; those gentlemen being by the wits of the university called sculls.

Gollumpus. A large clumsy fellow.

Gollup up. To drink down quickly. *Cant.*

Good. A place or person, which promises to be easily robbed, is said to be *good*, as, that house is *good upon the crack;* this shop is *good upon the star; the swell* is *good for* his *montra; &c.* A man who declares himself *good for* any favour or thing, means, that he has sufficient influence, or possesses the certain means to obtain it; *good as bread,* or, *good as cheese,* are merely emphatical phrases to the same effect. *See* Caz.

Good Man. A word of various imports, according to the place where it is spoken: in the city it means a rich man; at Hockley-in-the-Hole, or St. Giles's, an expert boxer; at a bagnio in Covent Garden, a vigorous fornicator; at an alehouse or tavern, one who loves his pot or bottle; and sometimes, though but rarely, a virtuous man.

Good Woman. A nondescript, represented on a famous sign in St. Giles's, in the form of a common woman, but without a head.

Goose. A tailor's goose; a smoothing iron used to press down the seams, for which purpose it must be heated: hence, it is a jocular saying, that a tailor, be he ever so poor, is always sure to have a goose at his fire. He cannot say boh to a goose; a saying of a bashful or sheepish fellow.

Gooseberry. He played up old gooseberry among them; said of a person who, by force or threats, suddenly puts an end to a riot or disturbance.

Gooseberry-eyed. One with dull grey eyes, like boiled gooseberries.

Gooseberry Wig. A large frizzled wig; perhaps, from a supposed likeness to a gooseberry bush.

Goosecap. A silly fellow or woman.

Go out. A person who has left his business to go a thieving; it is said, he has *gone out*. *Cant.*

Goree. Money, chiefly gold; perhaps, from the traffic carried on at that place, which is chiefly for gold dust. *Cant.*

Gorger. A gentleman. A well dressed man. Mung kiddey. Mung the gorger; beg, child, beg of the gentleman.

Gospel Shop. A church.

Gotch-gutted. Pot bellied: a gotch in Norfolk signifying a pitcher, or large round jug.

Gouge. To squeeze out a man's eye with the thumb: a cruel practice used by the Bostonians, in America.

Grab. To sieze, apprehend, take into custody; to make a *grab* at any thing, is to snatch suddenly, as at a gentleman's watch-chain, &c.

Grab. To sieze a man. The pigs grabbed the kiddey for a crack; the officers seized the youth for a burglary.

Grabbed. Taken, apprehended.

Grabble. To seize. To grabble the bit; to seize any one's money. *Cant.*

Grafted. Cuckolded; i. e. having horns grafted on his head.

Grannam. Corn.

Grannum's Gold. Hoarded money; supposed to have belonged to the grandmother of the possessor.

Granny. An abbreviation of grandmother: also, the name of an idiot, famous for licking her eye, who died, Nov. 14, 1719. Go teach your granny to suck eggs; said to such as would instruct any one in a matter he knows better than themselves.

Grapple the Rails. A cant name used in Ireland for whiskey.

Grappling-Irons. Handcuffs.

Grave Digger. Like a grave digger; up to the a–se in business, and don't know which way to turn.

Gravey-eyed. Blear-eyed, one whose eyes have a running humour.

Grawler. A beggar. *Scotch cant.*

Gray. A copper coin, having two heads and two tails, to answer the purposes of gamblers, who, by such deceptions, frequently win large sums.

Gray Beard. Earthen jugs, formerly used in public houses for drawing ale; they had the figure of a man with a large beard stamped on them, whence, probably, they took the name. *Vide Ben Jonson's Plays, Bartholomew Fair, &c. &c.* Dutch earthen jugs, used for smuggling gin on the coasts of Essex and Suffolk, are, at this time, called gray beards.

Gray Mare. The gray mare is the better horse; said of a woman who governs her husband.

Gray Parson. A farmer who rents the tithes of the rector or vicar.

Grease. To bribe. To grease a man in the fist; to bribe him. To grease a fat sow in the a–se; to give to a rich man. Greasy chin; a treat given to parish officers in part of commutation for a bastard: called, also, Eating a child.

Great Intimate. As great as shirt and shitten a–se.

Great Joseph. A surtout. *Cant.*

Greedy Guts. A covetous or voracious person.

Greek. St. Giles's Greek; the slang lingo, cant, or gibberish.

Green. Doctor Green; i. e. grass; a physician, or rather medicine, found very successful in curing most disorders to which horses are liable. My horse is not well; I shall send him to Doctor Green.

Green. Young, inexperienced, unacquainted, ignorant. How green the cull was not to stag how the old file planted the books; how ignorant the booby was not to perceive how the old sharper placed the cards in such a manner as to insure the game.

Green Bag. An attorney: those gentlemen carry their clients' deeds in a green bag; and, it is said, when they have no deeds to carry, frequently fill them with an old pair of breeches, or any other trumpery, to give themselves the appearance of business.

Green Gown. To give a girl a green gown; to tumble her on the grass, and pick the pins out of her frock.

Green Sickness. The disease of maids, occasioned by celibacy.

Greenhead. An inexperienced young man.

Greenhorn. A novice on the town, an undebauched young fellow, just initiated into the society of bucks and bloods.

Greenwich Goose. A pensioner of Greenwich Hospital.

Gregorian Tree. The gallows: so named from Gregory Brandon, a famous finisher of the law, to whom Sir William Segar, garter king of arms, (being imposed on by Brooke, a herald), granted a coat of arms. *Obsolete.*

Grig. A farthing. A merry grig, a fellow as merry as a grig: an allusion to the apparent liveliness of a grig, or young eel.

Grim. Old Mr. Grim; Death.

Grimalkin. A cat: mawkin signifies a hare, in Scotland.

Grin. To grin in a glass case; to be anatomized for murder: the skeletons of many criminals are preserved in glass cases, at Surgeon's Hall.

Grin. To "stand the grin," in the flash lingo, is to be ridiculed and laughed at.

Grind. To have carnal knowledge of a woman.

Grinders. Teeth. Gooseberry-grinder; the breech. Ask bogey, the gooseberry-grinder; ask mine a--se.

Groats. To save his groats; to come off handsomely: at the universities, nine groats are deposited in the hands of an academic officer, by every person standing for a degree, which if the depositer obtains with honour, the groats are returned to him.

Grocery. Halfpence. *Cant.*

Grog. Rum and water. Grog was first introduced into the navy about the year 1740, by Admiral Vernon, to prevent the sailors intoxicating themselves with their allowance of rum or spirits. Groggy, or groggified; drunk.

Grog-blossom. A carbuncle, or pimple in the face, caused by drinking.

Grogged. A grogged horse; a foundered horse.

Grogham. A horse. *Cant.*

Grog on Board. Nearly drunk.

Gropers. Blind men: also, midwives.

Ground Squirrel. A hog, or pig. *Sea term.*

Ground Sweat. A grave.

Grub. Victuals. To grub; dine.

Grub-Street. A street near Moorfields, formerly the supposed habitation of many persons who wrote for the booksellers; hence, a Grub-street writer means a hackney author, who manufactures books for the booksellers.

Grub-Street-News. Lying intelligence.

Grumbletonian. A discontented person; one who is always railing at the times or ministry.

Grunter. A hog. To grunt; to groan, or complain of sickness.

Grunters. Traps, officers of justice.

Grunter's gig. A smoaked hog's face.

Grunting Peck. Pork, bacon, or any kind of hog's flesh.

Gruts. Tea.

Gudgeon. One easily imposed on. To gudgeon; to swallow the bait, or fall into a trap; from the fish of that name, which is easily taken.

Gull. A simple credulous fellow, easily cheated.

Gulls. Novices at the university.

Gulled. Deceived, cheated, imposed on.

Gull-gropers. Usurers, who lend money to the gamesters.

Gum. Abusive language. Come, let's have no more of your gum.

Gummy. Clumsy: particularly applied to the ancles of men or women, and the legs of horses.

Gumption, or Rum Gumption. Docility, comprehension, and capacity.

Gun. He is in the gun; he is drunk: perhaps, from an allusion to a vessel called a gun, used for ale in the universities.

Gun. To *gun*, among flash people, is to be noticed. Do not you see we are *gunned?* an expression used by thieves when they think they are being watched.

Gundiguts. A fat, pursy fellow.

Gunner's Daughter. To kiss the gunner's daughter; to be tied to a gun and flogged on the posteriors: a mode of punishing boys on board a ship of war.

Gunpowder. An old woman. *Cant.*

Gutfoundered. Exceeding hungry.

Guts. My great guts are ready to eat my little ones; my guts begin to think my throat's cut; my guts curse my teeth: all expressions signifying the party is extremely hungry.

Guts and Garbage. A very fat man or woman. More guts than brains; a silly fellow. He has plenty of guts, but no bowels; said of a hard, merciless, or unfeeling person.

Gut Scraper, or Tormentor of Catgut. A fiddler.

Gutter-Lane. The throat, the swallow, the red lane. *See* Red Lane.

Gutting a Quart Pot. Taking out the lining of it; i. e. drinking it off. Gutting an oyster; eating it. Gutting a house; clearing it of its furniture. *See* Poulterer.

Guy. A dark lanthorn; in allusion to Guy Faux, the principal actor in the gunpowder plot. Stow the guy; conceal the lanthorn.

Guzzle. Liquor. To guzzle; to drink greedily.

Guzzle Guts. One greedy of liquor.

Gybe, or Jybe. Any writing or pass with a seal.

Gybing. Jeering, or ridiculing.

Gyles, or Giles. Hopping Giles; a nick-name for a lame person: St. Giles was the tutelar saint of cripples.

Gyp. A college runner or errand-boy at Cambridge, called at Oxford a scout. *See* Scout.

Gypsies. A set of vagrants, who, to the great disgrace of our police, are suffered to wander about the country. They pretend that they derive their origin from the ancient Egyptians, who were famous for their knowledge in astronomy and other sciences; and, under the pretence of fortune-telling, find means to rob or defraud the ignorant and superstitious. To colour their impostures, they artificially discolour their faces, and speak a kind of gibberish peculiar to themselves. They rove up and down the country in large companies, to the great terror of the farmers, from whose geese, turkeys, and fowls, they take very considerable contributions.

When a fresh recruit is admitted into the fraternity, he is to take the following oath, administered by the principal maunder, after going through the annexed forms:—

First, a new name is given to him, by which he is ever after to be called; then, standing up in the middle of the assembly, and directing his face to the dimber-damber, or principal man of the gang, he repeats the following oath, which is dictated to him by some experienced member of the fraternity:

I, Crank Cuffin, do swear to be a true brother, and that I will, in all things, obey the commands of the great tawney prince, and keep his counsel, and not divulge the secrets of my brethren.

I will never leave nor forsake the company, but observe and keep all the times of appointment, either by day or by night, in every place whatever.

I will not teach any one to cant, nor will I disclose any of our mysteries to them.

I will take my prince's part against all that shall oppose him, or any of us, according to the utmost of my ability; nor will I suffer him, or any one belonging to us, to be abused by any strange abrams, rufflers, hookers, pailliards, swaddler's, Irish toyles, swigmen, whip jacks, jarkmen, bawdy baskets, dommerars, clapper dogeons, patricoes, or curtals; but will defend him, or them, as much as I can, against all other outliers whatever. I will not conceal aught I win out of libkins or from the ruffmans, but will preserve it for the use of the company. Lastly, I will cleave to my doxy wap stiffly, and will bring her duds, marjery praters, goblers, grunting cheats, or tibs of the buttery, or any thing else I can come at, as winnings for her weppings.

The canters have, it seems, a tradition, that, from the three first articles of this oath, the first founders of a certain boastful, worshipful fraternity (who pretend to derive their origin from the earliest times) borrowed both the hint and form of their establishment; and that their pretended derivation from the first *Adam* is a forgery, it being only from the first *Adam Tiler: See* ADAM TILER. At the admission of a new brother, a general stock is raised for booze, or drink, to make themselves merry on the occasion. As for peckage, or eatables, they can procure without money; for, while some are sent to break the ruffmans, or woods and bushes, for firing, others are detached to filch geese, chickens, hens, ducks (or mallards), and pigs. Their morts are their butchers, who presently make bloody work with what living things are brought them; and having made holes in the ground under some remote hedge, in an obscure place, they make a fire, and boil or broil their food; and, when it is enough, fall to work, tooth and nail; and having eaten more like beasts than men, they drink more like swine than human creatures, entertaining one another all the time with songs in the canting dialect.

As they live, so they lie, together, promiscuously, and know not how to claim a property either in their goods or children; and this general interest ties them more firmly together than if all their rags were twisted into ropes, to bind them indissolubly from a separation; which detestable union is farther consolidated by the above oath.

They stroll up and down all summer-time in droves, and dexterously pick pockets, while they are telling of fortunes; and the money, rings, silver thimbles, &c., which they get, are instantly conveyed, from one hand to another, till the remotest person of the gang (who is not suspected, because they come not near the person robbed) gets possession of it; so that, in the strictest search, it is impossible to recover it; while the wretches, with imprecations, oaths, and protestations, disclaim the thievery.

That by which they are said to get the most money is, when young gentlewomen of good families and reputation have happened to be with child before marriage, a round sum is often bestowed among the gypsies, for some one mort to take the child; and, as that is never heard of more by the true mother and family, so the disgrace is kept concealed from the world; and, if the child lives, it never knows its parents.

H

HABERDASHER OF PRONOUNS. A schoolmaster, or usher.

HACKNEY WRITER. One who writes for attornies or booksellers.

HADDOCK. A purse. A *haddock stuffed with beans;* i. e. a purse full of gold.

HAIR SPLITTER. A thing *with* use *without* ornament.

HALBERT. A weapon carried by a sergeant of foot. To get a halbert; to be appointed a sergeant. To be brought to the halberts; to be flogged *à la militaire*: soldiers of the infantry, when flogged, being commonly tied to three halberts, set up in a triangle, with a fourth fastened across them. He carries the halbert in his face; a saying of one promoted from a sergeant to a commissioned officer.

HALF A BEAN. Half a guinea. *Cant.*

HALF A HOG. Sixpence.

HALF FLASH AND HALF FOOLISH. This phrase is applied, in a sarcastic manner, to those persons who have a *smattering* of the cant language, and also pretend to a knowledge of life, which they do not possess. The family of the *half flash and half foolish* are very numerous in London.

HALF SEAS OVER. Almost drunk.

HAMLET. A high constable. *Cant.*

HAMMERSMITH. *Milling:* a person that has received a severe beating is jocosely said to have been at Hammersmith.

HAMS, or HAMCASES. Breeches.

HAND. A sailor. We lost a hand; we lost a sailor. Bear a hand; make haste. Hand to fist; opposite: the same as tête-à-tête, or cheek by joul.

HAND BASKET PORTION. A woman whose husband receives frequent presents from her father or family is said to have a hand-basket portion.

HANDLE. To know how to handle one's fists; to be skilful in the art of boxing. The cove flashes a rare handle to his physog; the fellow has a large nose.

HANDSOME. He is a handsome-bodied man in the face; a jeering commendation of an ugly fellow. Handsome is that handsome does; a proverb frequently cited by ugly women.

HANDSOME REWARD. This, in advertisements, means a horse-whipping.

HANG AN A–SE. To hang back, to hesitate.

Hanger on. A dependant.

Hang Gallows Look. A thievish or villanous appearance.

Hang it on. Purposely to delay or protract the performance of any task or service you have undertaken, by dallying, and making as slow a progress as possible, either from natural indolence, or to answer some private end of your own. To *hang it on with* a woman, is to form a temporary connexion with her; to cohabit or keep company with her without marriage.

Hang it up. Score it up; speaking of a reckoning.

Hangman's Wages. Thirteen pence halfpenny; which, according to the vulgar tradition, was thus allotted: one shilling for the executioner, and three halfpence for the rope. N. B. This refers to former times; the hangmen of the present day having, like other artificers, raised their prices. The true state of this matter is, that a Scottish mark was the fee allowed for an execution, and the value of that piece was settled, by a proclamation of James I. at thirteen pence halfpenny.

Hang out. The traps scavey where we hang out; the officers know where we live.

Hank. He has a hank on him; i. e. an ascendancy over him, or a hold upon him. To have a person *at a good hank*, is to have made any contract with him very advantageous to yourself; or to be able, from some prior cause, to command or use him just as you please; to have the benefit of his purse or other services, in fact, upon your own terms. A Smithfield hank; an ox rendered furious by over-driving and barbarous treatment. *See* Bull Hank.

Hank. A spell or cessation from any work or duty, on the score of indisposition, or some other pretence.

Hanker. To hanker after any thing; to have a longing after or for it.

Hans in Kelder. Jack in the cellar; i. e. the child in the womb: a health frequently drank to breeding women or their husbands.

Hard. Stale beer, nearly sour, is said to be hard. Hard, also, means severe: as, hard fate, a hard master.

Hard at his A–se. Close after him.

Hare. He has swallowed a hare; he is drunk: more probably a *hair*, which requires washing down.

Harman. A constable. *Cant.*

Harman Beck. A beadle. *Cant.*

Harmans. The stocks. *Cant.*

Harp. To harp upon; to dwell upon a subject. Have among you, my blind harpers; an expression used in throwing or shooting at random among the crowd. Harp is also the Irish expression for woman, or tail, used in tossing up in Ireland: from Hibernia being represented with a harp on the reverse of the copper coins of that country; for which it is, in hoisting the copper, i. e. tossing up, sometimes likewise called music.

HARRIDAN. A hagged old woman; a miserable, scraggy, worn-out harlot, fit to take her bawd's degree: derived from the French word *haridelle*, a worn-out jade of a horse or mare.

HARRY. A country fellow. *Cant.* Old Harry; the Devil.

HARUM SCARUM. He was running harum scarum; said of any one running or walking hastily, and in a hurry, after they know not what.

HASH. To flash the hash; to vomit.

HAT. Old hat; the monosyllable, because frequently felt.

HATCHES. Under the hatches; in trouble, distress, or debt.

HATCHET FACE. A long, thin face.

HATCHWAY. The mouth. *Sea term.*

HAUL YOUR WIND. To get clear. *Sea term.*

HAVIL. A sheep. *Cant.*

HAWK. Ware hawk; the word to look sharp, a bye-word when a bailiff passes. Hawk also signifies a sharper, in opposition to pigeon. *See* PIGEON. *See* WARE HAWK.

HAZEL GILD. To beat any one with a hazel stick.

HEAD CULLY OF THE PASS, or PASSAGE BANK. The top tilter of that gang throughout the whole army, who demands and receives contribution from all the pass banks in the camp.

HEAD RAILS. Teeth. *Sea phrase.*

HEARING CHEATS. Ears. *Cant.*

HEART'S EASE. Gin.

HEARTY CHOAK. He will have a hearty choak and caper sauce for breakfast, i. e. he will be hanged.

HEATHEN PHILOSOPHER. One whose breech may be seen through his pocket-hole: this saying arose from the old philosophers, many of whom despised the vanity of dress to such a point as often to fall into the opposite extreme.

HEAVE. To rob. To heave a case; to rob a house. To heave a bough; to rob a booth. *Cant.*

HEAVER. The breast. *Cant.*

HEAVERS. Thieves who make it their business to steal tradesmen's shop-books. *Cant.*

HEAVY WET. Beer. *Cant.* Thus, in "The Ale-house Keeper's Lamentation," in Randall's Scrap Book, the bard says,

> "My caps were of the deepest mould
> That I could *bone* or get,
> And all the streams that in them roll'd
> Were *gin* or *heavy wet.*"

Hector. A bully, a swaggering coward. To hector; to bully: probably, from such persons affecting the valour of Hector, the Trojan hero.

Hedge. To make a hedge; to secure a bet or wager laid on one side, by taking the odds on the other; so that, let what will happen, a certain gain is secured, or hedged in, by the person who takes this precaution; who is then said to be on velvet.

Hedge Alehouse. A small, obscure alehouse.

Hedge Creeper. A robber of hedges.

Hedge Priest. An illiterate, unbeneficed curate, a patrico.

Hedge Whore. An itinerant harlot, who bilks the bagnios and bawdy-houses, by disposing of her favours on the way-side, under a hedge; a low beggarly prostitute.

Heels. To be laid by the heels; to be confined or put in prison. Out at heels; worn or diminished: his estate or affairs are out at heels. To turn up his heels; to turn up the knave of trumps at the game of all-fours.

Heel Tap. A peg in the heel of a shoe, taken out when it is finished. A person leaving any liquor in his glass is frequently called upon by the toast-master to take off his heel tap.

Hell. A tailor's repository for his stolen goods, called cabbage. *See* Cabbage. Little hell; a small, dark, covered passage, leading from London-wall to Bell-alley.

Hell-born Babe. A lewd, graceless youth, one naturally of a wicked disposition.

Hell Cat. A termagant, a vixen, a furious scolding woman. *See* Termagant and Vixen.

Hell fire Dick. The driver of the Cambridge Telegraph. He died lately (1822). He was the favourite companion of the University fashionables, and the only tutor to whose precepts they attended.

Hell Hound. A wicked abandoned fellow.

Hell, or Hells. Gambling-houses at the West End of the town. *Cant.*

Helter Skelter. To run helter skelter, hand over head, in defiance of order.

Hemp. Young hemp; an appellation for a graceless boy.

Hempen Fever. A man who was hanged is said to have died of a hempen fever; and, in Dorsetshire, to have been stabbed with a Bridport dagger; Bridport being a place famous for manufacturing hemp into cords.

Hempen Widow. One whose husband was hanged.

Hen. A woman. A cock and hen club; a club composed of men and women.

Hen-hearted. Cowardly.

Hen House. A house where the woman rules; called also a

she house, and *hen frigate*: the latter, a sea phrase, originally applied to a ship, the captain of which had his wife on board, supposed to command him.

HENPECKED. A husband governed by his wife, is said to be henpecked.

HERE AND THEREIAN. One who has no settled place of residence.

HERRING. The devil a barrel the better herring; all equally bad.

HERRING-GUTTED. Thin as a shotten herring.

HERRING-POND. The sea. To cross the herring-pond at the king's expense; to be transported.

HERTFORDSHIRE KINDNESS. Drinking twice to the same person.

HICK. A country hick; an ignorant clown. *Cant.*

HICKEY. Tipsey, quasi, hiccoughing.

HIDE AND SEEK. A childish game. He plays at hide and seek; a saying of one who is in fear of being arrested for debt, or apprehended for some crime, and therefore does not choose to appear in public, but secretly skulks up and down. *See* SKULK.

HIDEBOUND. Stingy, hard of delivery; a poet, poor in invention, is said to have a hidebound muse.

HIGGLEDY PIGGLEDY. Confusedly mixed.

HIGH AND DRY. Cast on shore. *Cant.*

HIGH EATING. To eat skylarks in a garret.

HIGH FLYERS. Dressy cyprians, such as sport bear-skin muffs, embroidered pelisses, hats and feathers.

HIGHGATE. Sworn at Highgate: a ridiculous custom formerly prevailed at the public-houses in Highgate, to administer a ludicrous oath to all travellers, of the middling rank, who stopped there. The party was sworn on a pair of horns, fastened on a stick: the substance of the oath was, never to kiss the maid when he could kiss the mistress, never to drink small-beer when he could get strong, with many other injunctions of the like kind; to all which was added the saving clause of "unless you like it best." The person administering the oath was always to be called father by the juror; and he, in return, was to style him son, under the penalty of a bottle.

HIGH JINKS. A gambler at dice, who, having a strong head, drinks to intoxicate his adversary, or pigeon. Under this head are also classed those fellows who keep Little Goes, take in insurances: also, attendants at the races, and at the E O Tables; chaps always on the look out to rob unwary countrymen at cards, &c.

HIGH LIVING. To lodge in a garret or cockloft.

HIGH PAD, or HIGH TOBY. A highwayman. *Cant.*

High Ropes. To be on the high ropes; to be in a passion.

High Shoon, or Clouted Shoon. A country clown.

High Water. It is high water with him; he is full of money.

Hike. To hike off; to run away. *Cant.*

Hind-Leg. To kick out a hind-leg; to make a rustic bow.

His Nabs. Him, or himself; a term used when speaking of a third person.

History of the Four Kings, or Child's best Guide to the Gallows. A pack of cards. He studies the history of the four kings assiduously; he plays much at cards.

Hoaxing. Bantering, ridiculing. Hoaxing a quiz; joking an odd fellow. *University wit.*

Hobberdehoy. Half a man and half a boy; a lad between both.

Hobbled. Impeded, interrupted, puzzled. To hobble; to walk lamely. Boned. *Cant.*

Hobbledygee. A pace between a walk and a run, a dog-trot.

Hobby. Sir Posthumous's hobby; one nice or whimsical in his clothes.

Hobby Horse. A man's favourite amusement, or study, is called his hobby horse: it also means a particular kind of small Irish horse; and also a wooden one, such as is given to children.

Hobby Horsical. A man who is a great keeper or rider of hobby horses; one that is apt to be strongly attached to his systems of amusement.

Hobnail. A country clodhopper: from the shoes of country farmers and ploughmen being commonly stuck full of hob-nails, and even often clouted, or tipped with iron. The Devil ran over his face with hobnails in his shoes; said of one pitted with the small-pox.

Hob, or Hobbinol. A clown.

Hob or Nob. Will you hob or nob with me? a question formerly in fashion at polite tables, signifying a request or challenge to drink a glass of wine with the proposer: if the party challenged answered Nob, they were to chuse whether white or red. This foolish custom is said to have orignated in the days of good queen Bess, thus: when great chimnies were in fashion, there was at each corner of the hearth, or grate, a small elevated projection, called hob, and behind it a seat. In winter time the beer was placed on the hob to warm: and the cold beer was set on a small table, said to have been called the nob: so that the question, Will you have hob or nob? seems only to have meant, Will you have warm or cold beer? i.e. beer from the hob, or beer from the nob.

Hobson's Choice. That or none; from old Hobson, a famous carrier of Cambridge, who used to let horses to the students; but never permitted them to chuse, always allotting each man the horse he thought most proper for his manner of riding and treatment.

Hockey. Drunk with strong stale beer, called old hock. *See* Hickey.

Hocking, or Houghing. A piece of cruelty practised by the butchers of Dublin on soldiers, by cutting the tendon of Achilles; this has by law been made felony.

Hocks. A vulgar appellation for the feet. You have left the marks of your dirty hocks on my clean stairs; a frequent complaint from a mop squeezer to a footman.

Hocus Pocus. Nonsensical words used by jugglers, previous to their deceptions, as a kind of charm, or incantation. A celebrated writer supposes it to be a ludicrous corruption of the words *hoc est corpus,* used by the popish priests in consecrating the host: also, Hell Hocus is used to express drunkenness: as, he is quite hocus; he is quite drunk.

Hod. Brother Hod; a familiar name for a bricklayer's labourer: from the hod which is used for carrying bricks and mortar.

Hoddy Doddy, all A–se and no Body. A short clumsy person, either male or female.

Hodge. An abbreviation of Roger: a general name for a country booby.

Hodge Podge. An irregular mixture for numerous things.

Hodmandods. Snails in their shells.

Hog. A shilling. To drive one's hogs; to snore: the noise made by some persons in snoring, being not much unlike the notes of that animal. He has brought his hogs to a fine market; a saying of any one who has been remarkably successful in his affairs, and is spoken ironically to signify the contrary. A hog in armour; an awkward or mean looking man or woman, finely dressed, is said to look like a hog in armour. To hog a horse's main; to cut it short, so that the ends of the hair stick up like hog's bristles. Jonian hogs; an appellation given to the members of St. John's College, Cambridge.

Hoggish. Rude, unmannerly, filthy.

Hog Grubber. A mean stingy fellow.

Hogo. Corruption of *haut goust,* high taste, or flavour; commonly said of flesh somewhat tainted. It has a confounded hogo; it stinks confoundedly.

Hoist. To go upon the hoist; to get into windows accidentally left open: this is done by the assistance of a confederate, called the hoist, who leans his head against the wall, making his back a kind of step or ascent.

Hoist. The *game* of shop-lifting is called *the hoist*: a person expert at this practice is said to be a *good hoist*.

Hoisting. A ludicrous ceremony formerly performed on every soldier, the first time he appeared in the field after being married; it was managed thus: As soon as the regiment, or company, had grounded their arms to rest awhile, three or four men of the same company to which the bridegroom belonged, seized upon him, and putting a couple of bayonets out of the two corners of his hat, to represent horns, it was placed on his head, the back part foremost. He was then hoisted on the shoulders of two strong fellows, and carried round the arms, a drum and fife beating and playing the pioneers call, named Round Heads and Cuckolds, but, on this occasion, styled the Cuckold's March; in passing the colours he was to take off his hat: this, in some regiments, was practised by the officers on their brethren.

Hoity-toity. A hoity-toity wench; a giddy, thoughtless, romping, girl.

Holborn-Hill. To ride backwards up Holborn-hill; to go to the gallows: the way to Tyburn, the place of execution for criminals condemned in London, was up that hill. Criminals going to suffer, always ride backwards, as some conceive, to increase the ignominy, but more probably to prevent them being shocked with a distant view of the gallows; as, in amputations, surgeons conceal the instruments with which they are going to operate. The last execution at Tyburn, and, consequently, the last of this procession, was in the year 1784, since which the criminals have been executed near Newgate.

Holiday. A holiday bowler; a bad bowler. Blind man's holiday; darkness, night. It is all holiday. *See* All Holiday.

Hollow. It was quite a hollow thing; i. e. certainty, or decided business.

Hollow. Among epicures, means poultry. Nothing but *hollow* for dinner.

Holy Ground, or Land. A well-known region of St. Giles's. An old *fancy* chaunt ends every verse thus:—

> "For we are the boys of the *Holy Ground*,
> And we'll dance upon nothing and turn us round."

Holy Lamb. A thorough-paced villain. *Irish.*

Holy Water. He loves him as the Devil likes holy water; i. e. hates him mortally. Holy water, according to the Roman Catholics, having the virtue to chase away the Devil and his imps.

Honest Man. A term frequently used by superiors to inferiors. As honest a man as any in the cards when all the kings are out; i. e. a knave. I dare not call thee rogue for fear of the law, said a quaker to an attorney; but I will give thee five pounds, if thou canst find any creditable person who wilt say thou art an honest man.

HONEST WOMAN. To marry a woman with whom one has cohabited as a mistress, is termed, making an honest woman of her.

HONEY MOON. The first month after marriage. A poor honey; a harmless, foolish, good-natured fellow. It is all honey, or all t—d, with them; said of persons who are either in the extremity of friendship or enmity, either kissing or fighting.

HOOD-WINKED. Blindfolded by a handkerchief, or other ligature, bound over the eyes.

HOOF. To beat the hoof; to travel on foot. He hoofed it or beat the hoof every step of the way from Chester to London.

HOOK AND SNIVEY, WITH NIX THE BUFFER. This rig consists in feeding a man and a dog for nothing, and is carried on thus: Three men, one of whom pretends to be sick and unable to eat, go to a public-house; the two well men make a bargain with the landlord for their dinner, and when he is out of sight, feed their pretended sick companion and dog gratis.

HOOKED. Over-reached, tricked, caught: a simile taken from fishing. * * * * hooks; fingers.

HOOKEE WALKER. An expression signifying that the story is not true, or that the thing will not occur.

HOOKERS. *See* ANGLERS.

HOOP. To run the hoop; an ancient marine custom. Four or more boys, having their left hands tied fast to an iron hoop, and each of them a rope, called a nettle, in their right, being naked to the waist, wait the signal to begin: this being made by a stroke with a cat of nine tails, given by the boatswain to one of the boys, he strikes the boy before him, and every one does the same: at first, the blows are but gently administered; but each, irritated by the strokes from the boy behind him, at length lays it on in earnest. This was anciently practised when a ship was wind-bound.

HOOP. To beat. I'll well hoop his or her barrel. I'll beat him or her soundly.

HOP. A dance. *Sea term.*

HOPKINS. Mr. Hopkins; a ludicrous address to a lame or limping man, being a pun on the word *hop*.

HOP MERCHANT. A dancing-master. *See* CAPER MERCHANT.

HOP-O'-MY-THUMB. A diminutive person, man or woman. She was such a hop-o'-my-thumb, that a pigeon, sitting on her shoulder, might pick a pea out of her a–se.

HOPPER-ARSED. Having large projecting buttocks; from their resemblance to a small basket, called a hopper or hoppet, worn by husbandmen, for containing seed-corn, when they sow the land.

HOPPER DOCKERS. Shoes. *Cant.*

HOPPING GILES. A jeering appellation given to any person who limps, or is lame: St. Giles was the patron of cripples, lepers, &c. Churches dedicated to that saint commonly stand out of town, many of them having been chapels to hospitals. *See* GYLES.

HOP THE TWIG. To run away. *Cant.*

HORN COLIC. A temporary priapism.

HORN FAIR. An annual fair held at Charlton, in Kent, on St. Luke's day, the 18th of October. It consists of a riotous mob, who, after a printed summons dispersed through the adjacent towns, meet at Cuckold's Point, near Deptford, and march from thence, in procession, through that town and Greenwich to Charlton, with horns of different kinds upon their heads; and at the fair there are sold rams horns, and every sort of toy made of horn; even the gingerbread figures have horns. The vulgar tradition gives the following history of the origin of this fair: King John, or some other of our ancient kings, being at the palace of Eltham, in this neighbourhood, and having been out hunting one day, rambled from his company to this place, then a mean hamlet; when entering a cottage to inquire his way, he was struck with the beauty of the mistress, whom he found alone; and having prevailed over her modesty, the husband returned suddenly, surprised them together, and threatened to kill them both; the king was obliged to discover himself, and to compound for his safety by a purse of gold, and a grant of the land from this place to Cuckold's Point, besides making the husband master of the hamlet. It is added, that, in memory of this grant, and the occasion of it, this fair was established, for the sale of horns, and all sorts of goods made with that material. A sermon is preached at Charlton church on the fair day.

HORNIFIED. Cuckolded.

HORN MAD. A person extremely jealous of his wife is said to be horn mad; also, a cuckold who does not cut or breed his horns easily.

HORNS. To draw in one's horns; to retract an assertion through fear: metaphor borrowed from a snail, who, on the apprehension of danger, draws in his horns, and retires to his shell.

HORN WORK. Cuckold-making.

HORSE BUSS. A kiss with a loud smack: also, a bite.

HORSE COSER. A dealer in horses; vulgarly and corruptly pronounced *horse courser*. The verb *to cose* was used, by the Scots, in the sense of bartering or exchanging.

HORSE GODMOTHER. A large masculine woman, a gentleman-like kind of lady.

HORSE'S MEAL. A meal without drinking.

HOSTELER. Oat-stealer. Hosteler was originally the name for an inn-keeper; inns being, in old English, styled hostels, from the French, signifying the same.

HOT POT. Ale and brandy made hot.

HOT STOMACH. He has so hot a stomach, that he burns all the clothes off his back; said of one who pawns his clothes to purchase liquor.

HOUSE, or TENEMENT, TO LET. A widow's weeds: also, an achievement marking the death of a husband, set up on the outside of a mansion; both supposed to indicate that the dolorous widow wants a male comforter.

HOXTER. An inside pocket. *Cant.*

HOYDON. A romping girl.

HOYS. Shoplifting. *Cant.*

HUBBLE-BUBBLE. Confusion. A hubble-bubble fellow; a man of confused ideas, or one thick of speech, whose words sound like water bubbling out of a bottle: also, an instrument used for smoking through water in the East Indies, called likewise a caloon, and hooker.

HUBBUB. A noise, riot, or disturbance.

HUCKLE MY BUFF. Beer, egg, and brandy, made hot.

HUCKSTERS. Itinerant retailers of provisions. He is in hucksters' hands; he is in a bad way.

HUE. To lash. The cove was hued in the naskin; the rogue was soundly lashed in bridewell. *Cant.*

HUFF. To reprove, or scold at, any one: also, to bluster, bounce, ding, or swagger. A captain huff; a noted bully. To stand the huff; to be answerable for the reckoning in a public house.

HUG. To hug brown bess; to carry a firelock, or serve as a private soldier. He hugs it as the Devil hugs a witch; said of one who holds any thing as if he were afraid of losing it.

HUGGER MUGGER. By stealth, privately, without making an appearance. They spent their money in a hugger mugger way.

HULKY, or HULKING. A great hulky fellow; an overgrown clumsy lout or fellow.

HUM, or HUMBUG. To deceive, or impose on any one by some story or device. A humbug; a jocular imposition, or deception. To hum and haw; to hesitate in speech: also, to delay, or be with difficulty brought to consent to any matter or business.

HUM BOX. A pulpit.

HUM CAP. Very old and strong beer; called, also, stingo. *See* STINGO.

HUM DRUM. A hum drum fellow; a dull tedious narrator, a bore: also, a set of gentlemen who (Bailey says) used to meet near the Charter-house, or at the King's Head, in St. John's Street, who had more of pleasantry, and less of mystery, than the Freemasons.

HUM DURGEON. An imaginary illness. He has got the hum durgeon, the thickest part of his thigh is nearest his a--se; i. e. nothing ails him except low spirits.

HUMMER. A great lie, a rapper. *See* RAPPER.

HUMMUMS. A bagnio, or bathing-house.

HUMP. To hump; once a fashionable term for copulation.

HUMPTY DUMPTY. A little humpty dumpty man or woman; a short, clumsy person of either sex: also, ale boiled with brandy.

HUMS. Persons at church. There is a great number of hums in the autem; there is a great congregation in the church.

HUMSTRUM. A musical instrument made of a mopstick, a bladder, and some packthread, thence also called a bladder and string and hurdy-gurdy: it is played on like a violin, which is sometimes ludicrously called a humstrum: sometimes, instead of a bladder, a tin canister is used.

HUNCH. To jostle or thrust.

HUNCH-BACKED. Hump-backed.

HUNG BEEF. A dried bull's pizzle. How the dubber served the cull with hung beef; how the turnkey beat the fellow with a bull's pizzle.

HUNKS. A covetous miserable fellow, a miser: also, the name of a famous bear mentioned by Ben Jonson.

HUNTING. Drawing in unwary persons to play or game. *Cant.*

HUNTSUP. The reveille of huntsmen, sounded on the French horn, or other instrument.

HURDY GURDY. A kind of fiddle, originally made, perhaps, out of a gourd. *See* HUMSTRUM.

HURLY BURLY. A rout, riot, bustle, or confusion.

HUSH. Hush the cull; murder the fellow.

HUSH MONEY. Money given to hush up or conceal a robbery, theft, or any other offence, or to take off the evidence from appearing against a criminal.

HUSSY. An abbreviation of housewife; but now always used as a term of reproach: as, How now, hussy? or, She is a light hussy.

HUZZA. Said to have been originally the cry of the huzzars, or Hungarian light horse; but now the national shout of the English, both civil and military: in the sea phrase termed a cheer; to give three cheers being to huzza thrice.

HYP. The hypochondriac; low spirits. He is hypped; he has got the blue devils, &c.

HYP, or HIP. A mode of calling to any one passing by. Hip, Michael, your head's on fire; a piece of vulgar wit to a red haired man.

I & J

JABBER. To talk thick and fast, as great praters usually do; to chatter like a magpie: also, to speak a foreign language. He jabbered to me in his damned outlandish parlez vous, but I could not understand him; he chattered to me in French, or some other foreign language, but I could not understand him.

JACK. A farthing. A small bowl, serving as the mark for bowlers. An instrument for pulling off boots.

JACK. A post-chaise. *Cant.*

JACK ADAMS. A fool. Jack Adams's parish; Clerkenwell.

JACKANAPES. An ape. A pert, ugly, little fellow.

JACKED. Spavined. A jacked horse.

JACKET. To *jacket* a person, or *clap a jacket* on him, is nearly synonymous with *bridging* him. *See* BRIDGE. But this term is more properly applied to removing a man by underhand and vile means from any birth or situation he enjoys, commonly with a view to supplant him; therefore, when a person is supposed to have fallen a victim to such infamous machinations, it is said to have been a *jacketting concern.*

JACK IN A BOX. A sharper, or cheat. A child in the mother's womb.

JACK IN AN OFFICE. An insolent fellow in authority.

JACK KETCH. The hangman. *Vide* DERRICK and KETCH.

JACKMEN. *See* JARKMEN.

JACK NASTY FACE. A sea term, signifying a common sailor.

JACK OF LEGS. A tall long-legged man: also, a giant said to be buried in Weston-church-yard, near Baldock, in Hertfordshire, where there are two stones fourteen feet distant, said to be the head and feet stones of his grave. This giant, says Salmon, as fame goes, lived in a wood here, and was a great robber, but a generous one; for he plundered the rich to feed the poor. He frequently took bread for this purpose from the Baldock bakers, who, catching him at an advantage, put out his eyes, and afterwards hanged him upon a knoll in Baldock-field. At his death, he made one request, which was, that he might have his bow and arrow put into his hand, and, on shooting it off, where the arrow fell they would bury him; which being granted, the arrow fell in Weston-church-yard. Above seventy years ago, a very large thigh-bone was taken out of the church chest, where it had lain many years for a show, and was sold by the clerk to Sir John Tradescant, who, it is said, put it among the rarities of Oxford.

JACK PUDDING. The merry-andrew, zany, or jester, to a mountebank.

JACK ROBINSON. Before one could say Jack Robinson; a saying to express a very short time; originating from a very volatile gentleman of that appellation, who would call on his neighbours, and begone before his name could be announced.

JACK SPRAT. A dwarf, or diminutive fellow.

JACK TAR. A sailor.

JACK WEIGHT. A fat man.

JACK WHORE. A large, masculine, overgrown wench.

JACKY. Gin. Speaking of the *Seven Dials*, the author of Randall (a Fragment) poetically says,

> " 'Tis
> Where *Jacky* 's drank until the senses reel;
> Where *Beauty* 's *bashful*, and where *Wit* 's *genteel*."
> *Vide Randall's Diary.*

JACOB. A soft fellow, a fool, a spooney, or innocent.

JACOB. A ladder; perhaps from Jacob's dream. *Cant.* Also, the common name for a jay; jays being usually taught to say, Poor Jacob! a cup of sack for Jacob.

JACOBITES. Sham or collar shirts: also, partizans for the Stuart family; from the name of the abdicated king, i. e. James, or Jacobus.

JADE. A term of reproach to women.

JAGUE. A ditch; perhaps, from jakes.

JAIL BIRDS. Prisoners.

JAKES. A house of office, a cacatorium.

JAMMED. Hanged. *Cant.*

JANIZARIES. The mob, sometimes so called: also, bailiffs, their setters, and followers.

JAPANNED. Ordained. To be japanned; to enter into holy orders, to become a clergyman, to put on the black cloth; from the colour of the japan ware, which is black.

JARK. A seal.

JARKMEN. Those who fabricate counterfeit passes, licenses, and certificates, for beggars.

JARVIS, or JARVY. A hackney coachman. *Cant.*

JASON'S FLEECE. A citizen cheated of his gold.

JAUN. To discover. *Scotch cant.*

JAW. Speech, discourse. Give us none of your jaw; let us have none of your discourse. A jaw-me-dead; a talkative fellow. Jaw work; a cry used in fairs by the sellers of nuts.

JAWING TACKLE ON BOARD. To be saucy or impudent. *Sea slang.*

JASEY. A bob wig.

IDEA-POT. The knowledge-box, the head. *See* KNOWLEDGE-BOX.

JEFFY. It will be done in a jeffy; it will be done in a short space of time, in an instant.

JEHU. To drive Jehu-like; to drive furiously; from a king of Israel of that name, who was a famous charioteer, and mentioned as such in the Bible.

JEM. A gold ring. *Cant.*

JEMMY. A crow. This instrument is much used by housebreakers. Sometimes called Jemmy Rook.

JEMMY FELLOW. A smart spruce fellow.

JENNY. An instrument for lifting up the grate or top of a show-glass, in order to rob it. *Cant.*

JERRY. A fog or mist. *Cant.*

JERRYCUMMUMBLE. To shake, towzle, or tumble about.

JERRY SNEAK. A henpecked husband; from a celebrated character in one of Mr. Foote's plays, representing a man governed by his wife.

JESSAMY. A smart, jemmy fellow, a fopling.

JESUIT. *See* BOX THE JESUIT.

JESUITICAL. Sly, evasive, equivocal. A jesuitical answer; an equivocal answer.

JET. A lawyer. Autem jet; a parson.

JEW. A tradesman who has no faith; i. e. will not give credit.

JEW'S EYE. "That's worth a Jew's eye;" a pleasant or agreeable sight: a saying taken from Shakspeare.

JIBBER THE KIBBER. A method of deceiving seamen, by fixing a candle and lanthorn round the neck of a horse, one of whose fore feet is tied up; this, at night, has the appearance of a ship's light. Ships bearing towards it, run on shore, and, being wrecked, are plundered by the inhabitants. This diabolical device, it is said, has been practised by the inhabitants of our western coasts.

JIG. A trick. A pleasant jig; a witty arch trick: also, a lock or door. The feather-bed jig; copulation.

JIGGER. A whipping-post: also, a door. *Sea cant.*

JILT. A tricking woman, who encourages the addresses of a man whom she means to deceive and abandon.

Jilted. Rejected by a woman who has encouraged a man's advances.

Jingle Boxes. Leathern jacks tipped with silver, and hung with bells, formerly in use among fuddle caps. *Cant.*

Jingle Brains. A wild, thoughtless, rattling, fellow.

Jinglers. Horse cosers, frequenting country fairs.

Ignoramus. A stupid fellow.

Impost takers. Usurers who attend the gaming-tables, and lend money at great premiums.

Impure. A modern term for a lady of easy virtue.

Inching. Encroaching.

India Wipe. A silk handkerchief.

Indies. Black Indies; Newcastle.

Indorser. A sodomite. To indorse with a cudgel; to drub or beat a man over the back with a stick, to lay *cane* upon Abel.

Inexpressibles. Breeches.

In it. To let another partake of any benefit or acquisition you have acquired by robbery, or otherwise, is called *putting* him *in it:* a *family-man* who is accidentally witness to a robbery, &c. effected by one or more others, will say to the latter, Mind, I'm *in it;* which is generally acceded to, being the established custom; but there seems more of courtesy than right in this practice.

Inkle Weavers. Supposed to be a very brotherly set of people; "as great as two inkle weavers" being a proverbial saying.

Inlaid. Well inlaid; in easy circumstances, rich or well to pass.

Innocents. One of the innocents; a weak or simple person, man or woman.

Inside and Outside. The inside of a **** and the outside of a gaol.

In the Wind. Drunk. *Sea term.*

In Town. Flush of money; *breeched.*

Job. A guinea. Any concerted robbery, which is to be executed at a certain time, is spoken of by the parties as *the job*, or having *a job* to do at such a place; and in this case as regular preparations are made, and as great debates held, as about any legal business undertaken by the industrious part of the community.

Job. Any robbery. To do a job; to commit some kind of robbery.

Job. To reprove or reprehend. *Cambridge term.*

Jobation. A reproof.

Jobbernole. The head.

Job's Comfort. Reproof instead of consolation.

Job's Comforter. One who brings news of some additional misfortune.

Job's Dock. He is laid up in Job's dock; i.e. in a salivation. The apartments for the foul or venereal patients in St. Bartholomew's hospital are called Job's ward.

Jock, or Crowdy-headed Jock. A jeering appellation for a north country seaman, particularly a collier; Jock being a common name, and crowdy the chief food, of the lower order of the people in Northumberland.

Jock, or Jockum-cloy. To enjoy a woman.

Jockum Gage. A chamber-pot, jordan, looking-glass, or member-mug. *Cant.*

Jogg-trot. To keep on a jogg-trot; to get on with a slow but regular pace.

Jogue. A shilling. *Cant.*

Johnny-Bum. A he or jack ass: so called by a lady that affected to be extremely polite and modest, who would not say Jack because it was vulgar, nor ass because it was indecent.

Johnny-Raw. A gawky countryman; as stupid as a waggon-horse.

Joint. To hit a joint in carving, the operator must think of a cuckold. To put one's nose out of joint; to rival one in the favour of a patron or mistress.

Jolly Dog. A merry facetious fellow; a *bon vivant*, who never flinches from his glass, nor cries to go home to bed.

Jolly, or Jolly Nob. The head. I'll lump your jolly nob for you; I'll give you a knock on the head.

Jolter Head. A large head; metaphorically a stupid fellow.

Jonnok. Game, up to the mark. He is *jonnok;* meaning a good man. *Lan. dialect.*

Jordan. A chamber-pot.

Jorum. A jug, or large pitcher.

Joseph. A woman's great coat: also, a sheepish bashful young fellow: an allusion to Joseph who fled from Potiphar's wife. You are Josephus rex; you are jo-king, i.e. joking.

Joskin. A countryman. The drop-cove maced the joskin of twenty quid; the ring-dropper cheated the countryman of twenty guineas.

Jowl. The cheek. Cheek by jowl; close together, or cheek to cheek. My eyes, how the cull sucked the blowen's jowl; he kissed the wench handsomely.

Irish Apricots. Potatoes. It is a common joke against the Irish vessels to say they are loaded with fruit and timber; that is, potatoes and broomsticks. Irish assurance; a bold forward behaviour: as, being dipped in the river Styx was formerly supposed to render persons invulnerable, so it is said that a dip in the river Shannon totally annihilates bashfulness; whence arises the saying of an impudent Irishman, that he has been dipped in the Shannon.

IRISH BEAUTY. A woman with two black eyes.

IRISH LEGS. Thick legs, jocularly styled the Irish arms. It is said of the Irish women, that they have a dispensation from the Pope to wear the thick end of their legs downwards.

IRON. Money in general. To polish the king's iron with one's eyebrows; to look out of grated or prison windows, or, as the Irishman expresses them, the iron glass windows. Iron doublet; a prison. *See* STONE DOUBLET.

IRONMONGER'S SHOP. To keep an ironmonger's shop by the side of a common, where the sheriff sets one up; to be hanged in chains. Iron-bound; laced. An iron-bound hat; a silver-laced hat.

ISLAND. He drank out of the bottle till he saw the island; the island is the rising bottom of a wine-bottle, which appears like an island in the centre, before the bottle is quite empty.

ISLE OF BISHOP. So named from the good orthodox mead, composed of port wine and roasted oranges or lemons. *Oxf. Univ. cant.*

ISLE OF BULL-DOGS. From the satellites in the proctor's hemisphere. *Oxf. Univ. cant.*

ISLE OF FLIP. From the generous fluid that springeth from eggs and sherry. *Oxf. Univ. cant.*

ISLE OF MATRICULATION. First entrance into the University. *Oxf. cant.*

ITCHLAND, or SCRATCHLAND. Scotland.

JUDGE. A *family-man*, whose talents and experience have rendered him a complete adept in his profession, and who acts with a systematic prudence on all occasions, is allowed to be, and called by his friends, a fine *judge*.

JUDGEMENT. Prudence; economy in acting; abilities (the result of long experience) for executing the most intricate and hazardous projects; any thing accomplished in a masterly manner is, therefore, said to have been done with *judgement:* on concerting or planning any operations, one party will say, I think it would be *judgement* to do so and so, meaning expedient to do it.

JUDY. A *blowen;* but sometimes used when speaking familiarly of any woman.

JUGELOW. A dog.

JUGGLER'S BOX. The engine for burning culprits in the hand. *Cant.*

JUKRUM. A license.

JUMBLEGUT-LANE. A rough road or lane.

Jump. The jump, or dining-room jump; a species of robbery effected by ascending a ladder placed, by a sham lamplighter, against the house intended to be robbed. It is so called because, should the lamp-lighter be put to flight, the thief who ascended the ladder has no means of escaping but that of jumping down.

Jumpers. Persons who rob houses by getting in at the windows: also, a set of Methodists established in South Wales: also, a ten-penny piece. *Scotch cant.*

Juniper Lecture. A round scolding bout.

Jury Leg. A wooden leg: in allusion to a jury mast, which is a temporary substitute for a mast carried away by a storm, or any other accident. *Sea phrase.*

Jury Mast. A *journiere* mast; i.e. a mast for the day or occasion.

Just-ass. A punning appellation for a justice.

Ivories. Teeth. How the swell flashed his ivories; how the gentleman showed his teeth. To sluice the ivories; to drink.

Ivy Bush. Like an owl in an ivy bush; a simile for a meagre or weasel-faced man, with a large wig, or very bushy hair.

K

KATE. A picklock. 'Tis a rum kate; it is a clever picklock. *Cant.*

Keel Bullies. Men employed to load and unload the coal vessels.

Keelhauling. A punishment in use among the Dutch seamen, in which, for certain offences, the delinquent is drawn once, or oftener, under the ship's keel: ludicrously defined, undergoing a great hard-ship.

Keep. To inhabit. L—d, where do you keep? i.e. where are your rooms? *Academical phrase.* Mother, your tit won't keep; your daughter will not preserve her virginity.

Keeping Cully. One who keeps a mistress, as he supposes, for his own use, but really for that of the public.

Keep it up. To prolong a debauch. We kept it up finely last night: metaphor drawn from the game of shuttlecock.

Keffel. A horse. *Welch.*

Kelp. A hat. To *kelp* a person, is to move your hat to him.

Kelter. Condition, order. Out of kelter; out of order.

Kelter. Money.

Kemp's Morris. William Kemp, said to have been the original Dogberry, in Much Ado about Nothing, danced a morris from London to Norwich in nine days; of which he printed the account, A. D. 1600, entitled, "*Kemp's Nine Days' Wonder*," &c.

Kemp's Shoes. Would I had Kemp's shoes to throw after you. *Ben Jonson.* Perhaps Kemp was a man remarkable for his good luck or fortune; throwing an old shoe or shoes after any one going on an important business, being, by the vulgar, deemed lucky. *Obsolete.*

Ken. A house. A bob ken, or a bowman ken; a well furnished house: also, a house that harbours thieves. Biting the ken; robbing the house. *Cant.*

Ken Miller, or Ken Cracker. A housebreaker. *Cant.*

Kent. A coloured pocket handkerchief of cotton or linen.

Kent-Street Ejectment. To take away the street door: a method practised by the landlords in Kent-street, Southwark, when their tenants are above a fortnight's rent in arrear.

Kerry Security. Bond, pledge, oath, and keep the money.

Ketch. Jack Ketch; a general name for the finishers of the law, or hangmen, ever since the year 1682, when the office was filled by a famous practitioner of that name, of whom his wife said, that any bungler might put a man to death, but only her husband knew how to make a gentleman die sweetly. This officer is mentioned in Butler's Ghost, page 54, published about 1682, in the following lines:

> "Till Ketch, observing he was chous'd,
> And in his profits much abus'd,
> In open hall the tribute dunn'd,
> To do his office, or refund."

Mr. Ketch had not long been elevated to his office; for the name of his predecessor, Dun, occurs in the former part of this poem, page 29:

> "For you yourself to act squire Dun,
> Such ignominy ne'er saw the sun.

The addition of "squire," with which Mr. Dun is here dignified, is a mark that he had beheaded some state criminal for high treason; an operation which, according to custom, for time out of mind, has always entitled the operator to that distinction. The predecessor of Dun was Gregory Brandon, from whom the gallows was called the Gregorian tree; by which name it is mentioned in the prologue to Mercurius Pragmaticus, tragi-comedy, acted at Paris, &c. 1641:

"This trembles under the black rod, and he
Doth fear his fate from the Gregorian-tree."

Gregory Brandon succeeded Derrick. *See* DERRICK.

KETTLE DRUMS. Cupid's kettle drums; a woman's breasts; called by sailors chest and bedding.

KETTLE OF FISH. When a person has perplexed his affairs in general, or any particular business, he is said to have made a fine kettle of fish of it.

KICK. A sixpence, when speaking of compound sums only: as, *three and a kick,* is three and sixpence, &c.

KICKERAPOO. Dead. *Negro word.*

KICKS. Breeches. A high kick; the top of the fashion. It is all the kick; it is the present mode. Tip us your kicks, we'll have them as well as your lour; pull off your breeches, for we must have them as well as your money. A kick in the guts; a dram of gin or any other spirituous liquor. A kick up; a disturbance: also, a hop, or dance. An odd kick in one's gallop; a strange whim or peculiarity.

KICKSEYS. Breeches.

KICKSHAWS. French dishes; corruption of *quelque chose.*

KICK THE BUCKET. To die. He kicked the bucket one day; he died one day. To kick the clouds before the hotel door; i. e. to be hanged.

KID. A little dapper fellow. A child. The blowen has napped the kid; the girl is with child: also, a child of either sex; but particularly applied to a boy who commences thief at an early age; and when, by his dexterity, he has become famous, he is called, by his acquaintance, *the kid* so and so, mentioning his sirname.

KID. To coax, or wheedle, to inveigle, to amuse a man, or divert his attention while another robs him. The sneaksman kidded the cove of the ken, while his pall frisked it; the thief amused the master of the house, while his companion robbed it.

KIDDER. A forestaller. *See* CROCKER. Kidders are also persons employed by the gardeners to gather peas.

KIDDY. A thief of the lower order, who, when he is *breeched,* by a course of successful depredation, dresses in the extreme of vulgar gentility, and affects a knowingness in his air and conversation, which renders him, in reality, an object of ridicule; such a one is pronounced, by his associates of the same class, a *flash kiddy,* or a *rolling kiddy. My kiddy* is a familiar term used by these gentry in addressing each other.

KIDDY NIPPERS. Tailors out of work, who cut off the waistcoat pockets of their brethren, when cross-legged on their board, thereby grabbling their bit. *Cant.*

KID LAY. Rogues who make it their business to defraud

young apprentices, or errand-boys, of goods committed to their charge, by prevailing on them to execute some trifling message, pretending to take care of their parcels till they come back: these are, in cant terms, said to be on the kid lay.

KIDNAPPER. Originally, one who stole or decoyed children or apprentices from their parents or masters, to send them to the colonies; called, also, spiriting: but now used for all recruiting crimps for the king's troops, or those of the East India Company; and agents for indenturing servants for the plantations, &c.

KIDNEY. Disposition, principles, humour. Of a strange kidney; of an odd or unaccountable humour. A man of a different kidney; a man of different principles.

KIDRIG. Meeting a child in the streets, who is going on some errand, and, by a false, but well fabricated, story, obtaining any parcel or goods it may be carrying: this *game* is practised by two persons, who have each their respective parts to play, and even porters and other grown persons are sometimes defrauded of their load by this artifice. To *kid* a person *out of* any thing, is to obtain it from him by means of a false pretence; as, that you were sent by a third person, &c.: such impositions are all generally termed *the kidrig*.

KID'S EYE. A fi'penny piece. *Scotch cant.*

KILKENNY. An old frieze coat.

KILL DEVIL. New still-burnt rum.

KILL PRIEST. Port wine.

KIMBAW. To trick, cheat, or cozen: also, to beat, or to bully. Let's kimbaw the cull; let's bully the fellow. To set one's arms a-kimbaw, vulgarly pronounced a-kimbo, is, to rest one's hands on the hips, keeping the elbows square, and sticking out from the body; an insolent, bullying attitude. *Cant.*

KINCHIN. A little child. Kinchin coves; orphan beggar boys, educated in thieving. Kinchin morts; young girls under the like circumstances and training. Kinchin morts, or coves in slates; beggars' children carried at their mother's backs in sheets. Kinchin cove; a little man. *Cant.*

KINGDOM COME. He is gone to kingdom come; he is dead.

KING JOHN'S MEN. He is one of King John's men, eight score to the hundred: a saying of a little undersized man.

KING OF THE GYPSIES. The captain, chief, or ringleader, of the gang of misrule: in the cant language called also the upright man.

KING'S BAD BARGAIN. One of the king's bad bargains; a malingeror, or soldier, who shirks his duty.

KING'S HEAD INN, or CHEQUER INN, IN NEWGATE STREET. The prison of Newgate.

KING'S PICTURES. Coin, money.

KING'S PLATE. Fetters.

KINGSWOOD LION. An ass. Kingswood is famous for the great number of asses kept by the colliers who inhabit that place.

KIP. The skin of a large calf, in the language of the excise-office.

KIPPING. Playing the truant. *Scotch term.*

KISSING CRUST. That part where the loaves have touched the oven.

KISS MINE A–SE. An offer, as Fielding observes, "very frequently made, but never, as he could learn, literally accepted." A kiss mine a--se fellow; a sycophant.

KIT. A dancing-master; so called from his kit or cittern, a small fiddle, which dancing-masters always carry about with them, to play to their scholars. The kit is likewise the whole of a soldier's necessaries, the contents of his knapsack; and is used also to express the whole of different commodities; as, Here, take the whole kit; i. e. take all.

KITCHEN PHYSIC. Food, good meat roasted or boiled. A little kitchen physic will set him up; he has more need of a cook than a doctor.

KITTLE PITCHERING. A jocular method of hobbling or bothering a troublesome teller of long stories: this is done by contradicting some very immaterial circumstance at the beginning of the narration, the objections to which being settled, others are immediately started to some new particular of like consequence; thus impeding, or, rather, not suffering him to enter into, the main story. Kittle pitchering is often practised in confederacy, one relieving the other, by which the design is rendered less obvious.

KITTYS. Effects, furniture, stock in trade. To seize one's kittys; to take his sticks.

KNACK SHOP. A toy-shop, a nick-nack-atory.

KNAP. To steal, take, receive, accept, according to the sense it is used in: as, to *knap a clout*, is to steal a pocket-handkerchief: to *knap the swag* from your *pall*, is to take from him the property he has just stolen, for the purpose of carrying it: to *knap seven or fourteen pen'-worth*, is to receive sentence of transportation for seven or fourteen years: to *knap the glim*, is to catch the venereal disease: in making a bargain, to *knap* the sum offered you, is to accept it; speaking of a woman, supposed to be pregnant, it is common to say, I believe *Mr. Knap* is *concerned*, meaning that she has *knapp'd*.

KNAPPERS POLL. A sheep's head. *Cant.*

KNAPPING A JACOB FROM A DUNAGAN-DRAG. This is a curious species of robbery, or, rather, borrowing without leave, for the purpose of robbery; it signifies taking away the short ladder from a nightman's cart, while the men are gone into a house, the privy of which they are employed in emptying, in order to effect an ascent to a one-pair-of-stairs window, to scale a garden-wall, &c. after which the ladder, of course, is left to rejoin its master as it can.

KNAVE IN GRAIN. A knave of the first rate: a phrase borrowed from the dyehouse, where certain colours are said to be in grain, to denote their superiority, as being died with cochineal, called grain. Knave in grain is likewise a pun applied to a cornfactor or miller.

KNIGHT AND BARROW PIG, more hog than gentleman. A saying of any low pretender to precedency.

KNIGHT OF THE BLADE. A bully.

KNIGHT OF THE POST. A false evidence, one that is ready to swear any thing for hire.

KNIGHT OF THE RAINBOW. A footman: from the variety of colours in the liveries and trimming of gentlemen of that cloth.

KNIGHT OF THE ROAD. A highwayman.

KNIGHT OF THE SHEARS. A tailor.

KNIGHT OF THE THIMBLE, or NEEDLE. A tailor, or staymaker.

KNIGHT OF THE TRENCHER. A great eater.

KNIGHT OF THE WHIP. A coachman.

KNOB. The head. *See* NOB.

KNOCK. To knock a woman; to have carnal knowledge of her. To knock off; to conclude: phrase borrowed from the blacksmith. To knock under; to submit.

KNOCK ME DOWN. Strong ale or beer, stingo.

KNOT. A crew, gang, or fraternity. He has tied a knot with his tongue, that he cannot untie with his teeth; i. e. he is married.

KNOWING ONES. Sportsmen on the turf, who, from experience, and an acquaintance with the jockeys, are supposed to be in the secret, that is, to know the true merits or powers of each horse; notwithstanding which, it often happens that the knowing ones are taken in.

KNOWLEDGE-BOX. The head.

KNUCKLE. To pick pockets, but chiefly applied to the more

refined branch of that art, namely, extracting notes, loose cash, &c. from the waistcoat or breeches pockets, whereas *buzzing* is used in a more general sense. *See* Buz.

Knuckle-dabs, or Knuckle-confounders. Ruffles.

Knuckle one's Wipe. To steal his handkerchief.

Knuckles. Pickpockets who attend the avenues to public places to steal pocket-books, watches, &c. a superior kind of pickpockets. To knuckle to; to submit.

Konoblin Rig. Stealing large pieces of coal from coal-sheds.

L

LACED Mutton. A cyprian.

Lacing. Beating. I'll lace your jacket handsomely.

Ladder. To go up the ladder to rest; to be hanged.

Lady. A crooked or hump-backed woman.

Ladybirds. Light or lewd women; generally applied to those who sport their *toggery* in the saloons.

Lady Dacre's Wine. Gin.

Lady of Easy Virtue. A woman of the town, an impure.

Lag. A man transported. The cove was lagged for a drag; the man was transported for stealing something out of a waggon.

Lag. Water. *Cant.*

Lag. A transport. *Cant.*

Lag. To drop behind, to keep back. Lag last; the last of a company.

Lag Fever. A term of ridicule applied to men who, being under sentence of transportation, pretend illness, to avoid being sent from gaol to the hulks.

Lagger. A sailor.

Lagging Dues. When a person is likely to be transported, the *flash* people observe, *lagging dues* will be concerned.

Lagging Matter. Crimes which render persons liable to be transported.

Lag of Duds. A buck of linen.

Lag Ship. A vessel chartered by government for the conveyance of convicts to *Botany Bay*.

Laid on the Shelf, or Laid up in Lavender. Pawned.

Lamb, or Lambaste. To beat. Lamb pye; a beating: from *lambo*.

Lambskin Men. The judges: from their robes lined and bordered with ermine.

Lamb's Wool. Apples roasted and put in strong ale.

Lame Ducks. Defaulters at the Stock Exchange.

Lamp. An eye. The cove has a queer lamp; the man has a blind or squinting eye.

Land. How lies the land? How stands the reckoning? Who has any land in Appleby? questions asked the man at whose door the glass stands long, or who does not circulate it in due time.

Land Lopers, or Land Lubbers. Vagabonds lurking about the country and who subsist by pilfering.

Land of Incumbents. Good livings. *Oxf. Univ. cant.*

Land of Promises. The fair expectation cherished by a steady novice at Oxford. *Univ. cant.*

Land of Sheepishness. School boy's bondage. *Oxf. Univ. cant.*

Land Pirates. Highwaymen.

Lank Sleeve. The empty sleeve of a one-armed man. A fellow with a lank sleeve; a man who has lost an arm.

Lansprisado. One who has only two pence in his pocket: also, a lance, or deputy corporal; that is, one doing the duty without the pay of a corporal. Formerly a lancier, or horseman, who, being dismounted by the death of his horse, served in the foot, by the title of lansprisado, or *lancepesato*, a broken lance.

Lanthorn-jawed. Thin visaged: from their cheeks being almost transparent. Or else, lenten jawed; i. e. having the jaws of one emaciated by a too rigid observation of Lent. Dark lanthorn; a servant or agent at court, who receives a bribe for his principal or master.

Lap. Butter-milk or whey. *Cant.*

Lark. A boat.

Lark. A piece of merriment. People playing together jocosely. Fun or sport of any kind, to create which it is termed, *knocking up a lark.*

Larry Dugan's Eye Water. Blacking: Larry Dugan was a famous shoe-black at Dublin. *Obsolete.*

Latch. Let in.

Lathy. Thin, slender. A lathy wench; a girl almost as slender as a lath.

Latitat. A nick name for an attorney; from the name of a writ.

Laugh. To laugh on the wrong side of the mouth; to cry. I'll make him laugh on the wrong (or t'other) side of his mouth.

Launch. The delivery, or labour, of a pregnant woman; a crying out or groaning.

Lavender. Laid up in lavender; pawned.

Law. To give law to a hare; a sporting term, signifying to give the animal a chance of escaping, by not setting on the dogs till the hare is at some distance: it is also more figuratively used for giving any one a chance of succeeding in a scheme or project.

Lawful Blanket. A wife.

Lawn. A white cambric handkerchief.

Lay. Enterprise, pursuit, or attempt: to be sick of the lay. It also means a hazard or chance. He stands queer lay; i. e. he is in danger. *Cant.*

Laystall. A dunghill about London, on which the soil brought from necessary houses is emptied; or, in more technical terms, where the old gold, collected at weddings by the Tom t—d-man, is stored.

Lazybones. An instrument like a pair of tongs, for old or very fat people to take any thing from the ground without stooping.

Leaf. To go off with the fall of the leaf; to be hanged: criminals in Dublin being turned off from the outside of the prison by the falling of a board, propped up, and moving on a hinge, like the leaf of a table. *Irish term.*

Leak. To make water.

Leaky. Apt to blab: one who cannot keep a secret is said to be leaky.

Leaping over the Sword. An ancient ceremonial, said to constitute a military marriage. A sword being laid down on the ground, the parties to be married join hands, when the corporal or serjeant of the company repeated these words:

> Leap rogue, and jump whore,
> And then you are married for evermore.

Whereupon the happy couple jumped, hand in hand, over the sword, the drum beating a ruffle; and the parties were ever after considered as man and wife.

Leary Cove. Knowing. Down. Not to be done. *Cant.*

Least in Sight. To play least in sight; to hide, keep out of the way, or make one's self scarce.

Leather. To lose leather; to be galled with riding on horseback, or, as the Scotch express it, to be saddle-sick. To leather, also, means to beat, perhaps originally with a strap: I'll leather you to your heart's content. Leather-headed; stupid. Leathern conveniency; term used by Quakers for a stage-coach.

Leather-Lane. Paltry. *Cant.*

Leave it all to the Cook. A bit of flash, intending to denote judgement: as the cook is supposed to be the *best judge* in dressing the meat, so a sporting man, when he refuses a bet that he thinks will not answer his purpose, he replies, in an ironical manner, "*I'll leave it all to the cook.*"

Lech. A whim of the amorous kind, out of the common way.

Leery. On one's guard. *See* **Peery.**

LEFT-HANDED WIFE. A concubine: an allusion to an ancient German custom, according to which, when a man married his concubine, or a woman greatly his inferior, he gave her his left hand.

LEG. To make a leg; to bow. To give leg-bail and land-security; to run away. To fight at the leg; to take unfair advantages: it being held unfair by back-sword players to strike at the leg. To break a leg: a woman who has had a bastard, is said to have broken a leg.

LEGGERS. Sham leggers; cheats who pretend to sell smuggled goods, but in reality only deal in shopkeepers old or damaged goods.

LENTEN FARE. Spare diet.

LET-LOOSE-MATCH. At a bull bait, the dogs run in succession at the bull; but the dog that continues to attack the bull the longest without turning his back towards him, receives the silver collar. *Cant.*

LETTER RACKET. Men or women of genteel address, going about to respectable houses with a letter or statement, detailing some case of extreme distress, as shipwreck, sufferings by fire, &c. by which many benevolent, but credulous, persons are induced to relieve the fictitious wants of the impostors, who thus unfold a plausible tale of affliction. This is termed the *Letter Racket*, which is daily practised in London.

LEVANTING, or RUNNING A LEVANT. An expedient practised by broken gamesters to retrieve themselves, and signifies to bet money at a race, cock-match, &c. without a shilling in their pocket to answer the event. The punishment for this conduct in a public cockpit is rather curious: the offender is placed in a large basket, kept on purpose, which is hoisted up to the ceiling or roof of the building, and the party is there kept suspended, and exposed to derision during the pleasure of the company.

LEVITE. A priest or parson.

LIB. To lie together. *Cant.*

LIBBEGE. A bed. *Cant.*

LIBBEN. A private dwelling-house. *Cant.*

LIBKEN. A house to lie in. *Cant.*

LICK. To beat: also, to wash, or to paint slightly over. I'll give you a good lick o'the chops; I'll give you a good stroke or blow on the face. Jack tumbled into a cow-t—d, and nastied his best clothes, for which his father stept up, and licked him neatly. I'll lick you! the dove-tail to which is, If you lick me all over, you won't miss ———.

LICK SPITTLE. A parasite, or talebearer.

LIFE. By this term is meant the various cheats and deceptions practised by the designing part of mankind; a person well versed in this kind of knowledge, is said to be one that knows *life;* in other words, that knows the world. This is what Goldsmith defines to be a knowledge of human nature on the wrong side.

LIFT. To give one a lift; to assist. A good hand at a dead lift; a good hand on an emergency. To lift one's hand to one's head; to drink to excess, or to drink drams. To lift or raise one's elbow; the same.

LIFT. *See* SHOPLIFTER, &c.

LIFTER. A crutch.

LIG. A bed. *See* LIB.

LIGHT BOB. A soldier of the Light Infantry Company.

LIGHT BLUE. *Gin. Cant.*

"Never again
I'll cultivate *light blue* or *brown* inebriety."
Vide "*The Fancy,*" *by* Peter Corcoran.

"Taste for *light blue* and heavy wet,
Both say, with frowns, I soon shall get
And both called that undoing."
Vide Randall's Scrap Book.

"Not *glass* with *Deady's light blue* bright'ning,
But *one* with rays, the hues of lightning."
Ibid.

"My *brain-box* is airy
With *Deady's light blue.*"
Ibid.

"Thus *strong* to my mind, tho' not to my sight,
Is this glass of *light blue* I now grasp in my fist."
Ibid.

LIGHT-FINGERED. Thievish, apt to pilfer.

LIGHT-HEELED. Swift in running. A light-heeled wench; one who is apt, by the flying up of her heels, to fall flat on her back. A willing wench.

LIGHT HOUSE. A man with a red fiery nose.

LIGHTMANS. The day. *Cant.*

LIGHTNING. Gin. A flash of lightning; a glass of gin.

LIGHT TROOPS. Lice: the light troops are in full march; the lice are crawling about.

LIGHT WEIGHTS. A pugilistic expression for gentlemen under twelve stone.

LIGHT WET. Gin. *Cant.*

"Pure and clear *rose the beads* on the glass of *light wet.*"
Vide Randall's Scrap Book.

"Oft with *light wet* have I fill'd my tumbler."
Ibid.

LIKENESS. A phrase used by thieves when the officers or turnkeys are examining their countenances; as, the traps are taking our likenesses; the officers are attentively observing us.

LILIPUTIAN. A diminutive man or woman: from Gulliver's Travels, written by Dean Swift, where an imaginary kingdom of dwarfs of that name is described.

LILL. A pocket-book.

LILY SHALLOW. A white driving hat. *Whip slang.*

LILY WHITE. A chimney-sweeper. A man of colour.

LIMBO. A prison, confinement.

LIMB OF THE LAW. An inferior or pettifogging attorney.

LIMBS. Duke of limbs; a tall awkward fellow.

LINE. A term for the act of coition between dog and bitch.

LINE. To get a man into a line; i. e. to divert his attention by a ridiculous or absurd story. To humbug.

LINE. To *get* a person *in a line,* or *in a string,* is to engage them in a conversation, while your confederate is robbing their person or premises. To banter or jest with a man by amusing him with false assurances or professions, is also termed *stringing* him, or *getting* him *in tow.* To keep any body in suspense on any subject without coming to a decision, is called *keeping* him *in tow, in a string,* or *in a tow-line.* To *cut the line,* or *the string,* is to put an end to the suspense in which you have kept any one, by telling him the plain truth, coming to a final decision, &c. A person, who has been telling another a long story, until he is tired, or conceives his auditor has been all the while secretly laughing at him, will say at last, I've just *dropped down,* you've had me in a fine *string,* I think it's time to *cut* it. On the other hand, the auditor, having the same opinion on his part, would say, Come, I believe you want to *string* me all night, I wish you'd *cut it;* meaning, conclude the story at once.

LINE OF THE OLD AUTHOR. A dram of brandy.

LINEN ARMOURERS. Tailors.

LINGO. Language. An outlandish lingo; a foreign tongue. The parlez-vous lingo; the French language.

LINK. To turn out a pocket. *Cant.*

LION. To tip the lion; to squeeze the nose of the party tipped flat to his face with the thumb. To show the lions and tombs; to point out the particular curiosities of any place, to act the cicerone: an allusion to Westminster Abbey, and the Tower, where the tombs and lions are shown. A lion is also a name given by the gownsmen of Oxford to an inhabitant or visiter. It is a standing joke among the city wits to send boys and country-folks, on the first of April, to the Tower-ditch to see the lions washed.

LIP. A house. *Cant.*

LISTENER. The ear. *Cant.*

LITTLE BARBARY. Wapping.

LITTLE BREECHES. A familiar appellation used to a little boy.

LITTLE CLERGYMAN. A young chimney-sweeper.

LITTLE EASE. A small dark cell in Guildhall, London, where disorderly apprentices are confined by the city-chamberlain: it is called Little Ease from its being so low that a lad cannot stand upright in it.

LITTLE GO VALE. Orderly step to the first examination. *Oxf. Univ. cant.*

LITTLE SNAKESMAN. A little boy who gets into a house through the sink-hole, and then opens the door for his accomplices: he is so called, from writhing and twisting like a snake, in order to work himself through the narrow passage.

LIVE LUMBER. A term used by sailors, to signify all landsmen on board their ships.

LIVE STOCK. Lice or fleas.

LOAF. To be in a bad loaf; to be in a disagreeable situation, or in trouble.

LOB. A till in a tradesman's shop. To frisk a lob; to rob a till. *See* FLASH PANNEY.

LOB. Going on the lob; going into a shop to get change for gold, and secreting some of the change.

LOBCOCK. A large relaxed penis: also, a dull inanimate fellow.

LOBKIN. A house to lie in: also, a lodging.

LOBLOLLY BOY. A nick-name for the surgeon's servant on board a man of war; sometimes for the surgeon himself: from the water-gruel prescribed to the sick, which is called loblolly.

LOBSCOUSE. A dish much eaten at sea, composed of salt beef, biscuit, and onions, well peppered, and stewed together.

LOB'S POUND. A prison. Dr. Grey, in his notes on Hudibras, explains it to allude to one Doctor Lob, a dissenting preacher, who used to hold forth when conventicles were prohibited, and had made himself a retreat by means of a trap-door at the bottom of his pulpit. Once, being pursued by the officers of justice, they followed him through divers subterraneous passages, till they got into a dark cell, whence they could not find their way out, but, calling to some of their companions, swore they had got into Lob's Pound.

LOBSTER. A nick-name for a soldier, from the colour of his clothes. To boil one's lobster, for a churchman to become a soldier; lobsters, which are of a bluish black, being made red by boiling. I will not make a lobster-kettle of my * * * *, a reply frequently made by the nymphs of the Point at Portsmouth, when requested by a soldier to grant him a favour.

Lock. A scheme, a mode. I must fight that lock; I must try that scheme.

Lock. Character. He stood a queer lock; he bore but an indifferent character. A lock is also a buyer of stolen goods as well as the receptacle for them.

Lockeram Jawed. Thin-faced, or lanthorn-jawed. *See* Lanthorn-Jawed.

Lock Hospital. A hospital for venereal patients.

Locksmith's Daughter. A key.

Lock-up-Chovey. A covered cart, used by travelling hawkers to convey their goods about the country, and which is secured by a door, lock, and key.

Lock-up-House. A spunging house; a public house kept by sheriffs' officers, to which they convey the persons they have arrested, where they practise every species of imposition and extortion with impunity: also, houses kept by agents, or crimps, who enlist, or rather trepan, men to serve the East India or African Companies as soldiers.

Lodging-Slum. Hiring ready-furnished lodgings, and stripping them of the plate, linen, and other valuable articles.

Loggerhead. A blockhead, or stupid fellow. We three loggerheads be; a sentence frequently written under two heads, and the reader by repeating it makes himself the third. A loggerhead is a double-headed, or bar shot of iron. To go to loggerheads; to fall to fighting.

Loll. Mother's loll; a favourite child, the mother's darling.

Loll Tongue. He has been playing a game at loll tongue; he has been salivated.

Lollipops. Sweet lozenges purchased by children.

Lollpoop. A lazy, idle drone.

Lombard Fever. Sick of the Lombard fever; i. e. of the idles.

Long. Great. A long price; a great price.

Long Gallery. Throwing, or, rather, trundling, the dice the whole length of the board.

Long Hope. Johnson defines "a hope" to be any sloping plain between the ridges of mountains. At Oxford, it is the symbol of long expectations in studying for a degree.

Long One. A hare: a term used by poachers.

Longs and Broads. Cards.

Long Meg. A jeering name for a very tall woman; from one famous in story, called Long Meg of Westminster.

Long Shanks. A long-legged person.

LONG STOMACH. A voracious appetite.

LONG-TONGUED. Loquacious, not able to keep a secret. He is as long-tongued as Granny; Granny was an idiot who could lick her own eye. *See* GRANNY.

LONG-WINDED. A long-winded parson; one who preached long tedious sermons. A long-winded paymaster; one who takes long credit.

LOO. For the good of the loo; for the benefit of the company or community.

LOOBY. An awkward ignorant fellow.

LOOK AT A PLACE. When a plan is laid for robbing a house, &c. *upon the crack*, or *the screw*, the parties will go a short time before the execution, to examine the premises, and make any necessary observations; this is called *looking at a place.*

LOOKING AS IF ONE COULD NOT HELP IT. Looking like a simpleton, or as if one could not say boh! to a goose.

LOOKING-GLASS. A chamber-pot, jordan, or member-mug.

LOOK-OUT-HOUSES. The look-out kept by ordained masters on defunct incumbents. *Oxf. Univ. cant.*

LOON, or LOUT. A country bumpkin, or clown.

LOONSLATE. Thirteen-pence-halfpenny.

LOOP-HOLE. An opening, or means of escape. To find a loop-hole in an act of parliament; i.e. a method of evading it.

LOPE. To leap, to run away. He loped down the dancers; he ran down stairs.

LOP-SIDED. Uneven, having one side larger or heavier than the other; boys' paper kites are often said to be lop-sided.

LORD. A crooked or hump-backed man. These unhappy people afford great scope for vulgar raillery: such as, "did you come strait from home? if so, you have got confoundedly bent by the way." "Don't abuse the gemman," adds a bystander, "he has been grossly insulted already; don't you see his back is up?" Or some one asks him if the show is behind; "because I see," adds he, "you have the drum at your back." Another piece of vulgar wit is let loose on a deformed person; if met by a party of soldiers on their march, one of them observes that that gentleman is on his march too, for he has got his knapsack at his back. It is said in the British Apollo, that the title of lord was first given to deformed persons in the reign of Richard III. from several persons labouring under that misfortune being created peers by him; but it is more probably derived from the Greek word λορδος, *crooked.*

LOUNGE. A loitering place, or gossiping shop.

LOUR. Money. *Cant.*

LOUSE. A gentleman's companion. He will never louse a gray head of his own; he will never live to be old.

Louse-Bag. A black bag worn to the hair or wig.

Louse-House. The round house, cage, or any other place of confinement.

Louse-Ladder. A stitch fallen in a stocking.

Louse-Land. Scotland.

Louse-Trap. A small toothed comb.

Lout. A clumsy stupid fellow.

Love-Begotten Child. A bastard.

Lowing Rig. Stealing oxen or cows.

Low Pad. A footpad.

Low Tide, or Low Water. When there is no money in the pocket.

Lowre. Money. *Cant.*

Lubber. An awkward fellow: a name given by sailors to landsmen.

Luck, or Good Luck. To tread in a sirreverence, to be bewrayed; an allusion to the proverb, Sh--tt--n luck is good luck.

Lud's Bulwark. Ludgate-prison.

Lugs. Ears, or wattles. *See* Wattles.

Luke. Nothing. *Cant.*

Lullaby Cheat. An infant. *Cant.*

Lullers. Wet linen. *Cant.*

Lully Priggers. Thieves who steal wet linen: also, the lowest and meanest order of thieves, who go about decoying little children to some bye corner, and then rob them of their clothes. *Cant.*

Lumb. Too much.

Lumber. A room.

Lumber. Live lumber; soldiers or passengers on board a ship are so called by the sailors.

Lumber. To lumber any property, is to deposit it at a pawnbroker's, or elsewhere, for present security; to retire to any house, or private place for a short time, is called *lumbering* yourself. A man apprehended and sent to jail, is said to be *lumbered*, to be *in lumber*, or to be *in Lombard-street.*

Lumber House. A house appropriated by thieves for the reception of their stolen property.

Lumber Troop. A club or society of citizens of London.

Lump. To beat: also, to include a number of articles under one head.

Lumpers. Persons who contract to unload ships: also, thieves who lurk about wharfs to pilfer goods from ships, lighters, &c.

Lumping. Great. A lumping pennyworth; a great quantity for the money, a bargain. He has got a lumping pennyworth; frequently said of a man who marries a fat woman.

Lump the Lighter. To be transported.

Lum. Harlequin.

Lurch. To be left in the lurch; to be abandoned by one's confederates, or party, to be left in a scrape.

Lurched. Those who lose a game of whist without scoring five, are said to be lurched.

Lurcher. A lurcher of the law; a bum bailiff, or his setter.

Lurries. Money, watches, rings, or other moveables.

Lush. Strong beer, or drink of any kind.

Lush. To drink: speaking of a person who is drunk, they say, *Alderman Lushington is concerned*, or, he has been *voting for the Alderman.*

Lush Crib, or Ken. A public-house. *Cant.*

> "Then blame me not *kids, swells*, or lads of the fancy,
> For opening a *lush-crib* in Chancery-lane," &c.
>
> *Randall's Farewell to the Ring, vide Randall's Diary.*

Lushey. Drunk. The rolling kiddeys had a spree, and got b——y lushey; the dashing lads went on a party of pleasure, and got very drunk.

Lushing Muzzle. A blow on the mouth. *Sea term.*

Lye. Chamber lye; urine.

M

MACCARONI. An Italian paste made of flour and eggs: also, a fop; which name arose from a club, called the Maccaroni Club, instituted by some of the most dressy travelled gentlemen about town, who led the fashions; whence a man foppishly dressed was supposed a member of that club, and, by contraction, stiled a Maccaroni.

Mace. To *mace* a shopkeeper, or *give it to* him *upon the mace,* is to obtain goods on credit, which you never mean to pay for; to run up a score with the same intention, or to spunge upon your acquaintance, by continually begging or borrowing from them, is termed *macing*, or *striking the mace.*

Mace Cove. A swindler, a sharper, a cheat. On the mace; to live by swindling.

Mackerel. A bawd: from the French word *maquereau.* Mackerel-backed; long-backed.

Madam. A kept madam; a kept mistress.

Madam Ran. A whore. *Cant.*

Made. Stolen. *Cant.*

Madge. The private parts of a woman.

Mad Tom, or Tom of Bedlam, otherwise an Abram Man. A rogue that counterfeits madness. *Cant.*

Mag. A halfpenny.

Mag. To chatter. Hold your mag; hold your tongue. *Cant.*

Maggot Boiler. A tallow chandler.

Maggotty. Whimsical, capricious.

Magnum Bonum. A bottle containing two quarts of wine. *See* Scotch Pint.

Mahometan Gruel. Coffee: because formerly used chiefly by the Turks.

Maiden Sessions. A sessions where none of the prisoners are capitally convicted.

Make. A halfpenny. *Cant.*

Make Weight. A small candle: a term applied to a little slender man.

Malkin, or Maulkin. A general name for a cat: also, a parcel of rags, fastened to the end of a stick, to clean an oven: also, a figure set up in a garden to scare the birds: likewise, an awkward woman. The cove's so scaly, he'd spice a malkin of his jazey; the fellow is so mean that he would rob a scarecrow of his old wig.

Malkintrash. One in a dismal garb.

Malmsey Nose. A red pimpled snout, rich in carbuncles and rubies.

Man *(Cambridge)*. Any under-graduate from fifteen to thirty: as, a man of Emanuel; young member of Emanuel.

Manchester. The tongue. *Cant.*

Mang. To boast. *Scotch cant.*

Manœuvring the Apostles. Robbing Peter to pay Paul; i. e. borrowing of one man to pay another.

Man of the Town. A rake, a debauchee.

Man of the Turf. A horse racer, or jockey.

Man of the World. A knowing man.

Man Trap. A woman's commodity.

Manufacture. Liquors prepared from materials of English growth.

Mare's Nest. He has found a mare's nest, and is laughing at the eggs; said of one who laughs without any apparent cause.

Margery Prater. A hen. *Cant.*

Marine Officer. An empty bottle: marine officers being held useless by the seamen. *Sea wit.*

Marplot. A spoil sport.

Marriage Music. The squalling and crying of children.

Married. Persons chained or handcuffed together, in order to be conveyed to gaol, or on board the lighters, for transportation, are, in the cant language, said to be married together.

Marrow Bones. The knees. To bring any one down on his marrow bones; to make him beg pardon on his knees: some derive this from Mary's bones; i. e. the bones bent in honour of the Virgin Mary; but this seems rather far-fetched. Marrow bones and cleavers; principal instruments in the band of rough music: these are generally performed on by butchers, at marriages, elections, riding skimmington, and other public or joyous occasions.

Martinet. A military term for a strict disciplinarian: from the name of a French general, famous for restoring military discipline to the French army. He first disciplined the French infantry, and regulated their method of encampment: he was killed at the siege of Doesbourg, in the year 1672.

Master of Impediment. Troublesome preparation for the schools. *Oxf. Univ. cant.*

Master of the Mint. A gardener.

Master of the Rolls. A baker.

Master of the Wardrobe. One who pawns his clothes to purchase liquor.

Matrimonial Peace-maker. The sugar-stick, or arbor vitæ.

Maudlin Drunk. Crying drunk: perhaps, from Mary Magdalene, called Maudlin, who is always painted in tears.

Mauled. Extremely drunk, or soundly beaten.

Maundering Broth. Scolding.

Maunding. Asking, or begging. *Cant.*

Mawkes. A vulgar slattern.

Mawley. A hand. Tip us your mawley; shake hands with me. Fam the mawley; shake hands.

Maw-Wallop. A filthy composition, sufficient to provoke vomiting.

Max. Gin.

May Bees. May bees don't fly all the year long; an answer to any one who prefaces a proposition with, It may be.

Mealy-mouthed. Over-modest or backward in speech.

Medlar. A fruit, vulgarly called an open a–se, of which it is more truly than delicately said, that it is never ripe till it is as rotten as a t—d, and then it is not wort a f—t.

Mellow. Almost drunk.

Melt. To spend. Will you melt a borde? will you spend a shilling? The cull melted a couple of decusses upon us; the gentleman spent a couple of crowns upon us. *Cant.*

Melting Moments. A fat man and woman in the amorous congress.

Member Mug. A chamber pot.

Men of Kent. Men born east of the river Medway, who are said to have met the Conqueror in a body, each carrying a green bough in his hand, the whole appearing like a moving wood; and thereby obtaining a confirmation of their ancient privileges. The inhabitants of Kent are divided into Kentish men and men of Kent: also, a society held at the Fountain Tavern, Bartholomew Lane, A.D. 1743.

Men of Straw. Hired bail; so called from having straw stuck in their shoes to distinguish them.

Merkin. Counterfeit hair for the monosyllable. *See Bailey's Dict.*

Merry Andrew, or Mr. Merryman. The jack pudding, jester, or zany, of a mountebank, usually dressed in a party-coloured coat.

Merry A--se Christian. A whore.

Merry-begotten. A bastard.

Mess John. A Scotch presbyterian teacher or parson.

Messmate. One who eats at the same mess, companion or comrade.

Mettle. The semen. To fetch mettle; the act of self-pollution. Mettle is also figuratively used for courage.

Mettlesome. Bold, courageous.

Michael. Hyp, Michael, your head's on fire. *See* Hyp.

Midshipman's Watch and Chain. A sheep's heart and pluck.

Milch Cow. One who is easily tricked out of his property: a term used by gaolers, for prisoners who have money, and bleed freely.

Mile-Stone. A country booby. *Cant.*

Milk and Water. Both ends of the busk.

Milk the Pigeon. To endeavour at impossibilities.

Mill. A chisel.

Mill. To rob: also, to break, beat out, or kill. I'll mill your glaze; I'll beat out your eye. To mill a bleating cheat; to kill a sheep. To mill a ken; to rob a house. To mill doll; to beat hemp in bridewell. *Cant.*

Mill-doll. An obsolete name for Bridewell house of correction, in Bridge-street, Blackfriars, London.

Miller. A prize-fighter. *Cant.*

Milling Cove. A boxer. How the milling cove served the cull out; how the boxer beat the fellow.

Mill Lay. To force open the doors of houses, in order to rob them.

Mill Twig. A shirt. *Scotch cant.*

Milvad. A blow. *Scotch cant.*

Milvadering. Boxing. *Scotch cant.*

Mine A--se on a Bandbox. An answer to the offer of any

thing inadequate to the purpose for which it is wanted, just as a bandbox would be if used for a seat.

MINE UNCLE'S. A pawnbroker's shop: also, a necessary house. Carried to my uncle's; pawned. New-married men are also said to go to their uncle's, when they leave their wives soon after the honey-moon.

MINIKIN. A little man or woman: also, the smallest sort of pin.

MINOR CLERGY. Young chimney-sweepers.

MINT. Gold. A mint of money: common phrase for a large sum.

MISCHIEF. A man loaded with mischief; i. e. a man with his wife on his back.

MISH. A shirt, smock, or sheet. *Cant.*

MISH TOPPER. A coat, or petticoat.

MISS. A miss, or kept mistress; a harlot.

MISS LAYCOCK. The monosyllable.

MITE. A nickname for a cheesemonger: from the small insect of that name found in cheese.

MITTENS. The hands.

MIX METAL. A silversmith.

MIZZLE. To elope, to run off. *Cant.*

MOABITES. Bailiffs, or Philistines.

MOB, or MAB. A wench, or harlot.

MOBILITY. A mob: a sort of opposite to nobility.

MOIETY. Half; but vulgarly used to signify a share or portion: as, he will come in for a small moiety.

MOLL. A whore.

MOLL PEATLY'S GIG. A rogering bout.

MOLL THOMPSON'S MARK. M. T. i.e. empty: as, Take away this bottle, it has Moll Thompson's mark upon it.

MOLLY. A Miss Molly; an effeminate fellow.

MONDAY. Saint Monday. *See* SAINT.

MONEY. A girl's monosyllable, commonly applied to little children: as, Take care, Miss, or you'll show your money.

MONEY DROPPERS. Cheats who drop money, which they pretend to find just before some country lad; and, by way of giving him a share of their good luck, entice him into a public-house, where they and their confederates cheat or rob him of what money he has about him.

MONGREL. A hanger on among cheats, a spunger: also, a child whose father and mother are of different countries.

MONKERY. A name given by *family people* to the country parts of England.

MONKEY. To suck the monkey; to suck or draw wine, or any other liquor, privately, out of a cask, by means of a straw, or small tube. Monkey's allowance; more kicks than halfpence. Who put that monkey on horseback without tying his legs? vulgar wit on a bad horseman. A padlock.

MONKS AND FRIARS. Terms used by printers: monks are sheets where the letters are blotted, or printed too black; friars, those letters where the ink has failed touching them, which are therefore white or faint.

MONOSYLLABLE. A woman's commodity.

MONTRA. A watch.

MOON CURSER. A link-boy: link-boys are said to curse the moon, because it renders their assistance unnecessary; these gentry frequently, under colour of lighting passengers over kennels, or through dark passages, assist in robbing them. *Cant.*

MOON-EYED HEN. A squinting wench.

MOON MEN. Gypsies.

MOON-RAKERS. Wiltshire men: because it is said that some men of that county seeing the reflection of the moon in a pond, endeavoured to pull it out with a rake.

MOONSHINE. A matter or mouthful of moonshine; a trifle, nothing. The white brandy smuggled on the coasts of Kent and Sussex, and the gin in the north of Yorkshire, are also called moonshine.

MOP. A kind of annual fair in the west of England, where farmers usually hire their servants

MOPED. Stupid, melancholy for want of society.

MOPPY. Drunk. *Cant.*

MOPSEY. A dowdy, or homely woman.

MOPSQUEEZER. A maid servant, particularly a housemaid.

MOP UP. To drink. To empty a glass or pot.

MOPUSSES. Money.

MORNING DROP. The gallows. He napped the king's pardon and escaped the morning drop; he was pardoned and was not hanged.

MORNING SNEAK. Slipping in at the door of a shop or house early in the morning unperceived, while the shopman or servant is employed in cleaning the steps, windows, &c.

MORRIS. Come, morris off; dance off, or get you gone: allusion to morris, i.e. *morisco*, or Moorish dance.

MORT. A woman or wench: also, a yeoman's daughter. To be taken all-a-mort; to be confounded, surprised, or motionless through fear.

MOSES. To stand Moses: a man is said to stand Moses when he has another man's bastard child fathered upon him, and he is obliged by the parish to maintain it.

MOSS. A cant term for lead, because both are found on the tops of buildings.

MOSSY FACE. The mother of all saints.

MOT. A girl, or wench. *See* MORT.

MOTHER OF ALL SAINTS. The Monosyllable.
MOTHER OF ALL SOULS. The same. *Irish.*
MOTHER OF ST. PATRICK. The same. *Irish.*
MOTHER OF THE MAIDS. A bawd.
MOTHER, or THE MOTHER. A bawd. Mother abbess; the same. Mother midnight; a midwife. Mother-in-law's bit; a small piece; mothers-in-law being supposed not apt to overload the stomachs of their husbands' children.
MOUNT. To give false evidence for the sake of money. To *mount* for a person is similar to *bonetting* for him.
MOUNTER. A person who lives by false swearing.
MOUSE. To speak like a mouse in a cheese; i.e. faintly or indistinctly.
MOUSETRAP. The parson's mousetrap; the state of matrimony.
MOUTH. A noisy fellow. Mouth half cocked; one gaping and staring at every thing he sees. To make any one laugh on the wrong, or t'other side of his mouth; to make him cry or grieve.
MOUTH. A silly fellow. A dupe. To stand mouth; i.e. to be duped.
MOVE. Any action or operation in life; the secret spring by which any project is conducted: as, there is a *move* in that business which you are not *down to.* To be *flash to every move upon the board,* is to have a general knowledge of the world, and all its numerous deceptions.
MOVEABLES. Watches, rings, or any toys of value.
MOW, to A Scotch word for the act of copulation.
MOWER. A cow.
MOW HEATER. A drover: from their frequent sleeping on hay mows. *Cant.*
MUCK. Money: also, dung.
MUCKED OUT. Lost all the cash. *Cant.*
MUCK TOPER FEEKER. An umbrella maker. *Scotch cant.*
MUCKWORM. A miser.
MUCKINDER. A child's handkerchief tied to the side.
MUD. A fool, or thick-sculled fellow: also, among printers the same as dung among journeymen tailors. *See* DUNGHILL.
MUD LARK. A fellow who goes about by the water-side picking up coals, nails, or other articles in the mud: also, a duck.
MUFF. The monosyllable. To the well wearing of your muff, mort; to the happy consummation of your marriage, girl; a health: also, a fool.
MUFFLERS. Boxing-gloves, used in sparring.
MUFFLING CHEAT. A napkin.
MUG. The mouth. *Cant.*

MUGGLETONIANS. The sect or disciples of Lodowick Muggleton.

MUGS, TO CUT. Theatrical expression for making comic faces.

MULLIGRUBS. Sick of the mulligrubs with eating chopped hay; low spirited, having an imaginary sickness.

MUM. An interjection directing silence. Mum for that; I shall be silent as to that. As mute as Mumchance, who was hanged for saying nothing; a friendly reproach to any one who seems low spirited and silent.

MUMCHANCE. An ancient game, like hazard, played with dice: probably so named from the silence observed in playing at it.

MUMMER. The mouth.

MUMPERS. Originally beggars of the genteel kind, but since used for beggars in general.

MUMPERS' HALL. An alehouse where beggars are harboured.

MUNDUNGUS. Bad or rank tobacco from *mondongo*, a Spanish word signifying tripes, or the uncleaned entrails of a beast, full of filth.

MUNG. To beg.

MUNS. The face, or rather the mouth: from the German word *mund*, the mouth. Tout his muns; look at his face.

MUNSTER HEIFER. An Irish woman. A woman with thick legs is said to be like a Munster heifer; i.e. beef to the heels.

MUNSTER PLUMS. Potatoes. *Irish.*

MURPHIES. Potatoes.

MURPHY'S COUNTENANCE. A pig's face.

MUSHROOM. A person or family suddenly raised to riches and eminence: an allusion to that fungus, which starts up in a night.

MUSIC. The watch-word among highwaymen, signifying the person is a friend, and must pass unmolested. Music is also an Irish term, in tossing up, to express the harp side, or reverse, of a farthing or half-penny, opposed to the head.

MUTE. An undertaker's servant, who stands at the door of a person lying in state: so named from being supposed mute with grief.

MUTTON. In her mutton; i.e. having carnal knowledge of a woman.

MUTTON-HEADED. Stupid.

MUTTON MONGER. A man addicted to wenching.

MUZZLE. A beard.

MUZZLER. A violent blow on the mouth. The milling cove tipped the cull a muzzler; the boxer gave the fellow a blow on the mouth.

MY NABS. Myself. *Cant.*

Myint. *See* **Mint.**
Myrmidons. The constable's assistants, watchmen, &c.
My Uncle. A pawnbroker. *Cant.*

N

NAB, or Nab Cheat. A hat. Penthouse nab; a large hat.
Nab. To seize or catch unawares. To nab the teaze; to be privately whipped. To nab the stoop; to stand in the pillory. To nab the rust; a jockey term for a horse that becomes restive. To nab the snow; to steal linen left out to bleach or dry. *Cant.*
Nab Girder, or Nob Girder. A bridle.
Nack. To have a nack; to be ready at any thing, to have a turn for it.
Nacky. Ingenious.
Nail. To *nail* a person is to over-reach, or take advantage of him in the course of trade or traffic: also, to rob or steal; as, I *nailed* him *for* (or *of*) his *reader;* I robbed him of his pocket-book. I *nailed the swell's montra in the push;* I picked the gentleman's pocket of his watch in the crowd, &c. A person of an over-reaching, imposing, disposition, is called a *nail*, a *dead nail*, a *nailing* rascal, a *rank needle*, or a *needle-pointer*.
Nailed. Secured, fixed. He offered me a decus, and I nailed him; he offered me a crown, and I struck, or fixed him.
Nail in your Coffin. To drink drams repeatedly, it is observed, is adding another *nail to your coffin*.
Nancy. The posteriors.
Nanny-House. A brothel.
Nap. To cheat at dice by securing one chance: also, to catch the **** disease. You've napt it; you are infected.
Napkin-Snatching, or Fogle-Hunting. Shaking pocket-handkerchiefs. An old chaunt runs thus:—

> "Come all you *napkin snatchers*,
> And listen unto me,
> And a song that I will sing you,
> It shall be full of glee.
> "With my foll de doll, &c."

Napper. The head: also, a cheat or thief.
Napper of Naps. A sheep stealer. *Cant.*
Napping. To take any one napping; i.e. to come upon him unexpectedly, to find him asleep: as, he caught him napping, as Morse caught his mare.
Nappy Ale. Strong ale.
Nap the Bib. To cry; as, the *mollisher napp'd* her *bib;* the woman fell a crying

Nash. To go away from, or quit, any place or company: speaking of a person who is gone, they say, he is *nashed*, or *Mr. Nash is concerned*.

Nask, or Naskin. A prison or bridewell. The new nask; Clerkenwell bridewell. Tothil-fields nask; the bridewell at Tothil-fields. *Cant.*

Nation. An abbreviation of damnation: a vulgar term used in Kent, Sussex, and the adjacent counties, for very. Nation good; very good. A nation long way; a very long way.

Natty Lads. Young thieves or pickpockets. *Cant.*

Natural. A mistress, a child: also, an idiot. A natural son or daughter; a love, or merry begotten, child, a bastard.

Navy Office. The Fleet prison. Commander of the Fleet; the warden of the Fleet prison.

Nay-Word. A bye-word, proverb.

Nazy. Drunken. Nazy cove or mort; a drunken rogue or harlot. Nazy nabs; drunken coxcombs.

Neb, or Nib. The bill of a bird, or the slit of a pen. Figuratively, the face and mouth of a woman; as, she holds up her neb; she holds up her mouth to be kissed.

Neck-Verse. Formerly the persons claiming the benefit of clergy were obliged to read a verse in a Latin manuscript psalter; this saving them from the gallows, was termed their neck-verse: it was the first verse of the fifty-first psalm, *Miserere mei*, &c.

Neck Weed. Hemp.

Ne-dash. Of no use. Nothing.

Needle. To *needle* a person is to haggle with him in making a bargain, and, if possible, take advantage of him, though in the most trifling article. *See* Nail.

Needle Point. A sharper.

Needy-Mizzler. A poor ragged object of either sex; a shabby-looking person.

Negligee. A woman's undressed gown, vulgarly termed a neggledigee.

Negroe. A black-a-moor: figuratively used for a slave. I'll be no man's negro; I will be no man's slave.

Negroes' Heads. Brown loaves delivered to the ships in ordinary.

Nescio. He sports a Nescio; he pretends not to understand any thing. After the senate-house examination for degrees, the students proceed to the schools to be questioned by the proctor. According to custom immemorial the answers *must* be *Nescio*. The following is a translated specimen:

Ques. What is your name?—*Ans.* I do not know.

Ques. What is the name of this University.—*Ans.* I do not know.

Ques. Who was your father?—*Ans.* I do not know.

This last is probably the only true answer of the three!

NETTLED. Teized, provoked, out of temper. He or she has pissed on a nettle: said of one who is peevish or out of temper.

NEW DROP. The scaffold used at Newgate for hanging criminals; which, dropping down, leaves them suspended. By this improvement, the use of that vulgar vehicle, a cart, is entirely left off.

NEWGATE BIRD. A thief or sharper, frequently caged in Newgate.

NEWGATE SOLICITOR. A petty-fogging and roguish attorney,

NEW GUINEA. First possession of income. *Oxf. Univ. cant.*

NEW LIGHT. One of the new light; a methodist.

who attends the gaols to assist villains in evading justice.

NEWMAN'S HOTEL. Newgate.

NEWMAN'S LIFT. The gallows.

NEWMAN'S TEA-GARDENS. Newgate.

NEW SETTLEMENTS. Final reckoning. *Oxf. Univ. cant.*

NIB. A gentleman, or person of the higher order. People who affect gentility or consequence, without any real pretensions thereto, are from hence vulgarly called *Half-nibs* or *Half-swells;* and, indeed, persons of low minds, who conceive money to be the only criterion of gentility, are too apt to stigmatize with the before-mentioned epithets any man, who, however well-bred and educated, may be reduced to a shabby external, but still preserves a sense of decorum in his manners, and avoids associating with the vagabonds among whom he may unfortunately be doomed to exist.

NIBBED. Taken in custody.

NIBBLE. To pilfer trifling articles, not having spirit to touch any thing of consequence.

NIBBLER. A pilferer, or petty thief.

NICK. To win at dice, to hit the mark just in the nick of time, or at the critical moment.

NICK. Old Nick; the Devil.

NICKIN, NIKEY, or NIZEY. A soft simple fellow: also, a diminutive of Isaac.

NICKNACKS. Toys, baubles, or curiosities.

NICKNACKATORY. A toy-shop.

NICK NAME. A name given in ridicule or contempt: from the French *nom de nique. Nique* is a movement of the head to mark a contempt for any person or thing.

NICK NINNY. A simpleton.

Nickumpoop, or Nincumpoop. A foolish fellow; a regular innocent.

Niffynaffy Fellow. A trifler.

Nig. The clippings of money. Nigging; clipping. Nigler, a clipper. *Cant.*

Niggling. Cutting awkwardly, trifling: also, accompanying with a woman.

Nightingale. A soldier who, as the term is, sings out at the halberts. It is a point of honour in some regiments, among the grenadiers, never to cry out, or become nightingales, whilst under the discipline of the cat of nine tails: to avoid which, they chew a bullet.

Night Magistrate. A constable.

Nightman. One whose business it is to empty necessary-houses in London, which is always done in the night; the operation is called a wedding. *See* Wedding.

Nigmenog. A very silly fellow.

Nim. To steal or pilfer: from the German *nemen*, to take. Nim a togeman; steal a cloak.

Nimgimmer. A physician or surgeon, particularly those who cure the enviable disease.

Nine Lives. Cats are said to have nine lives, and women ten cats lives.

Ninny, or Ninnyhammer. A simpleton.

Nip. A cheat. Bung-nipper; a cut-purse.

Nip Cheese. A nick-name for the purser of a ship: from those gentlemen being supposed sometimes to nip, or diminish, the allowance of the seamen in that and every other article: it is also applied to stingy persons in general.

Nipperkin. A small measure.

Nippers. Handcuffs. *Cant.*

Nipps. The shears used in clipping money.

Nit Squeeger, i.e. Squeezer. A hair-dresser.

Nix. Nothing.

Nob. A king. A man of rank.

Nob. The head.

Nob it. To act with such prudence and knowledge of the world, as to prosper and become independent without any labour or bodily exertion; this is termed *nobbing it*, or *fighting nob work*. To effect any purpose, or obtain any thing by means of good judgement and sagacity, is called *nobbing it for* such a thing.

Nob-Pitchers. A general term for those sharpers who attend at fairs, races, &c. To take in the *flats* at prick in the garter, cups and balls, and other similar artifices.

Nob-Thatcher. A peruke-maker.

No catchy no havy. If I am not caught, I cannot be hurt. *Negro saying.*

NOCK. The breech; from nock, a notch.

NOCKY BOY. A dull simple fellow.

NOD. He is gone to the land of Nod; he is asleep.

NODDLE. The head.

NODDY. A simpleton or fool: also, a kind of low cart, with a seat before it for the driver, used in and about Dublin, in the manner of hackney-coach. Knave noddy; the old-fashioned name for the knave of trumps.

NOISY DOG RACKET. Stealing brass knockers from doors.

NOKES. A ninny, or fool. John-a-Nokes and Tom-a-Stiles; two honest peaceable gentlemen, repeatedly set together by the ears by lawyers of different denominations: two fictitious names formerly used in law proceedings, but now very seldom, having for several years past been supplanted by two other honest peaceable gentlemen, namely, John Doe and Richard Roe.

NOLL. Old Noll; Oliver Cromwell.

NON-CON. A non-conformist, presbyterian, or any other dissenter.

NONE-SUCH. One that is unequalled: frequently applied ironically.

NONPAREIL CLUB. This club was established at the house of John Randall, the celebrated pugilist, at the Hole-in-the-Wall, Chancery-lane, in 1819: and named after him, from his being termed the NONPAREIL of the boxers. It is held every Monday evening during the season; and it is *free and easy*.

NONSENSE. Melting butter in a wig.

NOOZED. Married, hanged.

NORFOLK CAPON. A red herring.

NORFOLK DUMPLING. A nick-name, or term of jocular reproach to a Norfolk man; dumplings being a favourite food in that county.

NORTH ALLERTONS. Spurs; that place, like Rippon, being famous for making them.

NORTHUMBERLAND. Lord Northumberland's arms; a black eye: so called in the last century. *Obsolete.*

NORWAY NECKLOTH. The pillory, usually made of Norway fir.

NOSE. As plain as the nose on your face; evidently to be seen. He is led by the nose; he is governed. To follow one's nose; to go straight forward. To put one's nose out of joint; to rival one in the favour of any person. To make a bridge of any one's nose; to pass by him in drinking. To nose a stink; to smell it. He cut off his nose to be revenged of his face; said of one who, to be revenged on his neighbour, has materially injured himself.

NOSE. A thief who becomes an evidence against his accomplices: also, a person who, seeing one or more suspicious characters in the streets, makes a point of watching them, in order to frustrate any attempt they may make, or cause their apprehension: also, a spy or informer of any description.

NOSE. To give evidence. To inform. His pall nosed and he was twisted for a crack; his confederate turned king's evidence, and he was hanged for burglary.

NOSE. To *nose*, is to pry into any person's proceedings in an impertinent manner. To *nose upon* any one, is to tell of any thing he has said or done with a view to injure him, or to benefit yourself.

NOSE-BAG. A bag fastened to the horse's head, in which the soldiers of the cavalry put the oats given to their horses: whence the saying, I see the nose bag in his face; i. e. he has been a private man, or rode private.

NOSEDAY. A blow on the nose. *Pugilistic cant.*

NOSE-GENT. A nun.

NOT A FEATHER TO FLY WITH. Ruined, &c. *Cant.*

NOTCH. The monosyllable.

NOTE. He changed his note; he told another sort of a story.

NOTICE TO QUIT. A cant phrase. When a person is in danger of dying from bad health, it is said, he has received "a *notice to quit.*"

NOUS-BOX. The head.

NOZZLE. The nose of a man or woman.

NUB. The neck: also, coition.

NUBBING. Hanging. Nubbing cheat; the gallows. Nubbing cove; the hangman. Nubbing ken; the sessions house.

NUG. An endearing word: as, My dear nug; my dear love.

NUGGING-DRESS. An out-of-the-way old-fashioned dress, or rather a loose kind of dress, denoting a courtezan.

NUGGING-HOUSE. A brothel.

NULL. To beat: as, He nulled him heartily.

NULL-GROPERS. Persons who sweep the streets, in search of old iron, nails, &c. *Cant.*

NULLING COVE. A fighting man.

NUMBERS. To consult the book of numbers: a term used in the House of Commons, when, instead of answering or confuting a pressing argument, the minister calls for a division, i. e. puts the matter to the vote.

NUMBSCULL. A stupid fellow.

NUMMS. A sham collar, to be worn over a dirty shirt.

NUNNERY. A bawdy-house.

NURSE. To cheat: as, they nursed him out of it. An estate in the hands of trustees, for the payment of debts, is said to be at nurse.

Nut. To please a person by any little act of assiduity, by a present, or by flattering words, is called *nutting* him; as the present, &c. by which you have gratified them, is termed a *nut*.

Nutcrackers. The pillory: as, The cull peeped through the nutcrackers.

Nutmegs. Testicles.

Nuts. It was nuts for them; i. e. it was very agreeable to them.

Nuts. Fond, pleased. She's nuts upon her cull; she's pleased with her cully. The cove's nutting the blowen; the man is trying to please the girl.

Nuts upon it. To be very much pleased or gratified with any object, adventure, or overture; so a person who conceives a strong inclination for another of the opposite sex, is said to be quite *nutty*, or *nuts upon* him or her.

Nuts upon Yourself. A man who is much gratified with any bargain he has made, narrow escape he has had, or other event in which he is interested, will express his self-satisfaction or gladness by declaring that he is, or was, quite *nuts upon himself*.

Nyp, or Nip. A half pint, a nip of ale: whence the nipperkin, a small vessel.

Nypper. A cut-purse: so called by one Wotton, who, in the year 1585, kept an academy for the education and perfection of pickpockets and cut-purses: his school was near Billingsgate, London. As in the dress of ancient times many people wore their purses at their girdles, cutting them was a branch of the light-fingered art, which is now lost, though the name remains. Maitland, from Stow, gives the following account of this Wotton: This man was a gentleman born, and some time a merchant of good credit, but fallen by time into decay: he kept an ale-house, near Smart's Key, near Billinsgate, afterwards, for some misdemeanour, put down. He reared up a new trade of life, and in the same house he procured all the cut-purses about the city to repair to it; there was a school-house set up to teach boys to cut purses: two devices were hung up; one was a pocket, and another was a purse; the pocket had in it certain counters, and was hung about with hawks bells, and over the top did hang a little sacring bell. The purse had silver in it; and he that could take out a counter, without noise of any of the bells, was adjudged a judicial *nypper:* according to their terms of art, a *foyster* was a pick-pocket; a *nypper* was a pick-purse, or cut-purse.

Nyp-Shop. The Peacock, in Gray's-Inn-lane, where Burton ale is sold in nyps.

O

OAF. A silly fellow.

OAFISH. Simple.

OAK. A rich man, a man of good substance and credit. To sport oak; to shut the outward door of a student's room, at college. An oaken towel; an oaken cudgel. To rub a man down with an oaken towel; to beat him.

OAR. To put in one's oar; to intermeddle, or give an opinion unasked; as, To be sure, you must put in your oar!

OATHS. The favourite oaths of the thieves of the present day are, "God strike me blind!" "I wish my b——y eyes may drop out if it is not true!" "So help me G—d!" "B——y end to me!"

OATS. He has sowed his wild oats; he is staid, or sober, having left off his wild tricks.

O BE JOYFUL. I'll make you sing O be joyful, on the other side of your mouth; a threat, implying the party threatened will be made to cry. To sing O be easy; to appear contented when one has cause to complain, and dare not.

O BE JOYFUL. Good liquor; brandy. *Sea term.*

OBSTROPULOUS. Vulgar misnomer of *obstreperous:* as, I was going my rounds, and found this here gemman very obstropulous, whereof I comprehended him as an auspicious person.

OCCUPY. To occupy a woman; to have carnal knowledge of her.

ODD-COME-SHORTLY'S. I'll do it one of these odd-come-shortly's; I will do it some time or another.

ODD FELLOWS. A society of that name, that make use of signs and pass words, to recognize any one of their order. There are numerous lodges of Odd Fellows in all parts of the kingdom.

ODDS PLUT AND HER NAILS. A Welsh oath, frequently mentioned in a jocular manner by persons, it is hoped, ignorant of it's meaning; which is, By God's blood, and the nails with which he was nailed to the cross.

OFFICE. To give the office; to give information, or make signs to the officers to take a thief.

OGLES. Eyes. Rum ogles; fine eyes.

OIL OF BARLEY, or BARLEY BROTH. Strong beer.

OIL OF GLADNESS. I will anoint you with the oil of gladness; ironically spoken for, I will beat you.

OIL OF PALMS. Money. *Cant.*

Oil of Stirrup. A dose the cobbler gives his wife whenever she is obstreperous.

Οι πολλοι. (*Cambridge.*) The many; the multitude; who take degrees without being entitled for an honour. All that is *required*, are three books of Euclid, and as far as Quadratic Equations in Algebra. *See* Plucked.

Old Chap. A good-natured flash phrase. *Cant.*

Old Ding. *See* Hat.

Old Dog at it. Expert, accustomed.

Old Doss. Bridewell.

Old Hand. Knowing or expert in any business.

Old Harry. A composition used by vintners to adulterate their wines: also, the nick-name for the Devil.

Old Lag. A man or woman who has been transported, is so called on returning home, by those who are acquainted with the secret. *See* Lag.

Old Mr. Gory. A piece of gold.

Old Nick. The Devil: from *Neken*, the evil spirit of the north.

Old One. The Devil. Likewise, an expression of quizzical familiarity, as, "how d'ye do, Old one?"

Old Prog. Poor Yorkshire cheese, made of skimmed milk.

Old Poger. The Devil.

Old Stager. One accustomed to business, one who knows mankind.

Old Toast. A brisk old fellow. *Cant.*

Oliver. The moon.

Oliver is in Town. A phrase signifying that the nights are moonlight, and, consequently, unfavourable to depredation.

Oliver's Scull. A chamber pot.

Oliver's up. The moon has risen.

Oliver Whiddles. The moon shines.

Olli Compolli. The name of one of the principal rogues of the canting crew. *Cant.*

Omnium Gatherum. The whole together: jocular imitation of law Latin.

One in Ten. A parson: an allusion to his tithes.

One of Us, or one of my Cousins. A woman of the town, a harlot.

One Two. In boxing, two blows rapidly put in after each other. *Jem Belcher* was distinguished for his *one two*. Vide note to Randall's Diary, page 70.

One upon your Taw. A person who takes offence at the conduct of another, or conceives himself injured by the latter, will say, never mind, I'll be *one upon your taw;* or, I'll be *a marble on your taw;* meaning, I'll be even with you some time.

Onion. A seal. Onion hunters; a class of young thieves who are on the look out for gentlemen who wear their seals suspended on a ribbon, which they cut, and thus secure the seals or other trinkets suspended to the watch.

O.P. and P.S. Theatrical cant, for Opposite the Prompter, and Prompt Side.

Open Arse. A medlar. *See* Medlar.

Optime. The senior and junior optimes are the second and last classes of Cambridge honours conferred on taking a degree. That of wranglers is the first. The last junior optime is called the Wooden Spoon.

Order-Racket. Obtaining goods from a shopkeeper, by means of a forged order or false pretence.

Organ. A pipe. Will you cock your organ? will you smoke your pipe?

Ostler. Oatstealer.

Ottomised. To be ottomised; to be dissected. You'll be scragged, ottomised, and grin in a glass case; you'll be hanged, anatomised, and your skeleton kept in a glass case, at Surgeons' Hall.

Ottomy. The vulgar word for a skeleton.

Out and Outer. Complete, up to every thing: also, a desperate thief, who values not the laws, but bids defiance to every opposition.

Out at Heels, or Out at Elbows. In declining circumstances.

Out of Print. Slang made use of by booksellers. In speaking of any person that is dead, they observe, "he is out of print."

Out of the Way. A thief who knows that he is sought after by the *traps* on some information, and, consequently, goes out of town, or otherwise conceals himself, is said by his *palls* to be *out of the way for* so and so, naming the particular offence he stands charged with. *See* Wanted.

Out of Twig. To *put* yourself *out of twig*, is to disguise your dress and appearance, to avoid being recognised, on some particular account; a man reduced by poverty to wear a shabby dress is said by his acquaintance to be *out of twig*; to *put* any article *out of twig*, as a stolen coat, cloak, &c. is to alter it in such a way that it cannot be identified.

Outrun the Constable. A man who has lived above his means, or income, is said to have outrun the constable.

Outs. A gentleman of three outs. *See* Gentleman.

Oven. A great mouth; the old woman would never have looked for her daughter in the oven, had she not been there herself.

Overseer. A man standing in the pillory, is, from his elevated situation, said to be an overseer.

Owl. (To catch the) A trick practised upon ignorant country boobies, who are decoyed into a barn under pretence of catching an owl, where, after divers preliminaries, the joke ends in their having a pail of water poured upon their heads.

Owl in an Ivy Bush. He looks like an owl in an ivy bush; frequently said of a person with a large frizzled wig, or a woman whose hair is dressed à-la-blowze.

Oyster. A gob of thick phlegm, spit by a consumptive man; in law Latin, *unum viridum gobbum.*

P

P's. To mind one's P's and Q's; to be attentive to the main chance.

P.P.C. An inscription on the visiting cards of our modern fine gentleman, signifying that they have called *pour prendre congé,* i. e. 'to take leave.' This has of late been ridiculed by cards inscribed D.I.O. i. e. 'Damme, I'm off.'

Packet. A false report.

Packthread. To talk packthread: to use indecent language well wrapt up.

Pad. The highway, or a robber thereon: also, a bed. Foot-pads; foot robbers. To go out upon the pad; to go out in order to commit a robbery.

Pad Borrowers. Horse-stealers.

Paddy. The general name for an Irishman; being the abbreviation of Patrick, the name of the tutelar saint of that island.

Pad the Hoof. *See* Beat the Hoof.

Pailliards. Those whose fathers were clapperdogens, or beggars born, and who themselves follow the same trade: the female sort beg with a number of children, borrowing them if they have not a sufficient number of their own, and making them cry by pinching, in order to excite charity: the males make artificial sores on different parts of their bodies, to move compassion.

Painter. I'll cut your painter for you; I'll send you off: the painter being the rope that holds the boat fast to the ship. *Sea term.*

Pair of Wings. Oars. *Cant.*

Palaver. To flatter: originally, an African word for a treaty, talk, or conference.

Pall. A companion. One who generally accompanies another, or who commit robberies together.

Palm. To bribe, or give money, for the attainment of any object or indulgence; and it is then said that the party who receives it is *palmed*, or that *Mr. Palmer is concerned*.

PALMING RACKET. Secreting money in the palm of the hand; a game at which some are very expert.

PAM. The knave of clubs.

PANNAM. Bread.

PANNIER-MAN. A servant belonging to the Temple and Gray's Inn, whose office is to announce the dinner. This, in the Temple, is done by blowing a horn; and, in Gray's Inn, by proclaiming the word *Manger, Manger, Manger*, in each of the three courts.

PANNY. A house. To do a panny; to rob a house. *See* the Session's Papers. Probably, panny originally meant the butler's pantry, where the knives and forks, spoons, &c. are usually kept. The pigs frisked my panny, and nailed my screws; the officers searched my house, and seized my pick-lock keys. *Cant.*

PANTER. A hart; that animal is, in the Psalms, said to pant after the fresh water brooks: also, the human heart, which frequently pants in time of danger. *Cant.*

PANTILE-SHOP. A presbyterian, or other dissenting meeting-house, frequently covered with pantiles: called, also, a cock-pit.

PANTLER. A butler.

PAP. Bread sauce: also, the food of infants. His mouth is full of pap; he is still a baby.

PAPER-SCULL. A thin-sculled foolish fellow.

PARENTHESIS. To put a man's nose into a parenthesis; to pull it, the fingers and thumb answering the hooks or crotchets. A wooden parenthesis; the pillory. An iron parenthesis; a prison.

PARINGS. The chippings of money. *Cant.*

PARISH-BULL. A parson.

PARISH. His stockings are of two parishes; i. e. they are not fellows.

PARK-PALEING. Teeth.

PARSON. A guide post, hand or finger-post by the road side, for directing travellers: compared to a parson, because, like him, it sets people in the right way. *See* GUIDE POST.

PARSON PALMER. A jocular name, or term of reproach, to one who stops the circulation of the glass by preaching over his liquor; as it is said was done by a parson of that name whose cellar was under his pulpit.

PARSON'S JOURNEYMAN. A curate.

PARTIAL. Incliniug more to one side than the other, crooked, all o' one hugh.

PASS BANK. The place for playing at passage, cut into the ground almost like a cock-pit: also, the stock or fund.

Passage. A camp game with three dice: doublets making up ten, or more, to pass or win; any other chances lose.

Pat. Apposite, or to the purpose.

Pate. The head. Carrotty-pated; red-haired.

Patlander. An Irishman.

Patrico, or Pater-Cove. The fifteenth rank of the canting-tribe; strolling priests that marry people under a hedge without gospel or common prayer book: the couple, standing on each side of a dead beast, are bid to live together till death them does part: so, shaking hands, the wedding is ended: also, any minister or parson.

Pattering. The maundering or pert replies of servants: also, talk or palaver, in order to amuse one intended to be cheated. Pattering of prayers; the confused sound of a number of persons praying together.

Patter. To talk. To patter flash; to speak flash, or the language used by thieves. How the blowen lushes jackey and patters flash; how the wench drinks gin and talks flash.

Pavier's Workshop. The street.

Paum. To conceal in the hand. To paum a die; to hide a die in the palm of the hand. He paums; he cheats. Don't pretend to paum that upon me.

Paunch. The belly. Some think paunch was the original name of that facetious prince of puppets, now called Mr. Punch, as he is always represented with a very prominent belly: though the common opinion is, that both the name and character were taken from a celebrated Italian comedian, called Polichenello.

Paw. A hand or foot. Look at his dirty paws. Fore paw; the hand. Hind paw; the foot. To paw; to touch or handle clumsily.

Paw-paw Tricks. Naughty tricks: an expression used by nurses, &c. to children.

Pay. To smear over. To pay the bottom of a ship, or boat; to smear it over with pitch: the devil to pay and no pitch hot, or ready. *Sea term.* Also, to beat; as, I will pay you as Paul paid the Ephesians, over the face and eyes, and all your d—d jaws. To pay away; to fight manfully: also, to eat voraciously. To pay through the nose; to pay an extravagant price.

Peach. To impeach: called, also, to blow the gab, squeak, or turn stag.

Peak. Any kind of lace.

Peal. To ring a peal in a man's ears; to scold at him: his wife rang him such a peal!

Pear-Making. Taking bounties from several regiments and immediately deserting. The cove was fined in the steel for peer-making; the fellow was imprisoned in the house of correction for taking bounties from different regiments.

PECCAVI. To cry peccavi; to acknowledge one's self in an error, to own a fault: from the Latin, *peccavi*, I have sinned.

PECK. Victuals. Peck and booze; victuals and drink.

PECKISH. Hungry.

PECULIAR. A mistress.

PED. A basket. *Cant.*

PEDLAR'S FRENCH. The cant language. Pedlar's pony; a walking stick.

PEEL. To strip: allusion to the taking off the coat or rind of an orange or apple.

PEEPER. A spying-glass; also, a looking-glass. Track up the dancers and pike with the peeper: whip up stairs and run off with the looking-glass. *Cant.*

PEEPERS. Eyes. Single peeper; a one-eyed man.

PEEPING TOM. A nick-name for a curious prying fellow; derived from an old legendary tale, told of a tailor of Coventry, who, when Godiva, countess of Chester, rode at noon quite naked through that town, in order to procure certain immunities for the inhabitants, (notwithstanding the rest of the people shut up their houses,) slily peeped out of his window, for which he was miraculously struck blind. His figure, peeping out of a window, is still kept up in remembrance of the transaction.

PEEPY. Drowsy.

PEER. To look about, to be circumspect.

PEERY. Inquisitive, suspicious. The cull's peery; that fellow suspects something. There's a peery, 'tis 'snitch; we are observed, there's nothing to be done.

PEG. Old peg; poor hard Suffolk or Yorkshire cheese. A peg is, also, a blow with a straight arm: a term used by the professors of gymnastic arts. A peg in the day-light, the victualling office, or the haltering place; a blow in the eye, stomach, or under the ear.

PEG TRANTUM'S. Gone to Peg Trantum's; dead.

PELL-MELL. Tumultuously, helter-skelter, jumbled together.

PELT. A heat, chafe, or passion; as, What a pelt he was in! Pelt is also the skin of several beasts.

PENANCE-BOARD. The pillory.

PENNY WISE AND POUND FOOLISH. Saving in small matters, and extravagant in great.

PENTHOUSE-NAB. A broad brimmed hat.

PEPPERED. Infected with the venereal disease.

PEPPERY. Warm, passionate.

PERKIN. Water cyder.

PERRIWINKLE. A wig.

Persuaders. Spurs. The kiddey clapped his persuaders to his prad, but the traps boned him; the highwayman spurred his horse hard, but the officers seized him.

> "'Twas like using *persuaders* upon a dead *prad*."
> *Vide Crib's Memorial.*

Pet. In a pet; in a passion or miff.

Peter. A portmanteau or cloak-bag. Biter of peters; one that makes it a trade to steal boxes and trunks from behind stage coaches or out of waggons. To rob Peter to pay Paul; to borrow of one man to pay another: styled, also, manœuvring the apostles.

Peter-hunting. Traversing the streets or roads for the purpose of cutting away trunks, &c. from travelling carriages; persons who follow this *game* are thence called *peter-hunters*, whereas *the drag* more properly applies to robbing carts or waggons.

Peter-hunting-Jemmy. A small iron crow, particularly adapted for breaking the patent chain, with which the luggage is, of late years, secured to gentleman's carriages; and which, being of steel, case-hardened, is fallaciously supposed to be proof against the attempts of thieves.

Peter Lug. Who is Peter Lug? who lets the glass stand at his door, or before him?

Petticoat-hold. One who has an estate during his wife's life, called the apron-string hold.

Petticoat-Pensioner. A mean-spirited fellow who lives with a woman of the town, and suffers her to maintain him in idleness in the character of her *fancy-man*.

Pettish. Passionate.

Pettyfogger. A little dirty attorney, ready to undertake any litigious or bad cause: it is derived from the French words, *petit vogue*, of small credit, or little reputation.

Pewter. Silver. *Cant.*

Pharoah. Strong malt liquor.

Philistines. Bailiffs, or officers of justice: also, drunkards.

Phos Bottle. A bottle of phosphorous: used by housebreakers, to light their lanthorns. Ding the phos; throw away the bottle of phosphorous.

Phrase of Paper. Half a quarter of a sheet. *See* Vessel.

Physog. The face. A vulgar abbreviation of physiognomy.

Phyz. The face. Rum phyz; an odd face or countenance.

Picaroon. A pirate: also, a sharper.

Pickaniny. A young child, an infant. *Negro term.*

Picking. Pilfering, petty larceny.

Pickle. An arch waggish fellow. In pickle, or in the pickling tub; in a salivation. There are rods in brine, or pickle, for him; a punishment awaits him, or is prepared for him. Pickle herring; the Zany or Merry Andrew of a mountebank. *See* JACK PUDDING.

PICKTHANK. A tale-bearer or mischief-maker.

PICKT HATCH. To go to the manor of Pickt Hatch; a cant name for some part of the town noted for bawdy-houses in Shakspeare's time, and used by him in that sense.

PICK-UP. To enter into conversation with any person in the street, for the purpose of executing some design upon his personal property. Among sharpers, it is called *picking up a flat*, a *Johnny Raw*, a *muff*, &c.: also, by the *drop coves*, who act together; but this task is allotted to the best *gammoner* of the party, who can spin a *good yarn*, likewise interesting in his conversation, who is termed the *picker-up*. This latter personage is generally enabled to *suck* the *flat* out of what place he comes from, when he pretends he is also a native of the same town, but left it a long time: this has the desired effect, and they adjourn to a public-house, to take a glass together as old townsmen. The *rig* then commences; the associates of the *picker-up* drop in, as it were, by accident, and appear as perfect strangers, but all join together in order to *clean out* the *flat*. The women of the town call it *picking up a cull.*

PICTURE-FRAME. The sheriff's picture-frame; the gallows or pillory.

PIECE. A wench. A damned good or bad piece; a girl who is more or less active and skilful in the amorous congress. Hence the *(Cambridge)* toast, May we never have a *piece* (peace) that will injure the constitution. Piece likewise means, at Cambridge, a close, or spot of ground adjacent to any of the colleges, as Clare-hall-piece, &c. The spot of ground before King's College formerly belonged to Clare-hall. While Clare-piece belonged to King's, the master of Clare-hall proposed a swop, which being refused by the provost of King's, he erected before their gates a temple of *Cloacina*. It will be unnecessary to say that his arguments were soon acceded to.

PIG. A police officer. A China-street pig; a Bow-street officer. Floor the pig and bolt; knock down the officer and run away.

PIG. Sixpence. A sow's baby. Pig-widgeon; a simpleton. To pig together; to lie or sleep together, two or more in a bed. Cold pig; a jocular punishment inflicted by the maid servants, or other females of the house, on persons lying over long in bed: it consists in pulling off all the bed-clothes, and leaving them to pig or lie in the cold. To buy a pig in a poke; to purchase any thing without seeing it. Pig's eyes; small eyes. Pigsnyes; the same: a vulgar term of endearment to a woman. He can have boiled pig at home; a mark of being master of his own house: an allusion to a well known poem and story. Brandy is Latin for pig and goose; an apology for drinking a dram after either.

PIGEON. A weak silly fellow easily imposed on. To pigeon; to cheat. To milk the pigeon; to attempt impossibilities, to be put to shifts for want of money. To fly a blue pigeon; to steal lead off a church.

PIGEONS. Sharpers, who, during the drawing of the lottery, wait, ready mounted, near Guildhall, and, as soon as the first two or three numbers are drawn, which they receive from a confederate on a card, ride with them full speed to some distant insurance office, before fixed on, where there is another of the gang, commonly a decent looking woman, who takes care to be at the office before the hour of drawing; to her he secretly gives the number, which she insures for a considerable sum; thus biting the biter. *An obsolete trick.*

PIGEON'S MILK. Boys and novices are frequently sent, on the first of April, to buy pigeon's milk.

PIG-HEADED. Obstinate.

PIG-RUNNING. A piece of game frequently practised at fairs, wakes, &c. A large pig, whose tail is cut short, and both soaped and greased, being turned out, is hunted by the young men and boys, and becomes the property of him who can catch and hold him by the tail above the height of his head.

PIKE. To run away. Pike off; run away.

PILGRIM'S SALVE. A sirreverence, human excrement.

PILL, or PEEL GARLICK. Said originally to mean one whose skin or hair had fallen off from some disease, chiefly the venereal one; but now commonly used by persons speaking of themselves: as, there stood poor Pill Garlick; i. e. there stood I.

PILLALOO. The Irish cry or howl at funerals.

PIMP. A male procurer, or cock bawd: also, a small faggot used about London for lighting fires; named from introducing the fire to the coals.

PIMPLE. The head.

PIMP WHISKIN. A top trader in pimping.

PIN. In or to a merry pin; almost drunk: an allusion to a sort of tankard, formerly used in the north, having silver pegs or pins set at equal distances from the top to the bottom: by the rules of good fellowship, every person drinking out of one of these tankards was to swallow the quantity contained between two pins; if he drank more or less, he was to continue drinking till he ended at a pin: by this means, persons, unaccustomed to measure their draughts, were obliged to drink the whole tankard. Hence, when a person was a little elevated with liquor, he was said to have drunk to a merry pin.

PIN-BASKET. The youngest child.

PINCH. To go into a tradesman's shop under the pretence of purchasing rings or other light articles, and while examining them to shift some up the sleeve of the coat: also, to ask for change for a guinea, and when the silver is received, to change some of the good shillings for bad ones; then suddenly pretending to recollect that you had sufficient silver to pay the bill, ask for the guinea again, and return the change, by which means several bad shillings are passed.

PINCHERS. Rogues who, in changing money, by dexterity of hand, frequently secrete two or three shillings out of the change of a guinea. This species of roguery is called the pinch, or pinching-lay.

PINCH-GLOAK. A man who *works upon the pinch.*

PINCH ON THE PARSON'S SIDE. To defraud the parson of his tithe.

PINDARIC HEIGHTS. Study of Pindar's Odes. *Oxf. Univ. cant.*

PINK. To stab or wound with a small sword: probably derived from the holes formerly cut in both men and women's clothes, called pinking. Pink of the fashion; the top of the mode. To pink and wink; frequently winking the eyes through a weakness in them.

PINKING-DINDES. A sweater or mohawk. *Irish.*

PIN MONEY. An allowance settled on a married woman for her pocket expenses.

PINS. Legs. Queer pins; ill-shapen legs. *Cant.*

PIPER. A broken-winded horse.

PIPES. Boots.

PISCINARIANS. A club or brotherhood, A.D. 1743.

PISS. He will piss when he can't whistle; he will be hanged. He shall not piss my money against the wall; he shall not have my money to spend in liquor.

> He who once a good name gets,
> May piss a bed, and say he sweats.

PISS-BURNED. Discoloured: commonly applied to a discoloured gray wig.

PISSING DOWN ANY ONE'S BACK. Flattering him.

PISSING PINS AND NEEDLES. To have a gonorrhea.

PISS-MAKER. A great drinker, one much given to liquor.

PISS-POT-HALL. A house at Clapton, near Hackney, built by a potter chiefly out of the profits of chamber pots, in the bottom of which the portrait of Dr. Sacheverel was depicted.

PISS PROPHET. A physician who judges of the diseases of his patients solely by the inspection of their urine.

PISS-PROUD. Having a false erection. That old fellow thought he had an erection, but his —— was only piss-proud; said of any old fellow who marries a young wife.

PIT. A watch-fob. He drew a rare thimble from the swell's pit; he took a handsome watch from the gentleman's fob.

PIT. To lay pit and boxes into one; an operation in midwifery or copulation, whereby the division between the anus and vagina is cut through, broken, and demolished: a simile borrowed from the playhouse, when, for the benefit of some favourite player, the pit and boxes are laid together. The pit is also the hole under the gallows, where poor rogues, unable to pay the fees, are buried.

PIT-A-PAT. The palpitation of the heart; as, my heart went pit-a-pat. Pintledy-pantledy; the same.

PITCHER. Newgate, in London, is called by various names; as *the pitcher, the stone pitcher, the start,* and *the stone jug*, according to the humour of the speaker.

PITCHER. The miraculous pitcher, that holds water with the mouth downwards; a woman's commodity. She has cracked her pitcher, or pipkin; she has lost her maidenhead.

PIT-MAN. A pocket-book worn in the bosom-pocket.

PITT'S PICTURE. A window stopt up on the inside to save the tax imposed in that statesman's administration. *Party wit.*

PLAINS OF BETTERIS. The diversion of billiards. *Oxf. Univ. cant.*

PLANK. To conceal. *Scotch cant.*

PLANT. The place in the house of the fence where stolen goods are secreted. Any place where stolen goods are concealed.

PLANT. To hide, or conceal, any person or thing, is termed *planting* him or it; and any thing hid is called, *the plant;* when alluded to in conversation, such article is said to be *in plant;* the place of concealment is sometimes called *the plant,* as, I know of a fine *plant;* that is, a secure hiding-place. To *spring a plant,* is to find any thing that has been concealed by another. To *rise the plant,* is to take up and remove any thing that has been hid, whether by yourself or another. A person's money, or valuables, secreted about his house, or person, is called his *plant.* To *plant upon* a man, is to set somebody to watch his motions; also, to place any thing purposely in his way, that he may steal it and be immediately detected.

PLASTER OF WARM GUTS. One warm belly clapped to another; a receipt frequently prescribed for different disorders.

Plate. Money, silver, prize. He is in for the plate; he has won the *heat*, i.e. is infected with the venereal disorder: a simile drawn from horse-racing. When the plate fleet comes in; when money comes to hand.

Platter-faced. Broad-faced.

Play. To play booty; to play with an intention to lose. To play the whole game; to cheat. To play least in sight; to hide, or keep out of the way. To play the devil; to be guilty of some great irregularity or mismanagement.

Play a Cross. What is commonly termed playing booty; that is, purposely losing the game, or match, in order to take in the *flats* who have backed you (*see* Bridge) while the *sharps* divide the spoil in which you have a share. This sort of treachery extends to boxing, racing, and every other species of sport on which bets are laid; sometimes a sham match is made for the purpose of inducing strangers to bet, which is decided in such a manner that the latter will inevitably lose. *A cross* signifies generally any collusion or unfair dealing between several parties.

Pluck. Courage. He wants pluck; he is a coward. Against the pluck; against the inclination. Pluck the ribbon; ring the bell. To pluck a crow with one; to settle a dispute, to reprove one for some past transgression. To pluck a rose; an expression said to be used by women for going to the necessary-house, which, in the country, usually stands in the garden. To pluck, also, signifies to deny a degree to a candidate at one of the universities, on account of insufficiency. The first three books of Euclid, and as far as Quadratic Equations in Algebra, will save a man from being plucked. These unfortunate fellows are designated by many opprobrious appellations, such as the twelve apostles, the legion of honour, wise men of the East, &c.

Plug Tail. A man's penis.

Plumb. A hundred thousand pounds.

Plummy. It is all plummy; i.e. all is right, or, as it ought to be. *Cant.*

Plump. Fat, full, fleshy. Plump in the pocket; full in the pocket. To plump; to strike, or shoot. I'll give you a plump in the bread-basket, or victualling-office; I'll give you a blow in the stomach. Plump his peepers, or day-lights; give him a blow in the eyes. He pulled out his pops and plumped him; he drew out his pistols and shot him. A plumper; a single vote at an election. Plump, also, means directly, or exactly: as, it fell plump upon him; it fell directly upon him.

PLUMP CURRANT. I am not plump currant; I am out of sorts.

PLUMPERS. Contrivances said to be formerly worn by old maids, for filling out a pair of shrivelled cheeks.

PLYER. A crutch: also, a trader.

POACHING COUNTRY. Resort of all who go shooting. *Oxf. Univ. cant.*

POCKETS TO LET. Out of cash; done up. *Cant.*

POGUE. A bag. *Cant.*

POGY. Drunk.

POINT. To stretch a point; to exceed some usual limit, to take a great stride. Breeches were usually tied up with points, a kind of short laces, formerly given away by the church-wardens at Whitsuntide, under the denomination of tags: by taking a great stride these were stretched.

POINT FAILURE. Catastrophe of plucking. *Oxf. Univ. cant.*

POISONED. Big with child: that wench is poisoned, see how her belly is swelled. Poison-pated; red-haired.

POKE. A blow with the fist. I'll lend you a poke. A poke likewise means a sack; whence, to buy a pig in a poke; i.e. to buy any thing without seeing or properly examining it.

POKER. A sword. Fore-poker; aces and kings at cards. To burn your poker; to catch the venereal disease.

POLE. He is like a rope-dancer's pole, lead at both ends; a saying of a stupid sluggish fellow.

POLISH. To polish the king's iron with one's eyebrows; to be in gaol, and look through the iron-grated windows. To polish a bone; to eat a meal. Come and polish a bone with me; come and eat a dinner, or supper, with me. *Obsolete.*

POLL. The head, jolly nob, napper, or knowledge-box: also, a wig.

POLT. A blow. Lend him a polt in the muns; give him a knock in the face.

POMMEL. To beat: originally confined to beating with the hilt of a sword, the knob being, from its similarity to a small apple, called *pomelle;* in Spain it is still called the apple of the sword. As the clenched fist likewise somewhat resembles an apple, perhaps that might occasion the term pommelling to be applied to fisty-cuffs.

POMP. To save one's pomp at whist, is to score five before the adversaries are up, or win the game: originally derived from *pimp,* which is Welsh for five; and should be, I have saved my pimp.

PONTIUS PILATE. A pawn-broker. Pontius Pilate's guards, the first regiment of foot, or Royal Scots; so entitled from their supposed great antiquity. Pontius Pilate's counsellor;

one who, like him, can say, *Non invenio causam*, I can find no cause: also, (*Cambridge*) a Mr. Shepherd, of Trinity College; who, disputing with a brother parson on the comparative rapidity with which they read the liturgy, offered to give him as far as Pontius Pilate in the Belief.

PONY. Money. Post the pony; lay down the money.

POPE. A figure burned every fifth of November, in memory of the gunpowder-plot, which is said to have been carried on by the papists.

POPE'S NOSE. The rump of a turkey.

POPLERS. Pottage. *Cant.*

POPS. Pistols. Pop-shop; a pawn-broker's shop. To pop; to pawn: also, to shoot. I popped my tatler; I pawned my watch. I popped the cull; I shot the man. His means are two pops and a galloper; that is, he is a highwayman.

PORK. To cry pork; to give intelligence to the undertaker of a funeral; metaphor borrowed from the raven, whose note sounds like the word *pork*. Ravens are said to smell carrion at a distance.

PORKER. A hog: also, a Jew.

PORRIDGE. Keep your breath to cool your porridge; i.e. hold your tongue.

PORT FOR STUFFS. Assumption of a commoner's gown. *Oxf. Univ. cant.*

POSEY, or POESY. A nosegay. I shall see you ride backwards up Holborn-hill, with a book in one hand and a posey in t'other; i.e. I shall see you go to be hanged. Malefactors, who piqued themselves on being properly equipped for that occasion, had always a nosegay to smell to, and a prayer-book, although they could not read.

POSTILION OF THE GOSPEL. A parson who hurries over the service.

POST NOINTER. A house painter, who occasionally paints or anoints posts. Knight of the post; a false evidence, one ready to swear any thing for hire. From post to pillar; backwards and forwards.

POT. The pot calls the kettle black a–se; one rogue exclaims against another.

POT. On the pot; i.e. at stool.

POTATOE-TRAP. The mouth. Shut your potatoe-trap and give your tongue a holiday; i.e. be silent. *Irish wit.*

POT CONVERTS. Proselytes to the Romish church, made by the distribution of victuals and money.

POT-HUNTER. One who hunts more for the sake of the prey than the sport. Pot valiant; courage from drink. Pot-wallopers; persons entitled to vote in certain boroughs by having boiled a pot there.

POT-WABBLERS. Persons entitled to vote for members of

parliament in certain boroughs, from having boiled their pots therein. These boroughs are called pot-wabbling boroughs.

POULTERER. A person that guts letters; i. e. opens them and secretes the money. The kiddey was topped for the poultry rig; the young fellow was hanged for secreting a letter and taking out the contents.

POUND. To beat. How the milling cove pounded the cull for being nuts on his blowen; how the boxer beat the fellow for taking liberties with his mistress.

POUND. A prison. *See* LOB'S POUND. Pounded; imprisoned. Shut up in the parson's pound; married.

POUNDABLE Any event which is considered certain or inevitable, is declared to be poundable; as, the issue of a game, the success of a bet, &c.

POUND IT. To ensure or make a certainty of any thing; thus, a man will say, I'll pound it to be so; taken, probably, from the custom of laying, or rather offering, ten pounds to a crown at a cock-match, in which case, if no person takes this extravagant odds, the battle is at an end. This is termed pounding a cock.

POWDERING-TUB. The same as pickling-tub. *See* PICKLING-TUB.

POWDER-MONKEY. A boy on board a ship of war, whose business is to fetch powder from the magazine.

PRAD. A horse. The swell flashes a rum prad; the gentleman sports a fine horse.

> " And long before day-light, *gigs, rattlers,* and *prads,*
> Were in motion for Moulsey, brim full of the *lads.*"
>
> *Vide Crib's Memorial.*

> " And *prads* and *rattlers* rolled by,
> Full trot, in drunken revelry."
>
> *Vide Moulsey, a Poem at the end of Randall's Diary.*

PRAD COVE. A horse-dealer.

PRAD LAY. Cutting bags from behind horses. *Cant.*

PRANCER. A horse. Prancer's nob; a horse's head, used as a seal to a counterfeit pass. At the sign of the prancer's poll; i. e. the nag's head.

PRATE ROAST. A talkative boy.

PRATING CHEAT. The tongue.

PRATTLE BROTH. Tea. *See* CHATTER BROTH, SCANDAL BROTH, &c.

PRATTLING-BOX. The pulpit.

PRATTS. Buttocks: also, a tinder-box. *Cant.*

PRAY. She prays with her knees upwards; said of a woman much given to gallantry and intrigue. At her last prayers; saying of an old maid.

PRESERVE OF LONG BILLS. Stock of debts to be discharged. *Oxf. Univ. cant.*

Pricklouse. A tailor.

Priest-craft. The art of awing the laity, managing their conscieuces, and diviug into their pockets.

Priest-linked. Married.

Priest-ridden. Governed by a priest, or priests.

Prig. A thief, a cheat: also, a conceited coxcomical fellow.

Priggers. Thieves in general. Priggers of prancers; horse-stealers. Priggers of cacklers; robbers of hen-roosts.

Prigging. Riding: also, lying with a woman.

Prig Napper. A thief-taker.

Prigstar. A rival in love.

Prime. Bang up. Quite the thing. Excellent. Well done. She's a prime piece; she is very skilful in the venereal act. Prime post; she's a prime article.

Priminary. I had like to be brought into a priminary; i. e. into trouble: from *premunire.*

Prince Prig. A king of the gypsies: also, the head thief, or receiver general.

Princes. When the majesty of the people was a favourite term in the House of Commons, a celebrated wit, seeing chimney sweepers dancing on a May-day, styled them the young princes.

Princod. A pincushion. *Scotch.* Also, a round plump man or woman.

Princox. A pert, lively, forward, fellow.

Princum Prancum. Mrs. Princum Prancum; a nice, precise, formal, madam.

Prinking. Dressing over nicely: prinked up as if he came out of a bandbox, or fit to sit upon a cupboard's head.

Print. All in print; quite neat or exact, set, screwed up. Quite in print; set in a formal manner.

Priscian. To break Priscian's head; to write, or speak false grammar. Priscian was a famous grammarian, who flourished at Constantinople in the year 525; and who was so devoted to his favourite study, that to speak false Latin in his company was as disagreeable to him as to crack his head.*

Prittle Prattle. Insignificant talk: generally applied to women and children.

Prog. Provision. Rum prog; choice provision. To prog; to be on the hunt for provision: called, in the military term, to forage.

Property. To make a property of any one; to make him a conveniency, tool, or cat's paw; to use him as one's own.

* This is inserted for the benefit of country gentlemen.

Props. Crutches.

Proud. Desirous of copulation. A proud bitch; a bitch at heat, or desirous of a dog.

Provender. He from whom any money is taken on the highway: perhaps, providor or provider. *Cant.*

Province of Bacchus. Inebriety. *Oxf. Univ. cant.*

Prunella. Mr. Prunella; a parson: parsons' gowns being frequently made of prunella.

Pry. To examine minutely into a matter or business. A prying fellow; a man of impertinent curiosity, apt to peep and inquire into other mens' secrets.

Public Leger. A prostitute; because, like that paper, she is open to all parties.

Public Man. A bankrupt.

Pucker. All in a pucker; in a dishabille: also, in a fright; as, she was in a terrible pucker.

Pucker Water. Water impregnated with alum, or other astringents, used by old experienced traders to counterfeit virginity.

Pudding-headed Fellow. A stupid fellow, one whose brains are all in confusion.

Puddings. The guts. I'll let out your puddings.

Pudding Sleeves. A parson.

Pudding Time. In good time, or at the beginning of a meal: pudding formerly making the first dish. To give the crows a pudding; to die. You must eat some cold pudding to settle your love.

Puff, or Puffer. One who bids at auctions, not with an intent to buy, but only to raise the price of the lot: for which purpose, many are hired by the proprietor of the goods on sale. Puffing is at present greatly practised, and essentially necessary in all trades, professions, and callings. To puff and blow; to be out of breath.

Pug. A Dutch pug; a kind of lap-dog, formerly much in vogue: also, a general name for a monkey.

P.C. Pugilistic Club; a society of gentlemen, founded in 1814, expressly for the purpose of keeping alive the principles of courage and hardihood which have distinguished the British character, and to check the progress of that effeminacy which wealth is apt to produce. Men of rank, associating together, learn to prize the native and acquired powers of human nature. The incitement which they produce to noble deeds of hardihood and bravery, and the high respectability which they confer by the patronage of their rank and fortune, is of inestimable benefit. This club consists of about 120 subscribers.

Pug Drink. Watered cyder.

Pugnosed, or **Puggified.** A person with a snub or turned up nose.

Pull. To be pulled; to be arrested by a police officer. To have a pull is to have an advantage; generally where a person has some superiority at a game of chance or skill.

Pull: to have the Pull. Is a sort of advantage possessed by one person over another, either by talent or trick. In gambling, it is having such a knowledge of the cards that the odds are likely to be in your favour, and which is called *having the pull:* also, to have the power of injuring a person by the knowledge of anything erroneous in his conduct, which may, perhaps, leave his character or personal safety at your mercy, is likewise termed *having the pull upon him;* i. e. to have him under your thumb.

Pully Hauly. To have a game at pully hauly; to romp with women.

Pump. A thin shoe. To pump; to endeavour to draw a secret from any one without his perceiving it. Your pump is good but your sucker is dry; said by any one to a person who is attempting to pump him. Pumping was also a punishment for bailiffs who attempted to act in privileged places, such as the Mint, Temple, &c. It is also a piece of discipline administered to a pickpocket caught in the fact, when there is no pond at hand. To pump ship; to make water, and, sometimes, to vomit. *Sea phrase.*

Pump Water. He was christened in pump water; commonly said of a person that has a red face.

Punch. A liquor called, by foreigners, contradiction, from its being composed of spirits to make it strong, water to make it weak, lemon-juice to make it sour, and sugar to make it sweat. Punch is also the name of the prince of puppets, the chief wit and support of a puppet-show. To punch it is a cant term for running away. Punchable; old passable money, anno 1695. A girl that is ripe for man is called a punchable wench. Cobbler's punch; urine with a cinder in it.

Punished. Severely beaten. *Pugilistic cant.*

Punk. A whore: also, a soldier's trull. *See* **Trull.**

Puny. Weak. A puny child; a weak little child. A puny stomach; a weak stomach. Puny, or puisne, judge; the last made judge.

Pupil Mongers. Persons at the universities, who make it their business to instruct and superintend a number of pupils.

Pupil's Straits. Interval between restraint and liberty. *Oxf. Univ. cant.*

Puppy. An affected or conceited coxcomb.

Purblind. Dim-sighted.

Purl. Ale, in which wormwood has been infused, or ale and bitters drank warm.

Purl Royal. Canary wine, with a dash of tincture of wormwood.

Pursenets. Goods taken up at thrice their value, by young spendthrifts, upon trust.

Purse Proud. One that is vain of his riches.

Purser's Pump. A bassoon: from its likeness to a syphon, called a purser's pump.

Pursy, or Pursive. Short-breathed, or foggy, from being over fat.

Pushing-School. A fencing school: also, a brothel.

Put. A country put; an ignorant awkward clown. To put upon any one; to attempt to impose on him, or to make him the but of the company.

Putty Cove, or Covess. A man or woman upon whom no dependence can be placed; i. e. they are as liable as *putty*, which can be bent any way.

Put up Affair. A preconcerted plan to rob a house, at the suggestion of the porter, or servants belonging to it; they, possessing a knowledge of the premises, are the most competent to advise the best and safest mode to carry it into effect; pointing out all the places where the plate and other valuable articles are deposited, &c Instances of this kind are too frequent in London. The *putter-up*, as he is called, comes in for a share of the booty, although he may take no active part in the robbery.

Puzzle-Cause. A lawyer who has a confused understanding.

Puzzle-Text. An ignorant blundering parson.

Puzzling Sticks. The triangles to which culprits are tied up, to undergo the punishment of whipping.

Q

QUACK. An ungraduated ignorant pretender to skill in physic, a vender of nostrums.

Quacking Cheat. A duck.

Quack-Salver. A mountebank, a seller of salves.

Quail-Pipe. A woman's tongue: also, a device to take birds of that name by imitating their call. Quail-pipe boots; boots resembling a quail-pipe, from the number of plaits; they were much worn in the reign of Charles II.

Quaking Cheat. A calf or sheep.

Quandary. To be in a quandary; to be puzzled: also, one so over-gorged, as to be doubtful which he should do first, sh—e or spew. Some derive the term quandary from the French phrase *qu'en dirai je?* what shall I say of it? others, from an Italian word signifying a conjurer's circle.

Quarrel-picker. A glazier; from the small squares in casements, called *carreux*, vulgarly, quarrels.

Quartered. Divided into four parts; to be hanged, drawn, and quartered, is the sentence on traitors and rebels. Persons receiving part of the salary of an office from the holder of it, by virtue of an agreement with the donor, are said to be quartered on him. Soldiers billetted on a publican are likewise said to be quartered on him.

Quash. To suppress, annul, or overthrow; vulgarly pronounced *squash;* they squashed the indictment.

Quean. A slut, or worthless woman, a strumpet.

Queen Dick. To the tune of the life and death of Queen Dick. That happened in the reign of Queen Dick; i. e. never.

Queen-Street. A man governed by his wife, is said to live in Queen-street, or at the sign of the Queen's Head.

Queer, or Quire. Base, roguish, bad, naught, or worthless. How queerly the cull touts; how roguishly the fellow looks. It also means odd, uncommon. *Cant.*

Queer. A dealer in *queer* among sweeps, is an impostor, one who serves the farmer with a mixed-up article in imitation of *soot.*

Queer. To puzzle or confound. I have queered the old full bottom; i. e. I have puzzled the judge. To queer one's ogles among bruisers; to darken one's day lights.

Queer as Dick's Hatband. Out of order, without knowing one's disease.

Queer Bail. Insolvent sharpers, who make a profession of bailing persons arrested: they are generally styled Jew-bail, from that branch of business being chiefly carried on by the sons of Judah. The lowest sort of these, who borrow or hire clothes to appear in, are called mounters, from their mounting particular dresses suitable to the occasion. *Cant.*

Queer Birds. Rogues relieved from prison and returned to their old trade.

Queer Bitch. An odd out-of-the-way fellow.

Queer Bit-makers. Coiners. *Cant.*

Queer Bluffer. The master of a public-house the resort of rogues and sharpers, a cut-throat inn or ale-house keeper.

Queer Bung. An empty purse.

Queer Checkers. Among strolling players, door-keepers,

who defraud the company by falsely checking the number of people in the house.

QUEER COLE FENCER. A putter off, or utterer, of bad money.

QUEER COLE MAKER. A maker of bad money.

QUEER COVE. A rogue. *Cant.*

QUEER CUFFIN. A justice of the peace: also, a churl.

QUEER DEGEN. An ordinary sword, brass or iron hilted.

QUEER IT. To spoil it. *Cant.*

QUEER KEN. A prison. *Cant.*

QUEER KICKS. A bad pair of breeches.

QUEER MORT. A diseased strumpet. *Cant.*

QUEER NAB. A felt hat, or other bad hat.

QUEER PLUNGERS. Cheats who throw themselves into the water, in order that they may be taken up by their accomplices, who carry them to one of the houses appointed by the Humane Society for the recovery of drowned persons, where they are rewarded by the Society with a guinea each; and the supposed drowned persons, pretending he was driven to that extremity by great necessity, is also frequently sent away with a contribution in his pocket.

QUEER PRANCER. A bad worn-out foundered horse: also, a cowardly, or faint-hearted horse-stealer.

QUEER ROOSTER. An informer that pretends to be sleeping, and thereby overhears the conversation of thieves in night cellars.

QUEER SCREENS. Forged notes. *Cant.*

QUEER-STREET. Wrong. Improper. Contrary to one's wish. It is Queer-street, a cant phrase, to signify that it is wrong or different to our wish.

QUEER WEDGES. Large buckles.

QUIBBLE. To make subtle distinctions: also, to play upon words.

QUICK AND NIMBLE. More like a bear than a squirrel. Jeeringly said to any one moving sluggishly on a business or errand that requires despatch.

QUID. The quantity of tobacco put into the mouth at one time. To quid tobacco; to chew tobacco. *Quid est hoc? hoc est* quid; a guinea. Half a quid; half a guinea. The swell tipped me fifty quid for the prad; the gentleman gave fifty guineas for the horse.

QUIDNUNC. A politician; from a character of that name in the farce of the Upholsterer.

QUIDS. Cash, money. Can you tip me any quids? can you lend some money?

QUIFFING. Rogering. *See* ROGER.

QUILL DRIVER. A clerk, scribe, or hackney writer.

QUILT. To thrash. *Cant.*

> "Up with your hat in the Surrey air
> And turn to and *quilt* the Nonpareil."
> *Lines to Martin, the Baker, in Randall's Scrap Book.*

QUIM. The monosyllable: perhaps, from the Spanish *quemar*, to burn. *(Cambridge.) A piece's furbelow.*

QUINSEY. Choked by a hempen quinsey; hanged.

QUIPPS. Girds, taunts, jests.

QUIRE, or CHOIR BIRD. A complete rogue, one that has sung in different choirs or cages; i. e. gaols. *Cant.*

QUIRKS AND QUILLETS. Tricks and devices. Quirks in law; subtle distinctions and evasions.

QUI TAM. A qui tam horse; one that will both carry and draw. *Law wit.*

QUIZ. A strange-looking fellow, an odd dog. *Oxford.*

QUOD. Newgate, or any other prison. The dab's in quod; the poor rogue is in prison.

QUOD COVE. The keeper of a jail. *Cant.*

QUOTA. Snack, share, part, proportion, or dividend. Tip me my quota; give me part of the winnings, booty, or plunder. *Cant.*

R

RABBIT. A Welsh rabbit; bread and cheese toasted; i. e. a Welsh rare bit. Rabbits were also a sort of wooden cans to drink out of, now out of use.

RABBIT CATCHER. A midwife.

RABBIT SUCKERS. Young spendthrifts taking up goods on trust at great prices.

RACK RENT. Rent strained to the utmost value. To lie at rack and manger; to be in great disorder.

RACKET. Some particular kinds of fraud and robbery are so termed, when called by their *flash* titles, and others, [illegible]; as, *the Letter-racket; the Order-racket; the Kid-* [illegible] *the Cat and Kitten rig*, &c. but all these terms depend on the fancy of the speaker. In fact, any *game* may be termed a *rig, racket, suit, slum, &c.* by prefixing thereto the particular branch of depredation or fraud in question, many examples of which occur in this work.

RAFFS. An appellation given by the gownsmen of the university of Oxford to the inhabitants of that place.

RAG. Bank notes. Money in general. The cove has no rag the fellow has no money.

RAG. A farthing.

RAG. To abuse, and tear to rags the characters of the

persons abused. She gave him a good ragging, or ragged him off heartily.

RAGAMUFFIN. A ragged fellow, one all in tatters, a tatterdemalion.

RAG CARRIER. An ensign.

RAG FAIR. An inspection of the linen and necessaries of a company of soldiers, commonly made by their officers on Mondays or Saturdays.

RAG-GORGY. A rich or monied man, but generally used in conversation when a particular gentlemen, or person high in office, is hinted at; instead of mentioning his name, they say, *the Rag-gorgy*, knowing themselves to be understood by those they are addressing. *See* COVE, and SWELL.

RAG WATER. Gin, or any other common dram: these liquors seldom failing to reduce those that drink them to rags.

RAILS. *See* HEAD RAILS. A dish of rails; a lecture, jobation, or scolding from a married woman to her husband.

RAINBOW. Knight of the rainbow; a footman: from being commonly clothed in garments of different colours. A meeting of gentlemen, styled of the most ancient order of the rainbow, was advertised to be held at the Foppington's Head, Moorfields.

RAINY DAY. To lay up something for a rainy day; to provide against a time of necessity or distress.

RAKE, RAKEHELL, or RAKESHAME. A lewd, debauched fellow.

RALPH SPOONER. A fool.

RAM CAT. A he cat.

RAMMER. The arm. The busnapper's kenchin seized my rammer; i. e. the watchman laid hold of my arm. *Cant.*

RAMMISH. Rank. Rammish woman; a sturdy virago.

RAMP. To rob any person or place by open violence or suddenly snatching at something and running off with it; as, I *ramp'd* him *of* his *montra;* why did you not *ramp* his *castor?* &c. A man convicted of this offence is said to have *done* for a *ramp*. This audacious *game*, is called by *prigs, the ramp*, and is nearly similar to the RUSH, which see.

RAMSHACKLED. Out of repair. A ramshackled house; perhaps a corruption of *ransacked*, i. e. plundered.

RANDY. Obstreperous, unruly, rampant.

RANGLING. Intriguing with a variety of women.

RANK. Complete, absolute, downright, an emphatical manner of describing persons or characters, as, *a rank nose, a rank swell*, &c. &c.

RANK RIDER. A highwayman.

RANTALLION. One whose scrotum is so relaxed as to be

longer than his penis; i. e. whose shot-pouch is longer than the barrel of his piece.

RANTIPOLE. A rude romping boy or girl: also, a gadabout dissipated woman. To ride rantipole; the same as riding St. George. *See* ST. GEORGE.

RANTUM SCANTUM. Playing at rantum scantum; making the beast with two backs.

RAP. To take a false oath: also, to curse. He rapped out a volley; i.e. he swore a whole volley of oaths. To rap, means, also, to exchange or barter: a rap is likewise an Irish half-penny. Rap on the knuckles; a reprimand.

RAPPAREES. Irish robbers, or outlaws, who, in the time of Oliver Cromwell, were armed with short weapons, called in Irish *rapiers*, used for ripping persons up.

RAPPER. A swinging great lie.

RAREE SHOW MEN. Poor Savoyards, who subsist by showing the magic lantern and marmots about London.

RASCAL. A rogue or villain: a term borrowed from the chase; a rascal originally meant a lean shabby deer, at the time of changing his horns, penis, &c. whence, in the vulgar acceptation, rascal is conceived to signify a man without genitals: the regular vulgar answer to this reproach, if uttered by a woman, is the offer of an ocular demonstration of the virility of the party so defamed. Some derive it from *rascaglione*, an Italian word signifying a man without testicles, or an eunuch.

RAT. A drunken man or woman taken up by the watch, and confined in the watch-house. *Cant.* To smell a rat; to suspect some intended trick, or unfair design.

RATS. Of these there are the following kinds: a black rat and a grey rat, a py-rat and a cu-rat.

RATS. Men, in trade, who undermine each other, and who are not true to the cause in which they have embarked. This conduct is termed *ratting*.

RATTLE. A dice-box. To rattle; to talk without consideration: also, to move off, or go away. To rattle one off; to rate or scold him.

RATTLE-PATE. A volatile, unsteady, or whimsical, man or woman.

RATTLER. A coach. Rattle and prads; a coach and horses.

> "At a quarter past ten by Pat C—— h's tattler,
> Crib came on the ground in a four-in-hand *rattler*."
>
> *Vide Crib's Memorial.*

RATTLE-TRAPS. A contemptuous name for any curious portable piece of machinery, or philosophical apparatus.

RATTLING COVE. A coachman. *Cant.*

RATTLING MUMPERS. Beggars who ply coaches. *Cant.*

Raw Head and Bloody Bones. A bull beggar, scarechild, with which foolish nurses terrify crying brats.

Reader. A pocket-book. *Cant.*

Reader Merchants. Pick-pockets; chiefly young Jews, who ply about the Bank to steal the pocket-books of persons who have just received their dividends.

Ready. The ready rhino; money. *Cant.*

Rebus. A riddle, or pun, on a man's name, expressed in sculpture or painting, thus, a bolt, or arrow and a tun, for Bolton; death's head and a tun, for Morton.

Receiver-General. A prostitute: also, in boxing, a man who *takes* all the blows, and gives none in return.

Reckon. To reckon with one's host; to make an erroneous judgement in one's own favour. To cast up one's reckoning, or accounts; to vomit.

Recounters. The time of settlement between the bulls and bears at the Stock-Exchange, when the losers must pay their differences, or become lame ducks, and waddle out of the Alley.

Recruiting Service. Robbing on the highway.

Red Fustian. Port wine.

Red Lane. The throat. Gone down the red lane: swallowed.

Red Lattice. A public-house.

Red Letter Day. A saint's day, or holiday, marked in the calendars with red letters. Red-letter-men; Roman Catholics: from their observation of the saints' days marked in red letters.

Red Rag. The tongue. Shut your potatoe trap, and give your red rag a holiday; i.e. shut your mouth, and let your tongue rest. Too much of the red rag; too much tongue.

Red Ribbon. Brandy.

Red Sail-yard Dockers. Buyers of stores stolen out of the royal yards and docks.

Red Shank. A Scotch highlander.

Regulars. Share of the booty. The coves cracked the swell's crib, fenced the swag, and each cracksman napped his regular; some fellows broke open a gentleman's house, and, after selling the property which they had stolen, they divided the money between them.

Reign. The length or continuance of a man's career in a system of wickedness, which, when he is ultimately *bowled-out*, is said to have been a long or a short *reign*, according to its duration.

Religious Horse. One much given to prayer, or apt to be down upon his knees.

Religious Painter. One who does not break the commandment which prohibits the making of the likeness of any thing in heaven or earth, or in the waters under the earth.

Relish, the. The sign of the Cheshire cheese.

Relish. Carnal connection with a woman.

Remedy. A sovereign. *Cant.*

Remedy-Critch. A chamber-pot, or member-mug.

Remember Parson Melham. Drink about: a Norfolk phrase.

Rendezvous. A place of meeting. The rendezvous of the beggars were, about the year 1638, according to the Bellman, St. Quinton's, the Three Crowns in the Vintry, St. Tybs, and at Knapsbury: there were four barns within a mile of London. In Middlesex, were four other harbours, called Draw the Pudding out of the Fire; the Cross Keys, in Craneford parish; St. Julian's, in Isleworth parish; and the house of Pettie in Northall parish. In Kent, the King's Barn, near Dartford; and Ketbrooke, near Blackheath.

Rep. A woman of reputation.

Repository. A lock-up or spunging-house, a gaol: also, livery-stables where horses and carriages are sold by auction.

Resurrection Coves. Persons employed by the students in anatomy to steal dead bodies out of church-yards.

Reverence. An ancient custom, which obliges any person easing himself near the highway, or foot-path, on the word *reverence* being given him by a passenger, to take off his hat with his teeth, and, without moving from his station, to throw it over his head, by which it frequently falls into the excrement: this was considered as a punishment for the breach of delicacy. A person refusing to obey this law might be pushed backwards. Hence, perhaps, the term *sir-reverence.*

Reversed. A man set, by bullies, on his head, that his money may fall out of his breeches, which they afterwards, by accident, pick up. *See* Hoisting.

Review of the Black Cuirassiers. A visitation of the clergy. *See* Crow Fair.

Rheumatism in the Shoulder. To be arrested. *Cant.*

Rhino. Money. *Cant.*

Rib. A wife: an allusion to our common mother, Eve, made out of Adam's rib. A crooked rib; a cross-grained wife.

Ribaldry. Vulgar abusive language, such as was spoken by ribalds. Ribalds were originally mercenary soldiers, who travelled about, serving any master for pay, but afterwards degenerated into a mere banditti.

Ribbon. Money. The ribbon runs thick; i.e. there is plenty of money. *Cant.* Blue Ribbon. Gin. The cull lushes the blue ribbon; the silly fellow drinks common gin.

Ribbons. The reins.

Ribroast. To beat: I'll ribroast him to his heart's content.

Richard Snary. A dictionary. A country lad, having been reproved for calling persons by their Christian names, being sent by his master to borrow a dictionary, thought to show his breeding by asking for a Richard Snary.

RICH FACE, or NOSE. A red pimpled face.

RIDGE. Gold, whether in coin or any other shape, as a *ridge montra;* a gold watch. A *cly* full of *ridge;* a pocket full of gold.

RIDGE. A guinea. Ridge cully; a goldsmith. *Cant.*

RIDING ST. GEORGE. The woman uppermost in the amorous congress, that is, the dragon upon St. George. This is said to be the way to get a bishop.

RIDING SKIMMINGTON. A ludicrous cavalcade, in ridicule of a man beaten by his wife. It consists of a man riding behind a woman, with his face to the horse's tail, holding a distaff in his hand, at which he seems to work, the woman all the while beating him with a ladle; a smock, displayed on a staff, is carried before them as an emblematical standard, denoting female superiority: they are accompanied by what is called the *rough music,* that is, frying-pans, bulls' horns, marrow-bones and cleavers, &c. A procession of this kind is admirably described by Butler, in his Hudibras. He rode private; i.e. he was a private trooper.

RIFF RAFF. Low vulgar persons, mob, tag-rag and bob-tail.

RIG. Fun, game, diversion, or trick. To run one's rig upon any particular person; to make him a butt. I am up to your rig; I am a match for your tricks.

RIGGING. Clothing. I'll unrig the bloss; I'll strip the wench. Rum rigging; fine clothes. The cull has rum rigging, let's ding him, mill him, and pike; the fellow has good clothes. let's knock him down, rob him, and scour off, i.e. run away.

RIGHT. All right! A favourite expression among thieves, to signify that all is as they wish, or proper for their purpose. All right, hand down the jemmy; every thing is in proper order, give me the crow: also, said by the coachman to the guard before he starts from any place.

RIGMAROLE. Roundabout, nonsensical. He told a long rigmarole story.

RING. Money procured by begging: beggars so called it from its ringing when thrown to them: also, a circle formed for boxers, wrestlers, and cudgel-players, by men who go round the circle, striking at random with their whips, to prevent the populace from crowding in.

RING A PEAL. To scold: chiefly applied to women. His wife rung him a fine peal!

RINGING, or RINGING-IN. To *ring the changes,* is a fraud practised by *smashers,* who, with great dexterity, in getting good money in change, *ring-in* one or two bad shillings, or half-crowns, and then request the unsuspecting tradesman to change them.

Ringing Castors. This circumstance is often practised at churches and other public places, for the purpose of changing hats, by taking away a good, and leaving a shabby one in its stead.

Rip. A miserable rip; a poor, lean, worn-out horse. A shabby mean fellow.

Rippons. Spurs: Rippon is famous for a manufactory of spurs, both for men and fighting cocks.

River Tick. Standing debts, which only discharge themselves at the expiration of three years by leaving the Lake of Credit, and meandering through the haunts of 100 creditors. *Oxf. Univ. cant.*

Roaratorios and Uproars. Oratorios and operas.

Roarer. A broken-winded horse.

Roaring Boy. A noisy riotous fellow.

Roaring Trade. A quick trade.

Roast. To arrest. I'll roast the dab; I'll arrest the rascal: also, to jeer, ridicule, or banter. He stood the roast; he was the butt. Roast-meat clothes; Sunday or holiday clothes. To cry roast meat; to boast of one's situation. To rule the roast; to be master or paramount.

Roast and Boiled. A nick name for the Life Guards, who are mostly substantial house-keepers, and eat daily of roast and boiled.

Robert's Men. The third old rank of the canting crew, mighty thieves, like Robin Hood.

Roby Douglas, with one eye and a stinking breath; the breech.

Rochester Portion. Two torn smocks, and what nature gave.

Rocked. He was rocked in a stone kitchen; a saying meant to convey the idea that the person spoken of is a fool, his brains having been disordered by the jumbling of his cradle.

Roger A portmanteau: also, a man's yard. *Cant.*

Roger, or Tib of the Buttery. A goose. *Cant.* Jolly Roger; a flag hoisted by pirates.

Roger. To bull, or lie with a woman; from the name of Roger being frequently given to a bull.

Rogues. The fourth order of canters. A rogue in grain; a great rogue: also, a corn-chandler. A rogue in spirit; a distiller or brandy-merchant.

Rogum Pogum, or Dragrum Pogram. Goat's beard, eaten for asparagus; so called by the ladies who gather cresses, &c. who also deal in this plant.

Rollers. Horse and foot patrole, who parade the roads round about London during the night, for the prevention of robberies.

ROMANY. A gypsey: to *patter romany*, is to talk the gypsey *flash*.

ROMBOYLES. Watch and ward. Romboyled; sought after with a warrant.

ROME MORT. A queen.

ROMEVILLE. London. *Cant.*

ROMP. A forward wanton girl, a tomrig. Grey, in his notes to Shakspeare, derives it from *arompo*, an animal found in South Guinea; that is, a man eater. *See* HOYDEN.

ROOK. A cheat: probably from the thievish disposition of the birds of that name: also, the cant name for a crow used in house-breaking. To rook; to cheat, particularly at play.

ROOM. She lets out her fore room and lies backwards: a saying of a woman suspected of prostitution.

ROOST LAY. Stealing poultry.

ROPES. Upon the high ropes; elated, in high spirits, cock-a-hoop.

ROSE. Under the rose; privately or secretly. The rose was, it is said, sacred to Harpocrates, the god of silence, and therefore frequently placed in the ceilings of rooms destined for the receiving of guests; implying, that whatever was transacted there, should not be made public.

ROSY GILLS. One with a sanguine, or fresh-coloured countenance.

ROTAN. A coach, cart, or other wheeled carriage.

ROT GUT. Small beer; called beer-a-bumble—will burst one's guts before it will make one tumble.

ROUGH. To lie rough; to lie all night in one's clothes: called, also, roughing it. Likewise, to sleep on the bare deck of a ship, when the person is commonly advised to chuse the softest plank.

ROUGH-FAM, or ROUGH-FAMMY. The waistcoat-pocket.

ROUGH MUSIC. Saucepans, frying-pans, poker and tongs, marrow-bones and cleavers, bulls' horns, &c. beaten upon and sounded in ludicrous processions.

ROULEAU. A number of guineas, from twenty to fifty or more, wrapped up in paper, for the more ready circulation at gaming-tables: sometimes they are enclosed in ivory boxes, made to hold exactly 20, 50, or 100 guineas.

ROUND ABOUT. An instrument used in house-breaking. This instrument has not been long in use. It will cut a round piece, about five inches in diameter, out of a shutter or door.

ROUND DEALING. Plain, honest dealing.

ROUND HEADS. A term of reproach to the puritans and partizans of Oliver Cromwell, and the Rump Parliament, who, it is said, made use of a bowl as a guide to trim their hair.

Round Mouth. The fundament. Brother round mouth speaks: he has let a f—t.

Round Robin. A mode of signing remonstrances, practised by sailors on board the king's ships, wherein their names are written in a circle, so that it cannot be discovered who first signed it, or was, in other words, the ringleader.

Round Sum. A considerable sum.

Rout. A modern card-meeting at a private house: also, an order from the Secretary at War, directing the march and quartering of soldiers.

Rovers. Pirates, vagabonds.

Row. A disturbance; a term used by the students at Cambridge. A mob in the street,—" Here's a row!"

Row. To row in the same boat; to go snacks, or have a share in the benefit arising from any transaction to which you are privy. To let a person *row* with you, is to admit him to a share.

Rowland. To give a Rowland for an Oliver; to give an equivalent. Rowland and Oliver were two knights famous in romance: the wonderful achievements of the one could only be equalled by those of the other.

Royal Scamps. Highwaymen who never rob any but rich persons, and that without ill-treating them. *See* Scamp.

Royster. A rude boisterous fellow: also, a hound that opens on a false scent.

Rub. To run away. Don't rub us to the Whit; don't send us to Newgate. *Cant.* To rub up; to refresh, to rub up one's memory. A rub; an impediment. A rubber; the best two out of three. To win a rubber; to win two games out of three.

Ruby faced. Red-faced.

Ruff. An ornament formerly worn by men and women round their necks. Wooden ruff; the pillory.

Ruffian. The Devil. *Cant.* May the Ruffian nab the cuffin queer, and let the harmanbeck trine with his kinchins about his colquarren; may the Devil take the justice, and let the constable be hanged with his children about his neck. The Ruffian cly thee; the Devil take thee. Ruffian cook ruffian, who scalded the Devil in his feathers; a saying of a bad cook. Ruffian sometimes, also, means a justice.

Ruffian. In the pugilistic *cant*, is a fellow regardless of a knowledge of the science; one who hits away right or wrong, so that he can only obtain conquest.

Rufflers. The first rank of canters: also, notorious rogues pretending to be maimed soldiers or sailors.

RUFFLES. Handcuffs. *Cant.*
RUFFMANS. The woods, hedges, or bushes. *Cant.*
RUG. It is all rug; it is all right and safe, the game is secure. *Cant.*
RUG. Asleep. The whole gill is safe at rug; the people of the house are fast asleep.
RUGGINS'S. To go to bed, is called going to Ruggins's.
RUM. Fine, good, valuable.
RUM BEAK. A justice of the peace. *Cant.*
RUM BITE. A clever cheat, a clean trick.
RUM BLEATING CHEAT. A fat wether sheep. *Cant.*
RUM BLOWEN. A handsome wench. *Cant.*
RUM BLUFFER. A jolly host. *Cant.*
RUMBLE-TUMBLE. A stage-coach. *Cant.*
RUMBO. Rum, water, and sugar: also, a prison.
RUM BOB. A young apprentice: also, a sharp trick.
RUM BOOZE. Wine, or any other good liquor. Rum boozing welts; bunches of grapes. *Cant.*
RUMBOYLE. A ward or watch.
RUM BUBBER. A dexterous fellow at stealing silver tankards from inns and taverns.
RUM BUGHER. A valuable dog. *Cant.*
RUMBUMTIOUS. Obstreperous.
RUM BUNG. A full purse. *Cant.*
RUM CHANT. A song.
RUM CHUB. Among butchers, a customer easily imposed on, as to the quality and price of the meat. *Cant.*
RUM CLOUT. A fine silk, cambric, or holland, handkerchief. *Cant.*
RUM COD. A good purse of gold. *Cant.*
RUM COLE. New money, or medals.
RUM COVE. A dexterous or clever rogue.
RUM CULL. A rich fool, easily cheated, particularly by his mistress.
RUM DEGEN. A handsome sword. *Cant.*
RUM DELL. *See* RUM DOXY.
RUM DIVER. A dexterous pickpocket. *Cant.*
RUM DOXY. A fine wench. *Cant.*
RUM DRAWERS. Silk, or other fine stockings. *Cant.*
RUM DROPPER. A vintner. *Cant.*
RUM DUBBER. An expert picklock.
RUM DUKE. A jolly handsome fellow: also, an odd eccentric fellow: likewise, the boldest and stoutest fellows lately among the Alsatians, Minters, and Savoyards, and other inhabitants of privileged districts, sent to remove and guard the goods of such bankrupts as intended to take sanctuary in those places. *Cant.*

Rum File. *See* Rum Diver.

Rumford. To ride to Rumford; to have one's backside new bottomed: i. e. to have a pair of new leather breeches. Rumford was formerly a famous place for leather breeches. A like saying is current in Norfolk and Suffolk, of Bungay, and for the same reason. Rumford lion; a calf. *See* Essex Lion.

Rum Fun. A sharp trick. *Cant.*

Rum Gaggers. Cheats who tell wonderful stories of their sufferings at sea, or when taken by the Algerines. *Cant.*

Rum Glymmer. King or chief of the link-boys. *Cant.*

Rum Kicks. Breeches of gold or silver brocade, or richly laced with gold or silver. *Cant.*

Rum Mawnd. One that counterfeits a fool. *Cant.*

Rum Mort. A queen or great lady. *Cant.*

Rum Nab. A good hat.

Rum Nantz. Good French brandy.

Rum Ned. A very rich silly fellow. *Cant.*

Rump. To rump any one; to turn the back to him: an evolution sometimes used at court. Rump and a dozen; a rump of beef and a dozen of claret; an Irish wager: called, also, buttock and trimmings. Rump-and-kidney-men; fiddlers that play at feasts, fairs, weddings, &c. and live chiefly on the remnants.

Rum Pad. The highway. *Cant.*

Rum Padders. Highwaymen well mounted and armed. *Cant.*

Rumped. Flogged. *Cant.*

Rum Peepers. Fine looking-glasses. *Cant.*

Rum Prancer. A fine horse. *Cant.*

Rumpus. A riot, quarrel, or confusion: a masquerade.

Rum Quids. A great booty. *Cant.*

Rum Ruff Peck. Westphalia ham. *Cant.*

Rum Snitch. A smart fillip on the nose.

Rum Squeeze. Much wine, or good liquor, given among fiddlers. *Cant.*

Rumtitum. Synonymous with *prime twig;* in fine order or condition. A flash term for a *game* bull: one that is kept on purpose to be *baited:* and to try the courage of the dogs. Bill Gibbons, Caleb Baldwin, Pritchard, &c. were distinguished, in the *canine fancy,* for having, in their possession, such kind of animals.

Rum Tol. *See* Rum Degen.

Rum Topping. A rich commode, or woman's head-dress.

Rum Wiper. *See* Rum Clout.

Run Goods. A maidenhead, being a commodity never entered.

Running Horse, or **Nag.** A clap, or gleet.

Running Smobble. Snatching goods off a counter, and

throwing them to an accomplice, who brushes off with them.

RUNNING STATIONERS. Hawkers of newspapers, trials, and dying speeches.

RUNT. A short squat man or woman: from the small cattle, called Welsh runts.

RUSH. The *rush*, is nearly synonymous with the *ramp*; but the latter often applies to snatching at a single article, as a silk cloak, for instance, from a milliner's shop-door; whereas, a *rush* may signify a forcible entry by several men into a detached dwelling-house for the purpose of robbing its owners of their money, &c. A sudden and violent effort to get into any place, or, *vice versâ*, to effect your exit, as from a place of confinement, &c. is called *rushing them*, or *giving it to 'em upon the rush*.

RUSHERS. Thieves who knock at the doors of great houses in London, in summer time, when the families are gone out of town, and, on being opened by a woman, rush in and rob the house: also, housebreakers who enter lone houses by force.

RUSSIAN COFFEE-HOUSE, or HOTEL. The Brown Bear in Bow-street, Covent-garden, a house of call for thief-takers and runners of the Bow-street justices; a name given by some punster of the *family*.

RUSTICATION. Temporary dismissal for non-observance of college discipline.

RUSTY. Out of use. To nab the rust; to be refractory: properly applied to a restive horse, and figuratively to the human species. To ride rusty; to be sullen: called, also, to ride grub.

RUSTY GUTS. A blunt surly fellow: a jocular misnomer of *resticus*.

RUTTING. Copulating. Rutting time; the season when deer go to rut.

S

SACHEVEREL. The iron door, or blower, to the mouth of a stove: from a divine of that name, who made himself famous for blowing the coals of dissension in the latter end of the reign of queen Ann.

SACK. A pocket. To buy the sack; to get drunk. To dive into the sack; to pick a pocket. To break a bottle in an empty sack; a bubble bet, a sack with a bottle in it not being an empty sack.

Saddle. To saddle the spit; to give a dinner or supper. To saddle one's nose: to wear spectacles. To saddle a place or pension; to oblige the holder to pay a certain portion of his income to some one nominated by the donor. Saddle-sick; galled with riding, having lost leather.

Sad Dog. A wicked debauched fellow; one of the ancient family of the sad dogs. Swift translates it into Latin by the words *tristis canis.*

Saint. A piece of spoiled timber in a coach-maker's shop, like a saint, devoted to the flames. A hypocrite.

Saint Geoffrey's Day. Never, there being no saint of that name: to-morrow-come-never, when two Sundays come together.

Saint Luke's Bird. An ox: that evangelist being always represented with an ox.

Saint Monday. A holiday most religiously observed by journeyman shoemakers, and other inferior mechanics; a profanation of that day, by working, is punishable by a fine, particularly among the gentle craft. An Irishman observed, that this saint's anniversary happened every week.

Sal. An abbreviation of *salivation.* In a high sal; in the pickling tub, or under a salivation.

Salesman's Dog. A barker. *See* **Barker.**

Salmon, or Salamon. The beggars' sacrament or oath.

Salmon-Gundy. Apples, onions, veal or chicken, and pickled herrings, minced fine, and eaten with oil and vinegar: some derive the name of this mess from the French words *selon mon goût,* because the proportions of the different ingredients are regulated by the palate of the maker; others say it bears the name of the inventor, who was a rich Dutch merchant; but the general and most probable opinion is, that it was invented by the countess of Salmagondi, one of the ladies of Mary de Medecis, wife of King Henry IV. of France, and by her brought into France.

Salt. Lecherous. A salt bitch; a bitch at heat, or proud bitch. Salt eel; a rope's end, used to correct boys, &c. at sea: you shall have a salt eel for supper.

Salt-Box Cly. The outside coat-pocket, with a flap.

Salt-Boxes. The condemned cells in Newgate.

Salt-Pits. Store of attic wit. *Oxf. Univ. cant.*

Sammy. Foolish, silly.

Sand. Moist sugar. *Cant.*

Sandwich. Ham, dried tongue, or some other salted meat, cut thin, and put between two slices of bread and butter: said to be a favourite morsel with the Earl of Sandwich.

Sandy Pate. A red-haired man or woman.

SANK, SANKY, or CENTIPEES. A tailor employed by clothiers in making soldiers' clothing.

SAPSCULL. A simple fellow. Sappy, foolish.

SATYR. A libidinous fellow: those imaginary things are by poets reported to be extremely salacious.

SAUCE-BOX. A term of familiar raillery, signifying a bold or forward person.

SAUNTERER. An idle lounging fellow: by some derived from *sans terre*, applied to persons who, having no lands or home, lingered and loitered about. Some derive it from persons devoted to the Holy Land, *sainte terre*, who loitered about, as waiting for company.

SAVE-ALL. A kind of candlestick used by our frugal fore-fathers, to burn snuffs and ends of candles. Figuratively, boys running about gentlemen's houses in Ireland, who are fed on broken meats that would otherwise be wasted: also, a miser.

SAWNEY. A flitch of bacon. *Cant.*

SAWNY, or SANDY. A general nick-name for a Scotchman, as Paddy is for an Irishman, or Taffy for a Welshman; Sawny or Sandy being the familiar abbreviation or diminution of Alexander, a very favourite name among the Scottish nation.

SCAB. A worthless man or woman.

SCALDER. A clap. The cull has napped a scalder; the fellow has got a clap.

SCALY. Mean, sordid. How scaly the cove is; how mean the fellow is.

SCALY FISH. An honest, rough, blunt, sailor.

SCAMP. A highwayman. Royal scamp; a highwayman who robs civilly. Royal foot-scamp; a footpad who behaves in like manner. The game of highway robbery is called the scamp. To scamp a person is to rob him on the highway. Done for a scamp signifies convicted of a highway robbery.

SCANDAL-BROTH. Tea.

SCANDAL PROOF. One who has eaten shame and drank after it, or would blush at being ashamed.

SCAPEGALLOWS. One who deserves and has narrowly escaped the gallows: a slip-gibbet; one for whom the gallows is said to groan.

SCAPEGRACE. A wild dissolute fellow.

SCARCE. To make one's self scarce; to steal away.

SCARLET HORSE. A high red, hired or hack horse: a pun on the word *hired*.

SCAVEY. Sense, knowledge. "Massa, me no scavey;" master, I don't know, *(negro language,)* perhaps, from the French *sçavoir*.

Schism Monger. A dissenting teacher.

Schism Shop. A dissenting meeting-house.

School. A party of persons met together for the purpose of gambling.

School Butter. Cobbing, whipping.

School of Venus. A cyprian lodge.

Scold's Cure. A coffin. The blowen has napped the scold's cure; the wench is in her coffin.

Sconce. The head, probably, as being the fort and citadel of a man: from *sconce*, an old name for a fort, derived from a Dutch word of the same signification. To build a sconce: a military term for bilking one's quarters. To sconce or skonce; to impose a fine. *Academical phrase.*

Scot. A person of an irritable temper, who is easily put in a passion, which is often done by the company he is with to create fun; such a one is declared to be a fine *scot*. This diversion is called *getting* him *out*, or *getting* him *round the corner*, from these terms being used by *bull-hankers*, with whom, also, a *scot* is a bullock of a particular breed, which affords superior diversion when hunted.

Scotch Bait. A halt and a resting on a stick, as practised by pedlars.

Scotch Chocolate. Brimstone and milk.

Scotch Fiddle. The itch.

Scotch Greys. Lice. The head-quarters of the Scotch greys; the head of a man full of large lice.

Scotch Mist. A sober soaking rain; a Scotch mist will wet an Englishman to the skin.

Scotch Pint. A bottle containing two quarts.

Scotch Warming Pan. A wench: also, a f—t.

Scoundrel. A man void of every principle of honour.

Scour. To scour or score off; to run away: perhaps, from *score;* i. e. full speed, or as fast as legs would carry one: also, to wear: chiefly applied to irons, fetters, or handcuffs, because wearing scours them. He will scour the darbies; he will be in fetters. To scour the cramp ring; to wear bolts or fetters, from which, as well as from coffin-hinges, rings supposed to prevent the cramp are made.

Scourers. Riotous bucks, who amuse themselves with breaking windows, beating the watch, and assaulting every person they meet: called scouring the streets.

Scout. A college errand-boy at Oxford, called a gyp at Cambridge: also, a watchman or a watch. *Cant.*

Scout-ken. The watch-house. *Cant.*

Scrag. To hang.

Scragged. Hanged.

Scragg'em Fair. A public execution.

Scragging-Post. The gallows. *Cant.*

Scraggy. Lean, bony.

Scrap. A villanous scheme or plan. He whiddles the whole scrap; he discovers the whole plan or scheme.

Scrape. To get into a scrape; to be involved in a disagreeable business.

Scraper. A fiddler: also, one who scrapes plates for mezzotinto prints.

Scraping. A mode of expressing dislike to a person, or sermon, practised at Oxford by the students, in scraping their feet against the ground during the preachment; frequently done to testify their disapprobation of a proctor who has been, they think, too rigorous.

Scratch. Old Scratch; the Devil: probably from the long and sharp claws with which he is frequently delineated.

Scratch. A line made across the prize ring: up to which the boxers are brought when they *set-to.*

Scratch Land. Scotland.

Screave. A bank note. *Scotch cant.*

Screen. A bank note. Queer screens; forged bank notes. The cove was twisted for smashing queer screens; the fellow was hanged for uttering forged bank notes.

Screeve. A letter; or written paper. *Cant.*

Screw. A skeleton key used by house-breakers to open a lock. To stand on the screw signifies that a door is not bolted, but merely locked. A turnkey. *Cant.*

Screw. To copulate. A female screw; a common prostitute. To screw one up; to exact upon one in a bargain or reckoning.

Screw Jaws. A wry-mouthed man or woman.

Screw loose. This is a complete flash phrase; meaning something is wrong. For instance, if people quarrel, who have been hitherto friends, it is observed, a *screw is loose* among them, &c.

Scrip. A scrap or slip of paper. The cully freely blotted the scrip, and tipped me forty hogs; the man freely signed the bond, and gave me forty shillings. Scrip is also a Stock Exchange phrase for the last loan or subscription. What does scrip go at for the next recounters? what does scrip sell for delivered at the next day of settling?

Scroby. To be tipped the scroby; to be whipped before the justices.

Scroof. A sponge: one who endeavours to live at other people's expense, so that he can save his own pockets.

Scrope. A farthing. *Cant.*

Scrub. A low mean fellow, employed in all sorts of dirty work.

Scrubbado. The itch.

Scull. A head of a house, or master of a college, at the universities.

Scull, or **Sculler.** A boat rowed by one man with a light kind of oar, called a scull: also, a one-horse-chaise or buggy.

Scull Thatcher. A peruke-maker.

Scum. The riff-raff, tag-rag, and bob-tail, or lower order of people.

Scurfed. Laid hold of; taken up: an allusion to the head. It is a cant phrase to say such an one is *scurfed:* i. e. he has been pulled.

Scurrick. A halfpenny. *Cant.*

Scut. The tail of a hare or rabbit: also, that of a woman.

Scuttle. To scuttle off; to run away. To scuttle a ship; to make a hole in her bottom in order to sink her. To scuttle a nob; to break a head.

> " See the *Captain* and *Caleb* are chuckling around him,
> As he offered *to scuttle a nob* o'er again."
> *Lines on Randall's Fight with Turner, vide Randall's Diary.*

Sea Crab. A sailor.

Sea Lawyer. A shark.

Sealer, or **Squeeze Wax.** One ready to give bond and judgement for goods or money.

Seat of Magistracy. Proctor's authority. *Oxf. Univ. cant.*

Secret. He has been let into the secret: he has been cheated at gaming or horse-racing. He or she is in the grand secret, i. e. dead.

Seedy. Poor, pennyless, stiver-cramped, exhausted.

Sees. The eyes. *See* **Daylights.**

Sell. To sell, or to betray a man for interest, is termed, that he has been sold like a beast in a market.

Send. To drive or break in. Hand down the jemmy and send it in; apply the crow to the door, and drive it in.

Seraglio. A house full of lady-birds; the name of that part of the Great Turk's palace where the women are kept.

Serve. To *serve* a person, or place, is to rob them; as, I *serv'd* him *for* his *thimble;* I robb'd him of his watch: that *crib* has been *serv'd* before, that shop has been already robbed, &c. To *serve* a man, also, sometimes signifies to maim, wound, or do him some bodily hurt; and to *serve* him *out and out,* is to kill him. To *serve a fellow out,* is to mill him. *Ex. gr.*

> And all the lads looked gay and bright,
> And *gin* and *genius* flashed about,
> And whosoe'er grew unpolite,
> The well-bred Champion *serv'd him out.*
> *Vide Crib's Memorial.*

Served. Found guilty. Convicted. Ordered to be punished or transported. To serve a cull out; to beat a man soundly.

Set. A dead set: a concerted scheme to defraud a person by gaming.

Setter. A bailiff's follower, who, like a setting dog, follows and points out the game for his master: also, sometimes an exciseman.

Settle. To knock down or stun any one. We settled the cull by a stroke on his nob; we stunned the fellow by a blow on the head.

Set-to. Sparring.

Seven-sided Animal. A one-eyed man or woman, each having a right side and a left side, a fore side and a back side, an outside and an inside, and a blind side.

Shabbaroon. An ill-dressed shabby fellow: also, a mean-spirited person.

Shag. To copulate. He is but bad shag; he is no able woman's man.

Shag-bag, or Shake-bag. A poor sneaking fellow; a man of no spirit: a term borrowed from the cock-pit.

Shake. To shake one's elbow; to game with dice. To shake a cloth in the wind; to be hanged in chains.

Shake. To draw any thing from the pocket. He shook the swell of his fogle; he robbed the gentleman of his silk handkerchief. To steal, or rob; as, I *shook* a chest of *slop*, I stole a chest of tea; I've been *shook* of my *skin*, I have been robbed of my purse. A thief, whose *pall* has been into any place for the purpose of robbery, will say, on his coming out, Well, is it all right? have you *shook?* meaning, did you succeed in getting any thing? When two persons rob in company, it is generally the province, or part, of one to *shake*, (that is, to obtain *the swagg,)* and the other to carry, (that is, to bear it to a place of safety).

Shallow. A *whip* hat, so called from the want of depth in the crown. **Lilly Shallow.** A *white* whip hat.

Shallow Pate. A simple fellow.

Sham. A cheat, or trick. To cut a sham; to cheat or deceive. Shams; false sleeves to put on over a dirty shirt, or false sleeves with ruffles to put over a plain one. To sham Abram; to counterfeit sickness.

Shamble. To walk awkwardly. Shamble-legged; one that walks wide, and shuffles about his feet.

Shan. Bad money. *Cant.*

Shanks. Legs, or gams.

Shanks's Naggy. To ride Shanks's naggy; to travel on foot. *Scotch.*

Shannon. A river in Ireland: it is said, persons dipped in that river are perfectly and for ever cured of bashfulness.

Shapes. To show one's shapes; to be stripped, or made to peel at the whipping-post.

Shappo, or Shap. A hat: corruption of *chapeau*. *Cant.*

Shark. A sharper: perhaps from his preying upon any one he can lay hold of: also, a custom-house officer, or tide-waiter. Sharks; the first order of pick-pockets. *Bow-street term*, A.D. 1785.

Sharp. Subtle, acute, quick-witted; also, a sharper or cheat, in opposition to a flat, dupe, or gull. Sharp's the word and quick's the motion with him; said of any one very attentive to his own interest, and apt to take all advantages. Sharp set; hungry.

Sharper. A cheat, one that lives by his wits. Sharpers' tools; a fool and false dice; any *cross-cove*, in general, is called *a sharp* in opposition to *a flat*, or *square cove*; but this is only in a comparative sense in the course of conversation.

Shaver. A cunning shaver; a subtle fellow, one who trims close, an acute cheat. A young shaver; a boy. *Sea term.*

Shavings. The clippings of money.

She House. A house where the wife rules; or, as the term is, wears the breeches.

She Napper. A woman thief-catcher; also, a bawd or pimp.

Sheep's Head. Like a sheep's head, all jaw; saying of a talkative man or woman.

Sheepish. Bashful. A sheepish fellow; a bashful or shamefaced fellow. To cast a sheep's eye at any thing; to look wishfully at it.

Sheepskin Fiddler. A drummer.

Shelf. On the shelf, i.e. pawned.

Shelling-out. Clubbing money together. Come, shell out. *Cant.* To shell out the shiners; to produce the guineas.

Sheriff's Journeyman. The hangman.

Sheriff's Ball. An execution. To dance at the sheriff's ball, and loll out one's tongue at the company; to be hanged, or go to rest in a horse's night cap, i.e. a halter.

Sheriff's Bracelets. Handcuffs.

Sheriff's Hotel. A prison.

Sheriff's Picture Frame. The gallows.

Sherk. To evade or disappoint: to sherk one's duty.

Sherry. To run away: sherry off.

Shewing a Leg. To bolt; to run away. *Cant.*

Shifting. Shuffling; tricking. Shifting cove, i.e. a person who lives by tricking.

Shifting Ballast. A term used by sailors, to signify soldiers, passengers, or any landsmen on board.

Shillaley. An oaken sapling, or cudgel: from a wood of that name famous for its oaks. *Irish.*

Shilly-shally. Irresolute. To stand shilly-shally; to hesitate, or stand in doubt.

Shindy. A dance. *Sea phrase.*

Shine. It shines like a sh–tt–n barn-door.

Shiner. A looking-glass. *Cant.*

Ship blown up at Point Nonplus exemplifies the *quietus* of a man when plucked pennyless; or genteelly expelled. *Oxf. Univ. cant.*

Ship Shape. Proper, as it ought to be. *Sea phrase.*

Sh-t-ng through the Teeth. Vomiting. Hark ye, friend, have you got a padlock on your a–se, that you sh-te through your teeth? Vulgar address to one vomiting.

Sh-t Sack. A dastardly fellow: also, a non-conformist. This appellation is said to have originated from the following story:—After the restoration, the laws against the non-conformists were extremely severe. They sometimes met in very obscure places: and there is a tradition that one of their congregations were assembled in a barn, the rendezvous of beggars and other vagrants, where the preacher, for want of a ladder or tub, was suspended in a sack fixed to the beam. His discourse that day being on the Last Judgement, he particularly attempted to describe the terrors of the wicked at the sounding of the trumpet, on which a trumpeter to a puppet-show, who had taken refuge in that barn, and lay hid under the straw, sounded a charge. The congregation, struck with the utmost consternation, fled in an instant from the place, leaving their affrighted teacher to shift for himself. The effects of his terror are said to have appeared at the bottom of the sack, and to have occasioned that opprobrious appellation by which the non-conformists were vulgarly distinguished.

Shod all round. A parson who attends a funeral is said to be shod all round, when he receives a hat-band, gloves, and scarf; many shoeings being only partial.

Shoole. To go skulking about.

Shoot the Cat. To vomit from excess of liquor: called, also, catting.

Shoplifter. One that steals whilst pretending to purchase goods in a shop.

Short. A dram unlengthened by water. *Cant.*

"I'll take a drop of *short.*"

Short-heeled Wench. A girl apt to fall on her back.

Shot. To pay one's shot; to pay one's share of reckoning. Shot betwixt wind and water; poxed or clapped.

Shotten Herring. A thin meagre fellow.

Shoulder Clapper. A bailiff, or member of the hold-fast club. Shoulder-clapped; arrested.

Shoulder Feast. A dinner given after a funeral, to those who have carried the corpse.

Shoulder Sham. A partner to a file. *See* File.

Shoving the Moon. Moving goods by moonlight to prevent their being siezed by the landlord. *Cant.*

Shove in the Mouth. A dram.

Shovel. To be put to bed with a shovel; to be buried. He or she was fed with a fire-shovel; a saying of a person with a large mouth.

Shove the Tumbler. To be whipped at the cart's tail.

Shred. A tailor.

Shrimp. A diminutive person.

Shuffle. To make use of false pretences, or unfair shifts. A shuffling fellow; a slippery shifting fellow.

Shutter Racket. The practice of robbing houses, or shops, by boring a hole in the window-shutters, and taking out a pane of glass.

Shy Cock. One who keeps within doors for fear of bailiffs.

Shy for it. "I must have a *shy for it*, if I lose my stick," i. e. I will have a fight before I give up my right. *Cant.*

Sice. Sixpence.

Sick as a Horse. Horses are said to be extremely sick at their stomachs, from being unable to relieve themselves by vomiting. Bracken, indeed, in his Farriery, gives an instance of that evacuation being procured, but by a means which, he says, would make the Devil vomit. Such as may have occasion to administer an emetic either to the animal or the fiend, may consult his book for the recipe.

Side Pocket. He has as much need of a wife as a dog of a side-pocket; said of a weak old debilitated man. He wants it as much as a dog does a side-pocket; a simile used for one who desires any thing by no means necessary.

Sidledywry. Crooked.

Sign of a House to Let. A widow's weeds.

Sign of the { **Five Shillings.** The crown. / **Ten Shillings.** The two crowns. / **Fifteen Shillings.** The three crowns. }

Silence. To silence a man; to knock him down, or stun him. Silence in the court, the cat is p—ing; a gird upon any one requiring silence unnecessarily.

Silent Flute. Synonymous with Sugar Stick, &c.

Silk Port. Assumption of a gentleman commoner's gown. *Oxf. Univ. cant.*

Silk Snatchers. Thieves who snatch hoods or bonnets from persons walking in the streets.

SIX

SILVER LACED. Replete with lice. The cove's kickseys are silver laced; the fellow's breeches are covered with lice.

SIMEONITES, (at Cambridge,) the followers of the Rev. Charles Simeon, fellow of King's College, author of Skeletons of Sermons, and preacher at Trinity church; they are, in fact, rank methodists.

SIMKIN. A foolish fellow.

SIMON. Sixpence. Simple Simon; a natural, a silly fellow; Simon Suck-egg sold his wife for an addle duck-egg.

SIMPER. To smile: to simper like a firmity kettle.

SIMPLES. Physical herbs: also, follies. He must go to Battersea, to be cut for the simples—Battersea is a place famous for its garden grounds, some of which were formerly appropriated to the growing of simples for apothecaries, who, at a certain season, used to go down to select their stock for the ensuing year, at which time the gardeners were said to cut their simples; whence it became a popular joke to advise young people to go to Battersea, at that time, to have their simples cut, or to be cut for the simples.

SIMPLETON. Abbreviation of simple Tony or Anthony, a foolish fellow.

SING. To call out; the coves sing out beef; they call out stop thief.

SING SMALL. To be humbled, confounded, or abashed, to have little or nothing to say for one's self, to eat humble pie. *Cant.*

SINGLE PEEPER. A person having but one eye.

SINGLETON. A corkscrew, made by a famous cutler of that name, who lived in a place called Hell, in Dublin; his screws are remarkable for their excellent temper.

SIR JOHN. The old title for a country parson: as Sir John of Wrotham, mentioned by Shakspeare. *Obsolete.*

SIR JOHN BARLEYCORN. Strong beer.

SIR LOIN. The sur, or upper loin,

SIR REVERENCE. Human excrement, a t—d.

SIR SYDNEY. A clasp knife. *Cant.*

SIR TIMOTHY. One who, from a desire of being the head of the company, pays the reckoning, or, as the term is, stands squire. *See* SQUIRE.

SITTING BREECHES. One who stays late in company, is said to have his sitting breeches on, or that he will sit longer than a hen.

SIX AND EIGHT-PENCE An attorney, whose fee on several occasions is fixed at that sum.

SIX AND TIPS. Whisky and small beer. *Irish.*

SIX BOB BIT. A six-shilling-piece. *Scotch cant.*

SIXES AND SEVENS. Left at sixes and sevens: i. e. in confusion; commonly said of a room where the furniture, &c. is scattered about; or of a business left unsettled.

SIZE OF ALE. Half a pint. Size of bread and cheese; a certain quantity. Sizings; Cambridge term for the college allowance from the buttery, called, at Oxford, battles.

SIZE. *(Cambridge.)* To sup at one's own expense. If a *man* asks you to *sup*, he treats you; if to *size*, you pay for what you eat—liquors *only* being provided by the inviter.

SIZAR. *(Cambridge.)* Formerly students, who came to the university for purposes of study and emolument. But at present they are just as gay and dissipated as their fellow collegians. About fifty years ago, they were on a footing with the servitors at Oxford; but, by the exertions of the present Bishop of Llandaff, who was himself a sizar, they were absolved from all marks of inferiority or of degradation. The chief difference at present between them and the pensioners, consists in the less amount of their college fees. The saving thus made induces many extravagant fellows to become sizars, that they may have more money to lavish on their dogs, pieces, &c.

SKEW. A cup, or beggar's wooden dish.

SKEWVOW, or ALL ASKEW. Crooked, inclining to one side.

SKIN. In a bad skin; out of temper, in an ill humour. Thin-skinned; touchy, peevish.

SKIN. A purse. Frisk the skin of the stephen; empty the money out of the purse. Queer skin; an empty purse. To *strip* a man of all his money at play, is termed *skinning* him.

SKIN FLINT. An avaricious man or woman.

SKINK. To skink, is to wait on the company, ring the bell, stir the fire, and snuff the candles; the duty of the youngest officer in the military mess. *See* BOOTS.

SKINS. A tanner.

SKIP JACKS. Youngsters that ride horses on sale, horse-dealers' boys: also, a plaything made for children with the breast-bone of a goose.

SKIP KENNEL. A footman.

SKIPPER. A barn. *Cant.* Also, the captain of a Dutch vessel.

SKIT. To wheedle. *Cant.*

SKIT. A joke. A satirical hint.

SKULKER. A soldier who, by feigned sickness, or other pretences, evades his duty; a sailor who keeps below in time of danger: in the civil line, one who keeps out of the way when any work is to be done. To skulk; to hide one's self, to avoid labour or duty.

SKY BLUE. Gin.

SKY FARMERS. Cheats who pretend they were farmers

in the isle of Sky, or some other remote place, and were ruined by a flood, hurricane, or some such public calamity: or else, called sky farmers from their farms being *in nubibus*, (in the clouds).

SKY PARLOUR. The garret, or upper story.

SLABBERING BIB. A parson's or lawyer's band.

SLAG. A slack-mettled fellow, one not ready to resent an affront.

SLAM. A trick: also, a game at whist lost without scoring one. To slam to a door; to shut it with violence.

SLAMKIN. A female sloven, one whose clothes seem hung on with a pitch-fork, a careless trapes.

SLANG. A fetter. Double-slanged; double-ironed. Now double-slanged into the cells for a crop he is knocked down; he is double-ironed in the condemned cells, and ordered to be hanged.

SLANG. To defraud a person of any part of his due, is called *slanging* him: also, to cheat by false weights or measures, or other unfair means.

SLANGING-DUES. When a man suspects that he has been curtailed of any portion of his just right, he will say, there has been *slanging-dues concerned.*

SLAP-BANG SHOP. A petty cook's shop, where there is no credit given, but what is had must be paid for *down with the ready slap-bang*, i. e. immediately. This is a common appellation for a night-cellar frequented by thieves, and sometimes for a stage-coach or caravan.

SLAPDASH. Immediately, instantly, or suddenly.

SLAP UP. Synonymous with *bang-up:* as, " To morrow, *please the pigs*, I'll take a *prime slap up* walk."

SLASHER. A bullying, riotous fellow. *Irish.*

SLAT. Half a crown. *Cant.*

SLATE. A sheet. *Cant.*

SLATER'S PAN. The gaol at Kingston, in Jamaica; Slater is the deputy provost-marshal.

SLAVEY. A servant of either sex. *Cant.*

SLEEK WIPES. Silk handkerchiefs. *Cant.*

SLEEPING PARTNER. A partner in a trade, or shop, who lends his name and money, for which he receives a share of the profit, without doing any part of the business.

SLEEPY. Much worn: the cloth of your coat must be extremely sleepy, for it has not had a nap this long time.

SLEEVELESS ERRAND. A fool's errand, in search of what it is impossible to find.

SLICE. To take a slice; to intrigue, particularly with a married woman, because a slice off a cut loaf is not missed.

SLIP. The slash pocket in the skirt of a coat behind.

SLIPGIBBET. See SCAPEGALLOWS.

Slippery Chap. One on whom there can be no dependance, a shuffling fellow.

Slipslops. Tea, water-gruel, or any innocent beverage taken medicinally.

Slip the Wind. To die. *Cant.*

Slop. Tea. How the blowens lush the slop; how the wenches drink tea!

Slope it. To eat it or drink it. *Cant.*

Slop-Feeder. A tea-spoon. *Cant.*

Slops. Wearing apparel and bedding used by seamen.

Slop-Seller. A dealer in those articles, who keeps a slop-shop.

Slop-Tubs. Tea-things. Come, Moll, *cut* the *slop-tubs;* come, Mary, put away the tea-things. *Cant.*

> "Our *slop-tubs* being *clean* away,
> And all our *chatter-broth* mopp'd up,
> We," &c. &c.
>
> *Extract from a Westminster Ditty.*

Slouch. A stooping gait, a negligent slovenly fellow. To slouch; to hang down one's head. A slouched hat; a hat whose brims are let down.

Slour. To lock up; to fasten; to button up one's coat; to make all secure. *Cant.*

Slubber de Gullion. A dirty nasty fellow.

Slug. A piece of lead of any shape, to be fired from a blunderbuss. To fire a slug; to drink a dram.

Slug-a-bed. A drone, one that cannot rise in the morning.

Sluicery. A gin-shop. *Cant.*

Sluice your Gob. Take a hearty drink.

Slum. A room. *Cant.*

Slum. *Gammon.*

> "And thus, without more *slum*, began."
>
> *Vide Randall's Diary.*

Slum (Up to). Not to be gammoned.

Slur. To slur, is a method of cheating at dice: also, to cast a reflection on any one's character, to scandalize.

Slush. Greasy dish-water, or the skimmings of a pot where fat meat has been boiled.

Slush Bucket. A foul feeder, one that eats much greasy food.

Sly. Under the rose; transacting business privately, is frequently said to be done "*upon the sly.*" *Cant.*

Sly Boots. A cunning fellow, under the mask of simplicity.

Smabbled, or Snabbled. Killed in battle.

Smack. To kiss. I had a smack at her muns; I kissed her mouth. To smack calf's skin; to kiss the book, i. e. to take an oath. The queer cuffin bid me smack calf's skin, but I only bussed my thumb; the justice bid me kiss the book, but I only kissed my thumb.

SMACKING COVE. A coachman.

SMACK SMOOTH. Level with the surface, every thing cut away.

SMALL CLOTHES. Breeches: a gird at the affected delicacy of the present age; a suit being called coat, waistcoat, and articles, or small clothes.

SMART MONEY. Money allowed to soldiers or sailors for the loss of a limb, or other hurt received in the service.

SMASH. Leg of mutton and smash; a leg of mutton and mashed turnips. *Sea term.*

SMASH. To break: also, to kick down stairs. *Cant.* To smash; to pass counterfeit money.

> " She *smash'd* the lamp that gave them light,
> Which down in discord fell."
> *Vide Randall's Scrap Book.*

SMASHER. A person who lives by passing base coin. The cove was fined in the steel for smashing; the fellow was ordered to be imprisoned in the house of correction for uttering base coin.

SMASHING. Passing of counterfeit coin. *Cant.*

SMEAR. A plasterer.

SMEAR GELT. A bribe. *German.*

SMELLER. A nose. Smellers; a cat's whiskers.

SMELLING CHEAT. An orchard, or garden: also, a nosegay. *Cant.*

SMELTS. Half guineas. *Cant.*

SMICKET. A smock, or woman's shift.

SMIRK. A finical spruce fellow. To smirk; to smile, or look pleasantly.

SMISH. A shirt. *Cant.*

SMITER. An arm. To smite one's tutor; to get money from him. *Academic term.*

SMITHFIELD BARGAIN. A bargain whereby the purchaser is taken in. This is likewise frequently used to express matches or marriages contracted solely on the score of interest, on one or both sides, where the fair sex are bought and sold like cattle in Smithfield.

SMOCK-FACED. Fair-faced.

SMOKE. To observe, to suspect.

SMOKER. A tobacconist.

SMOKY. Curious, suspicious, inquisitive.

SMOUCH. Dried leaves of the ash-tree, used by the smugglers for adulterating the black or bohea teas.

SMOUS. A German Jew.

SMUG. A nick name for a blacksmith: also, neat and spruce.

SMUG LAY. Persons who pretend to be smugglers of lace

and valuable articles; these men borrow money of publicans by depositing these goods in their hands: they shortly afterwards decamp, and the publican discovers too late that he has been duped, and, on opening the pretended treasure, he finds trifling articles of no value.

Smuggling Ken. A bawdy-house.

Smush. To snatch, or seize suddenly.

Smut. Bawdy. Smutty story; an indecent story.

Smut. A copper. A grate. Old iron. The cove was lagged for a smut; the fellow was transported for stealing a copper.

Snabble. To rifle or plunder: also, to kill.

Snack. A share. To go snacks; to be partners.

Snaffle. To steal. To snaffle any one's poll; to steal his wig.

Snaffler. A highwayman. Snaffler of prancers; a horse stealer.

Snaggs. Large teeth: also, snails.

Snap Dragon. A Christmas gambol: raisins and almonds being put into a bowl of brandy, and the candles extinguished, the spirit is set on fire, and the company scramble for the raisins.

Snappers. Pistols.

Snap the Glaze. To break shop-windows or show-glasses.

Snatch Cly. A thief who snatches women's pockets.

Sneak. A pilferer. Morning sneak; one who pilfers early in the morning, before it is light. Evening sneak; an evening pilferer. Upright sneak; one who steals pewter pots from the alehouse boys employed to collect them. To go upon the sneak; to steal into houses whose doors are carelessly left open. *Cant.*

Sneaker. A small bowl.

Sneaking Budge. One that robs alone.

Sneaksby. A mean-spirited fellow, a sneaking cur.

Sneering. Jeering, flickering, laughing in scorn.

Sneezer, or Sneezing-Coffer. A snuff-box.

Snib. A prig. *Scotch cant.*

Snicker. A glandered horse.

Snicker, or Snigger. To laugh privately, or in one's sleeve.

Snilch. To eye, to look at any thing attentively: the cull snilches. *Cant.*

Snipes. Scissors. *Cant.*

Snitch. To turn snitch, or snitcher; to turn informer. A person who becomes king's evidence on such an occasion, is said to have turned *snitch;* an informer, or tale-bearer, in general, is called a *snitch*, or a *snitching* rascal, in which sense *snitching* is synonymous with *nosing*, or *coming it.*

Sniv. Hold your tongue: or, *sniv* that. *Cant.*

Snivel. To cry, or throw the snot or snivel about. Snivelling; crying. A snivelling fellow; one that whines or complains.

Snoach. To speak through the nose, to snuffle.

Snob. A nick name for a shoemaker.

Snooze, or Snoodge. To sleep. To snooze with a mort; to sleep with a wench. *Cant.*

Snoozing Ken. A brothel. The swell was spiced in a snoosing-ken of his screens; the gentleman was robbed of his bank-notes in a brothel.

Snoozy. A night-constable. *Cant.*

Snout. A hogshead. *Cant.*

Snow. Linen hung out to dry or bleach. Spice the snow; to steal the linen.

Snowball. A jeering appellation for a negro.

Snub. To check, or rebuke.

Snub Devil. A parson.

Snub Nose. A short nose turned up at the end.

Snudge. A thief who hides himself under a bed, in order to rob the house.

Snuff. To take snuff; to be offended.

Snuffing. Going into a shop on some pretence, watching an opportunity to throw a handful of snuff in the eyes of the shop-keeper, and then running off with any valuable article you can lay hands on; this is called *snuffing* him, or *giving it to him on the snuff-racket.*

Snuffle. To speak through the nose.

Snuffles. A cold in the head, attended with a running at the nose.

Snuffy. Drunk. *Cant.*

Snug. All's snug; all's quiet.

Soak. To drink. An old soaker; a drunkard, one that moistens his clay to make it stick together.

Socket-Money. A whore's fee, or hire: also, money paid for a treat, by a married man caught in an intrigue.

Soft. Bank-notes. *Cant.*

Soldier. A red herring.

Soldier's Bottle. A large one.

Soldier's Mawnd. A pretended soldier, begging with a counterfeit wound, which he pretends to have received at some famous siege or battle.

Soldier's Pomatum. A piece of tallow candle.

Solfa. A parish-clerk.

Solomon. The mass. *Cant.*

Solo Player. A miserable performer on any instrument, who always plays alone, because no one will stay in the room to hear him.

Son of Prattlement. A lawyer.

Song. He changed his song; he altered his account or evidence. It was bought for an old song, i. e. very cheap. His morning and his evening songs do not agree; he tells a different story.

Sop. A bribe. A sop for Cerberus; a bribe for a porter, turnkey, or gaoler.

Soph. *(Cambridge.)* An under graduate in his second year.

Sorrel. A yellowish red. Sorrel-pate; one having red hair.

Sorrow shall be his Sops. He shall repent this. Sorrow go by me; a common expletive used by the Presbyterians in Ireland. *Obsolete.*

Sorry. Vile, mean, worthless. A sorry fellow, or hussy; a worthless man or woman.

Sot-Weed. Tobacco.

Sou. Not a sou; not a penny. *French.*

Soul-case. The body. He made a hole in his soul-case; he wounded him.

Soul in Soak. Drunk. *Sea term.*

Sound, or Sounding, means generally to draw from a person, in an artful manner, any particulars you want to become acquainted with; for instance, to sound a kid, a porter, &c. is to pump out of him the purport of his errand, the bundle, or load, &c. that your pall may know how to accost him, in order to nap the swag. To sound a cly is to touch a person's pocket gently on the outside, in order to ascertain the nature of its contents. *Cant.*

Sounders. A herd of swine.

South Jeopardy. Terrors of insolvency. *Oxf. Univ. cant.*

Sow. A fat woman. He has got the wrong sow by the ear; he mistakes his man. Drunk as David's sow; *See* David's Sow.

Sow's Baby. A sucking pig.

Sow Child. A female child.

Spado. A sword. *Spanish.*

Spangle. A seven-shilling-piece.

Spanish. The Spanish; ready money.

Spanish Coin. Fair words and compliments.

Spanish Faggot. The sun.

Spanish Padlock. A kind of girdle contrived by jealous husbands of that nation to secure the chastity of their wives.

Spanish, or King of Spain's Trumpeter. An ass when braying.

Spank. *(Whip.)* To run neatly along, between a trot and gallop. The tits spanked it to town; the horses went merrily along all the way to town.

Spank is, among the thieves, to break a pane of glass in a shop-window, and make a sudden snatch at some article of value, having previously tied the shop-door with a strong cord on the outside, so as to prevent any pursuit, or the shopman from getting out till you have had full time to escape with the booty.

Spanking. Large.

Spanks, or Spankers. Money: also, blows with the open hand.

Spark. A spruce, trim, or smart fellow. A man that is always thirsty, is said to have a spark in his throat.

Sparking Blows. Blows given by cocks before they close, or, as the term is, mouth it: used figuratively for words previous to a quarrel.

Sparkish. Fine; gay.

Sparrow. Mumbling a sparrow; a cruel sport, frequently practised at wakes and fairs: for a small premium, a booby having his hands tied behind him, has the wing of a cock-sparrow put into his mouth; with this hold, without any other assistance than the motion of his lips, he is to get the sparrow's head into his mouth; on attempting to do which, the bird defends itself surprisingly, frequently pecking the mumbler till his lips are covered with blood, and he is obliged to desist: to prevent the bird from getting away, he is fastened by a string to a button of the booby's coat.

Sparrow-mouthed. Wide-mouthed, like the mouth of a sparrow: it is said of such persons, that they do not hold their mouths by lease, but have it from year to year; i. e. from ear to ear. One whose mouth cannot be enlarged without removing their ears, and who, when they yawn, have their heads half off.

Spatch Cock. [Abbreviation of *despatch cock.*] A hen just killed from the roost, or yard, and immediately skinned, split, and broiled: an Irish dish upon any sudden occasion.

Speak. Any thing stolen. He has made a good speak; he has stolen something considerable.

Speak with. To rob. I spoke with the cull on the cherry-coloured prancer; I robbed the man on the black horse. *Cant.*

Speckled Wipe. A coloured handkerchief. *Cant.*

Spell. A playhouse. *Cant.*

Spice. To rob. Spice the swell; rob the gentleman. The spice is the game of footpad robbery: describing an exploit of this nature, a rogue will say, I spiced a swell of so much, naming the booty obtained. A spice is a footpad robbery.

Spice Gloak. A footpad robber.

Spice Islands. A privy. Stink-hole bay, or Dilberry-creek. The fundament.

Spider-shanked. Thin-legged.

Spiflicate. To confound, silence, or dumbfound.

Spilt. A small reward or gift.

Spilt. Thrown from a horse, or overturned in a carriage. "Pray, Coachee, don't spill us."

Spindle-shanks. Slender legs.

Spirit away. To kidnap, or inveigle away.

Spiritual Flesh-Broker. A parson.

Spit. He is as like his father as if he was spit out of his mouth: said of a child much resembling his father.

Spit. A sword.

Spitfire. A violent pettish, or passionate person.

Spliced. Married; an allusion to joining two ropes ends by splicing. *Sea term.*

Split Crow. The sign of the spread eagle, which being represented with two heads on one neck, gives it somewhat the appearance of being split.

Split-Cause. A lawyer.

Split Fig. A grocer

Spoil Iron. The nick-name for a smith.

Spoil it. To throw some obstacle in the way of any project or undertaking, so as to cause its failure, is termed spoiling it. In like manner, to prevent another person from succeeding in his object, either by a wilful obstruction, or by some act of imprudence on your part, subjects you to the charge of having spoiled him. Speaking of some particular species of fraud or robbery, which, after a long series of success, is now become stale or impracticable from the public being guarded against it, the *family* will say, that *game* is *spoiled* at last. So having attempted the robbery of any particular house or shop, and by miscarrying caused such an alarm as to render a second attempt dangerous or impolitic, they will say, that place is spoiled, it is useless to try it on any more.

Spoil Pudding. A parson who preaches long sermons, keeping his congregation in church till the puddings are overdone.

Spunge. A thirsty fellow, a great drinker. To spunge; to eat and drink at another's cost. Spunging-house; a bailiff's lock-up-house, or repository, to which persons arrested are taken till they find bail, or have spent all their money: a house where every species of fraud and extortion is practised under the protection of the law.

Spunk. Rotten touchwood, or a kind of fungus prepared for tinder; figuratively, spirit, courage.

Spoon Hand. The right hand.

Spoony. Foolish, half-witted, nonsensical; a man who has been drinking till he becomes disgusting by his very ridiculous behaviour, is said to be spoony drunk; and from hence it is usual to call a very prating shallow fellow, a rank spoon.

SPORT. To exhibit; as Jack Jehu sported a new gig yesterday, I shall sport a new suit next week. To sport or flash one's ivories; to show one's teeth. To sport timber; to keep one's outside door shut: this term is used in the inns of court to signify denying one's self. N.B. The word *sport* was in great vogue in the years 1783 and 1784.

SPOUT. To pledge any property at a pawnbroker's is termed spouting it, or shoving it up the spout.

SPOUTING CLUB. A meeting of apprentices and mechanics to rehearse different characters in plays: thus forming recruits for the strolling companies.

SPOUTED. Pawned.

SPREAD. Butter.

SPREAD. Twig his spread; i.e. umbrella. *Cant.*

SPREAD EAGLE. A soldier tied to the halberts in order to be whipped; his attitude bearing some likeness to that figure, as painted on signs.

SPREE. A frolic. Fun. A drinking bout. A party of pleasure.

SPRING-ANKLE WAREHOUSE. Newgate; any gaol. *Irish.*

SQUAB. A fat man or woman; from their likeness to a well-stuffed couch, called also a squab. A new-hatched chicken.

SQUARE. All fair, upright, and honest, practices are called the square, in opposition to the cross. Any thing you have bought or acquired honestly is termed a square article; and any transaction which is fairly and equitably conducted is said to be a square concern. A tradesman, or other person, who is considered by the world to be an honest man, and who is unacquainted with family people, and their system of operation, is, by the latter, emphatically styled a square cove: whereas an old thief who has acquired an independence, and now confines himself to square practices, is called, by his old palls, a flash cove, who has tyed up prigging. *See* CROSS and FLAT. In making a bargain or contract, any overture considered to be really fair and reasonable, is declared to be a square thing, or to be upon the square. To be upon the square with any person is to have mutually settled all accounts between you both up to that moment. To threaten another that you will be upon the square with him some time, signifies that you will be even with him for some supposed injury, &c.

SQUARE CRIB. A respectable house, of good repute, whose inmates, their mode of life and connexions, are all perfectly on the square. *See* CROSS CRIB.

Square-Toes. An old man: square-toed shoes were anciently worn in common, and long retained by old men.

Squeak. A narrow escape, a chance: he had a squeak for his life. To squeak; to confess, to peach, or turn stag. They squeak beef upon us; they cry out thieves after us. *Cant.*

Squeaker. A bar-boy: also, a bastard or any other child. To stifle the squeaker; to murder a bastard, or throw it into the necessary house. Organ-pipes are likewise called squeakers. The squeakers are meltable; the small pipes are silver. *Cant.*

Squeal. An informer. *Scotch cant.*

Squeeze. The neck. *Cant.*

Squeeze-Crab. A sour-looking, shrivelled, diminutive fellow.

Squeeze-Wax. A good-natured foolish fellow, ready to become security for another, under hand and seal.

Squib. A small satirical or political temporary jeu d'esprit, which, like the fire-work of that denomination, sparkles, bounces, stinks, and vanishes.

Squint-a-pipes. A squinting man or woman; said to be born in the middle of the week, and looking both ways for Sunday; or born in a hackney-coach, and looking out of both windows: fit for a cook, one eye in the pot, and the other up the chimney: looking nine ways at once.

Squire of Alsatia. A weak profligate spendthrift, the squire of the company; one who pays the whole reckoning, or treats the company, is called standing squire.

Squirish. Foolish.

Squirrel. A prostitute: because she, like that animal, covers her back with her tail. *Meretrix corpore corpus alit.* Menagiana, ii. 128.

Squirrel-hunting. *See* Hunting.

Stag. To turn stag; to impeach one's confederates: from a herd of deer, who are said to turn their horns against any of their number who is hunted.

Stag. To find, discover, or observe.

Staggering Bob with his Yellow Pumps. A calf just dropped and unable to stand, killed for veal in Scotland: the hoofs of a young calf are yellow.

Stale Drunk. A person is said to be *stale drunk* when they feel languid after a night's debauch.

Staines. A man who is in pecuniary distress is said to be *at Staines, or at the Bush,* alluding to the Bush Inn at that town. *See* Bushed.

Stake. A booty acquired by robbery, or a sum of money won at play, is called a *stake;* and, if considerable, a *prime stake*, or a *heavy stake*. A person alluding to any thing difficult to be procured, or which he obtains as a great favour, and is therefore comparatively invaluable, would say I consider it a *stake* to get it all: a valuable or acceptable acquisition of any kind is emphatically called a *stake*, meaning a great prize.

STALL WHIMPER. A bastard. *Cant.*

STALL OFF. A term variously applied; generally, it means a pretence, excuse, or prevarication: as, a person charged with any fault, entering into some plausible story, to excuse himself, his hearers or accusers would say, O yes, that's a good *stall off*, or, Aye, aye, *stall it off* that way if you can. To extricate a person from any dilemma, or save him from disgrace, is called, *stalling* him *off*: as, an accomplice of yours being detected in a robbery, &c. and about to be given up to justice, you will step up as a stranger, interfere in his behalf, and, either by vouching for his innocence, recommending lenity, or some other artifice, persuade his accusers to forego their intention, and let the prisoner escape: you will then boast of having *stalled him off in prime twig*. To avoid or escape any impending evil or punishment by means of artifice, submission, bribe, or otherwise, is also called *stalling* it *off*. A man walking the streets, and passing a particular shop, or encountering a certain person, which or whom he has reasons for wishing to avoid, will say to any friend who may be with him, I wish you'd *stall* me *off from* that *crib*, (or from that cove, as the case may be,) meaning, walk in such a way as to cover or obscure me from notice, until we are past the shop or person in question.

STALL UP. To *stall* a person up, (a term used by pickpockets,) is to surround him in a crowd, or violent pressure, and even sometimes in the open street, while walking along, and by violence force his arms up, and keep them in that position while others of the gang rifle his pockets at pleasure, the cove being unable to help or defend himself; this is what the newspapers denominate hustling, and is universally practised at the doors of public theatres, at boxing matches, ship launches, and other places where the general anxiety of all ranks, either to push forward, or to obtain a view of the scene before them, forms a pretext for jostling, and every other advantage which the strength or numbers of one party gives them over a weaker one, or a single person. It is not unusual for the buz-coves, on particular occasions, to procure a formidable squad of stout fellows of the lower class, who, though not expert at *knuckling*, render essential service by violently pushing and squeezing in the crowd, and, in the confusion excited by this conduct, the unconcerned *prigs* reap a plentiful harvest, and the *stallers up* are gratified with such part of the gains acquired as the liberality of the *knuckling* gentlemen may prompt them to bestow. This *coup de guèrre* is termed making a regular stall at such a place, naming the scene of their operations. *See* STALL.

STALLING. Making or ordaining. Stalling to the rogue; an ancient ceremony of instituting a candidate into the society of rogues, somewhat similar to the creation of a herald at arms. It is thus described by Harman: the upright man taking a gage of bowse, i.e. a pot of strong drink, pours it on the head of the rogue to be admitted, saying, I, A B, do stall thee, B C, to the rogue; and from henceforth it shall be lawful for thee to cant for thy living in all places.

STALLING KEN. A broker's shop; or, a receiver of stolen goods.

STALLION. A man kept by an old lady for secret services.

STAM FLESH. To cant. *Cant.*

STAMMEL, or STRAMMEL. A coarse brawny wench.

STAMMER. An indictment. *Cant.*

STAMP. A particular manner of throwing the dice out of the box, by striking it with violence against the table.

STAMP DRAWERS. Stockings. *Cant.*

STAMPERS. Shoes.

STAMPS. Legs.

STAND-STILL. He was run to a stand-still: i.e. till he could no longer move.

STAND THE PATTER. To be tried for an offence. *Cant.*

STAR. The star is a game chiefly practised by young boys, often under ten years of age, although the offence is capital. It consists in cutting a pane of glass in a shop-window, by a peculiar operation called *starring the glaze*, which is performed very effectually by a common penknife; the depredators then take out such articles of value as lie within reach of their arm, which, if they are not interrupted, sometimes includes half the contents of a window. A person convicted of this offence is said to have been *done for a star*.

STARCHED. Stiff, prim, formal, affected.

STAR GAZER. A horse who throws up his head: also, a hedge whore.

STARING QUARTER. An ox cheek.

STARK NAKED. Gin. *Cant.*

STAR LAG. Breaking shop-windows, and stealing some article thereout.

START, or THE OLD START. Newgate: he is gone to the Start, or the Old Start. *Cant.*

P

STARTER. One who leaves a jolly company, a milksop. He is no starter; he will sit longer than a hen.

STAR THE GLAZE. To break and rob a jeweller's show glass. *Cant.*

STARVE'EM, ROB'EM, and CHEAT'EM. Stroud, Rochester, and Chatham; so called by soldiers and sailors, and not without good reasons.

STASH. To *stash* any practice, habit, or proceeding, signifies to put an end to, relinquish, or quash the same; thus, a thief determined to leave off his vicious courses will declare that he means to *stash* (or stow) *prigging*. A man in custody for felony will endeavour, by offering money, or other means, to induce his prosecutor's forbearance, and compromise the matter, so as to obtain his liberation; this is called *stashing the business*. To *stash* drinking, card-playing, or any other employment you may be engaged in, for the time present, signifies to *stow* it, *knife* it, *cheese* it, or *cut* it, which are all synonymous, that is, to desist or leave off. *See* WANTED.

STATE. To lie in state; to be in bed with three regular harlots.

STATES OF INDEPENDENCY. Frontiers of Extravagance. *Oxf. Univ. cant.*

STAY. A cuckold.

STAYTAPE. A tailor; from that article, and its coadjutor buckram; which formerly made no small figure in the bills of those knights of the needle.

STEAMER. A pipe. A swell steamer; a long pipe, such as is used by gentlemen to smoke.

STEEL. The house of correction.

STEEL BAR. A needle. A steel bar flinger; a tailor, staymaker, or any other person using a needle.

STEENKIRK. A muslin neckcloth carelessly put on, from the manner in which the French officers wore their cravats when they returned from the battle of Steenkirk.

STEEPLE-HOUSE. A name given to the church by dissenters.

STEPHEN. Money. Stephen's at home; i.e. he has money.

STEPNEY. A decoction of raisins of the sun and lemons in conduit water, sweetened with sugar, and bottled up.

STEWED QUAKER. Burnt rum, with a piece of butter: an American remedy for a cold.

STICK FLAMS. A pair of gloves.

STICKS. Household furniture.

STICKS. Pops or pistols. Stow your sticks; hide your pistols. *Cant. See* POPS.

STIFF, or THICK. Giving a bill instead of money is denominated, in the mercantile world, taking "*the stiff.*" *Mercantile cant.*

STIFF ONES. Of no use, dead men.

STIFF-RUMPED. Proud, stately.

STING. To rob or defraud a person or place is called *stinging* them: as, that cove is too fly; he has been *stung* before; meaning that that man is upon his guard, he has already been tricked.

STINGBUM. A niggard.

STINGO. Strong beer, or other liquor.

STINK. When any robbery of moment has been committed which causes much alarm, or of which much is said in the daily papers, the *family people* will say, there is a great *stink* about it. *See* WANTED.

STINKER. A black eye. *Cant.*

STIRRUP CUP. A parting cup or glass drunk on horseback by the person taking leave.

STITCH. A nickname for a tailor: also, a term for lying with a woman.

STIVER-CRAMPED. Needy, wanting money. A stiver is a Dutch coin, worth somewhat more than a penny sterling.

STOCK. A good stock; i.e. of impudence. Stock and block; the whole: he has lost stock and block.

STOCK DRAWERS. Stockings.

STOCK JOBBERS. Persons who gamble in the Stock Exchange, by pretending to buy and sell the public funds, but in reality only betting that they will be at a certain price at a particular time; possessing neither the stock pretended to be sold, nor money sufficient to make good the payments for which they contract. These gentlemen are known under the different appellations of bulls, bears, and lame ducks.

STOMACH WORM. The stomach worm gnaws; I am hungry.

STONE. Two stone under weight, or wanting; an eunuch. Stone doublet; a prison. Stone dead; dead as a stone.

STONE JUG. Newgate, or any other prison.

STONE TAVERN. Ditto.

STOOP. The pillory. The cull was served for macing, and napped the stoop; he was convicted of swindling, and put in the pillory.

STOOPING-MATCH. The exhibition of one or more persons in the pillory. *See* PUSH.

STOOP-NAPPERS, or OVERSEERS OF THE NEW PAVEMENT. Persons set in the pillory. *Cant.*

STOTER. A great blow. Tip him a stoter in the haltering place; give him a blow under the left ear.

STOUP. A vessel to hold liquor: a vessel containing a size, or half a pint, is so called at Cambridge.

STOW. Stow you; be silent, or hold your peace. Stow your whidds and plant'en, for the cove of the ken can cant'em; you have said enough, the man of the house understands you.

STRAIT-LACED. Precise, over nice, puritanical.

STRAIT WAISTCOAT. A tight waistcoat, with long sleeves coming over the hand, having strings for binding them behind the back of the wearer: these waistcoats are used in madhouses for the management of lunatics when outrageous.

STRANGER. A guinea.

STRANGLE GOOSE. A poulterer.

STRAP. To work. The kiddy would not strap, so he went on the scamp; the lad would not work, and therefore robbed on the highway.

STRAPPER. A large man or woman.

STRAPPING. Lying with a woman. *Cant.*

STRAW. A good woman in the straw; a lying-in woman. His eyes draw straw; his eyes are almost shut, or he is almost asleep: one eye draws straw, and t'other serves the thatcher.

STRETCH. A yard. The cove was lagged for prigging a peter with several stretch of dobbin from a drag; the fellow was transported for stealing a trunk, containing several yards of riband, from a waggon.

STRETCHING. Hanging. He'll stretch for it; he will be hanged for it: also, telling a great lie: he stretched stoutly.

STRIKE. Twenty shillings. *Cant.*

STRIP ME NAKED. Gin. Speaking of Randall having opened a gin-shop, the bard says,

> "Then shall young Bacchus see his glittering shrine
> Delug'd with *strip me naked* 'stead of wine."
>
> *Randall's Diary.*

STROKE. To take a stroke; to take a bout with a woman.

STROLLERS. Itinerants of different kinds. Strolling morts; beggars or pedlars pretending to be widows.

STROMMEL. Straw. *Cant.*

STRONG MAN. To play the part of the strong man, i.e. to push the cart and horses too; to be whipped at the cart's tail.

STRUM. A perriwig. Rum strum; a fine large wig. *(Cambridge.)* To *do* a piece. Fœminam subagitare. *Cant.*

STRUM. To have carnal knowledge of a woman: also, to play badly on the harpsichord, or any other stringed instrument. A strummer of wire; a player on any instrument strung with wire.

STRUMMEL. The hair of the head.

Strumpet. A harlot.
Stubble it. Hold your tongue. *Cant.*
Stubbs. Nothing. *Cant.*
Stub-faced. Pitted with the small-pox: the Devil ran over his face with horse-stubs (horse-nails) in his shoes.
Stuff. Gammon. "What *stuff* it is." "I will not be imprisoned upon by such *stuff*." *Cant.*
Stuling Ken. *See* Stalling Ken.
Stum. The flower for fermenting wine, used by vintners to adulterate their wines.
Stump. Money. *Cant.*
Stumped. Poor, destitute of money. *Cant.*
Stumps. Legs. To stir one's stumps; to walk fast.
Sturdy Beggars. The fifth and last of the most ancient order of canters; beggars that rather demand than ask. *Cant.*
Suck. Strong liquor of any sort. To suck the monkey. (*See* Monkey.) Sucky; drunk.
Suck. A breast pocket. *Cant.*
Suck. To pump. To draw from a man all he knows. The file sucked the noodle's brains; the deep one drew out of the fool all he knew.
Sucking Chicken. A young chicken.
Suds. In the suds; in trouble, in a disagreeable situation, or involved in some difficulty.
Sugar Stick. The virile member.
Suit. In general, synonymous with game: as, what suit did you give it to 'em upon? in what manner did you rob them, or upon what pretence, &c. did you defraud them? One species of imposition is said to be a prime suit, another a queer suit: a man describing the pretext he used to obtain money from another, would say, I drawed him of a quid upon the suit of so and so, naming the ground of his application. (*See* Draw.) A person having engaged with another on very advantageous terms to serve or work for him, will declare that he is upon a good suit. To use great submission and respect in asking any favour of another, is called giving it to him upon the humble suit.
Suit and Cloak. Good store of brandy, or other strong liquor, let down gutter-lane.
Suit of Mourning. A pair of black eyes. *Cant.*
Sulky. A one-horse chaise or carriage, capable of holding but one person: called by the French a *désobligeante.*
Sun. To have been in the sun; said of one that is drunk.
Sunburnt. Clapped: also, having many male children.
Sunday Man. One who goes abroad on that day only, for fear of arrests.
Sunny Bank. A good fire in winter.

SUPERNACULUM. Good liquor, of which there is not even a drop left sufficient to wet one's nail.

SURVEYOR OF THE HIGHWAYS. One reeling drunk.

SURVEYOR OF THE PAVEMENT. One standing in the pillory.

SUSPENSE. One in a deadly suspense; a man just turned off the gallows.

SUS. PER COLL. Hanged: persons who have been hanged are thus entered into the jailer's books.

SUTLER. A camp publican: also, one that pilfers gloves, tobacco boxes, and such small moveables.

SWABBERS. The ace of hearts, knave of clubs, ace and duce of trumps at whist: also, the lubberly seamen, put to swab and clean the ship.

SWAD, or SWADKIN. A soldier. *Cant.*

SWADDLE. To beat with a stick.

SWADDLERS. The tenth order of the canting tribe, who not only rob, but beat, and often murder passengers. *Cant.* Swaddlers is, also, the Irish name for methodists.

SWAG. A bundle, parcel, or package; as a *swag* of *snow, &c.* *The swag*, is a term used in speaking of any booty you have lately obtained, be it of what kind it may, except money; as where did you *lumber the swag?* that is, where did you deposit the stolen property? To carry *the swag* is to be the bearer of the stolen goods to a place of safety. *A swag* of any thing, signifies, emphatically, a great deal. To have *knapp'd* a good *swag*, is to have got a good booty.

SWAG. Wearing-apparel, linen, piece-goods, &c. are all comprehended under the name of *swag*, (when describing any *speak* lately *made, &c.*) in order to distinguish them from plate, jewellery, or other more portable articles.

SWAGGER. To bully, brag, or boast: also, to strut.

SWANNERY. He keeps a swannery, i.e. all his geese are swans.

SWAP. To exchange or barter one article for another. *Irish cant.*

SWEATING. A mode of diminishing the gold coin, practised chiefly by the Jews, who corrode it with aqua regia. Sweating was, also, a diversion practised by the bloods of the last century, who styled themselves Mohocks: these gentlemen lay in wait to surprise some person late in the night, when, surrounding him, they with their swords pricked him in the posteriors, which obliged him to be constantly turning round; this they continued till they thought him sufficiently sweated.

SWEET. Easy to be imposed on, or taken in: also, expert, dexterous, clever. Sweet's your hand; said of one dexterous at stealing.

SWEETEN. A grawler. To give money to a beggar. *Cant.*

SWEET HEART. A term applicable to either the masculine or feminine gender, signifying a girl's lover, or a man's mistress: derived from a sweet cake in the shape of a heart.

SWEETNERS. Guinea droppers, cheats, sharpers. To sweeten; to decoy, or draw in. To be sweet upon; to coax, wheedle, court, or allure. He seemed sweet upon that wench; he seemed to court that girl.

SWELL. A gentleman; but any well-dressed person is emphatically termed a *swell*, or a *rank swell*. A *family man* who appears to have plenty of money, and makes a genteel figure, is said, by his associates, to be *in Swell-street*. Any thing remarkable for its beauty or elegance is called *a swell article;* so a *swell crib* is a genteel house; *a swell mollisher*, an elegantly dressed woman, *&c.* Sometimes, in alluding to a particular gentleman, whose name is not requisite, he is styled *the swell*, meaning the person who is the object of your discourse, or attention; and whether he is called *the swell*, *the cove*, or *the gory*, is immaterial, as in the following (in addition to many other) examples:—I was *turned up* at *China-street*, because *the swell* would not appear; meaning, of course, the prosecutor: again, speaking of a person whom you were on the point of robbing, but who has taken the alarm, and is therefore on his guard, you will say to your *pall*, it's of no use, *the cove* is as *down as a hammer;* or, we may as well *stow it, the gory's leary*. *See* COVE and DOWN.

SWELLED HEAD. A disorder to which horses are extremely liable, particularly those of the subalterns of the army. This disorder is generally occasioned by remaining too long in one livery-stable or inn, and often arises to that height that it prevents their coming out at the stable door. The most certain cure is the *unguentum aureum*—not applied to the horse, but to the palm of the master of the inn or stable. N. B. Neither this disorder, nor its remedy, is mentioned by either Bracken, Bartlet, or any of the modern writers on farriery.

SWIG. A hearty draught of liquor.

SWIGMEN. Thieves who travel the country under colour of buying old shoes, old clothes, &c. or selling brooms, mops, &c. *Cant.*

SWILL. To drink greedily.

SWILL TUB. A drunkard, a sot.

SWIMMER. A counterfeit old coin.

SWIMMER. A ship. I shall have a swimmer; a cant phrase used by thieves to signify that they will be sent on board the tender.

SWIMMER. A guard-ship in the river. A thief who, in order to avoid prosecution, when before a magistrate, on condition of being sent on board the receiving ship to serve the king, is denominated by his *palls*, to have been *swimmered*. *Cant.*

SWINDLER. One who obtains goods on credit by false pretences, and sells them for ready money at any price, in order to make up a purse. This name is derived from the German word *schwindlin*, to totter, to be ready to fall; these arts being generally practised by persons on the totter, or just ready to break. The term *swindler* has since been used to signify cheats of every kind.

SWING. To be hanged. He will swing for it; he will be hanged for it.

SWINGE. To beat stoutly.

SWINGING. A great swinging fellow; a great stout fellow A swinging lie; a lusty lie.

SWING TAIL. A hog.

SWIPE. To drink.

"*Flue faker's* and *swoddies* may *eye-water swipe*."
Vide Randall's Scrap Book.

SWIPES. Purser's swipes; small beer: so termed on board the king's ships, where it is furnished by the purser.

SWISH TAIL. A pheasant; so called by the persons who sell game for the poachers.

SWISHED. Married.

SWIVE. To copulate.

SWIVEL-EYED. Squinting.

SWODDY. A soldier.

SWORD RACKET. To enlist in different regiments, and, on receiving the bounty, to desert immediately.

SYEBUCK. Sixpence.

SYNTAX. A schoolmaster.

T

TABBY. An old maid; either from Tabitha, a formal antiquated name, or else from a tabby cat, old maids being often compared to cats. To drive tab; to go out on a party of pleasure with a wife and family.

TACE. Silence, hold your tongue. *Tace* is Latin for a candle; a jocular admonition to be silent on any subject.

TACKLE. A mistress: also, good clothes. The cull has tipt his tackle rum gigging; the fellow has given his mistress good clothes. A man's tackle; the genitals.

TAFFY, i. e. Davy. A general name for a Welshman, St. David being the tutelar saint of Wales. Taffy's day. The first day of March, St. David's day.

Tag-rag and Bob-tail. An expression meaning an assemblage of low people, the mobility of all sorts. To tag after one like a tantony pig; to follow one wherever one goes, just as St. Anthony is followed by his pig.

Tail. A prostitute: also, a sword.

Tailor. Nine tailors makes a man; an ancient and common saying, originating from the effeminancy of their employment; or, as some have it, from nine tailors having been robbed by one man; according to others, from the speech of a woollen-draper, meaning that the custom of nine tailors would make or enrich one man. A London tailor, rated to furnish half a man to the trained bands, asking how that could possibly be done? was answered, by sending four journeymen and an apprentice. Put a tailor, a weaver, and a miller into a sack, shake them well, and the first that puts out his head is certainly a thief. A tailor is frequently styled pricklouse, from their assaults on those vermin with their needles.

Tailor's Goose. An iron with which, when heated, they press down the seams of clothes.

Tale Tellers. Persons said to have been formerly hired to tell wonderful stories of giants and fairies, to lull their hearers to sleep. Talesman; the author of a story or report: I'll tell you my tale and my talesman. Tale-bearers; mischief makers, incendiaries in families.

Tally Men. Brokers that let out clothes to the women of the town. *See* Rabbit Suckers.

Tame. To run tame about a house; to live familiarly in the family with which one is upon a visit. Tame army; the city trained bands.

Tandem. A two-wheeled chaise, buggy, or noddy, drawn by two horses, one before the other; that is, *at length*.

Tanner. A sixpence. The kiddy tipt the rattling cove a tanner for luck; the lad gave the coachman sixpence for drink.

Tantrums. Pet, or passion; madam was in her tantrums.

Tap. A gentle blow. A tap on the shoulder; an arrest. To tap a girl; to be the first seducer: in illusion to a beer barrel. To tap a guinea; to get it changed.

Tape. Red tape; brandy. Blue or *white tape; gin.*

"In this dim foggy clime they think if they cram one
With *tape* in the morning and *punch* in the night,
They do the thing neat," &c. &c.

Vide Randall's Scrap Book.

ALSO,

"Open your throats, lads, *wide* as you handle
The *tape* I pour into the glass in each *dandle.*"

Ibid.

Tappers. Shoulder tappers: bailiffs.

Taplash. Thick and bad beer.

Tar. Don't lose a sheep for a halfpenny worth of tar: tar is used to mark sheep. A jack tar; a sailor.

Taradiddle. A fib, or falsity.

Tarpawlin. A coarse cloth tarred over: also, figuratively, a sailor.

Tarring and Feathering. A punishment lately inflicted by the good people of Boston, in America, on any person convicted or suspected of loyalty: such delinquents being stripped naked, were daubed all over with tar, and afterwards put into a hogshead of feathers.

Tart. Sour, sharp, quick, pert.

Tartar. To catch a Tartar; to attack one of superior strength or abilities. This saying originated from a story of an Irish soldier in the Imperial service, who, in a battle against the Turks, called out to his comrade that he had caught a Tartar. 'Bring him along then,' said he. 'He won't come,' answered Paddy. 'Then come along yourself,' replied his comrade. 'Arrah,' cried he, 'but he won't let me.' A Tartar is also an adept at any feat or game; he is quite a Tartar at cricket or billiards.

Tat. Tit for tat; an equivalent.

Tatler. A watch. To flash a tatler: to wear a watch.

Tatmonger. One that uses false dice.

Tats. False dice.

Tat Shop. A place for gamblers to meet and play at hazard.

Tat's Man. One who lives by gambling with dice.

Tatterdemallion. A ragged fellow, whose clothes hang all in tatters.

Tattoo. A beat of the drum, or signal for soldiers to go to their quarters, and a direction to the sutlers to close the tap, and draw no more liquor for them; it is generally beat at nine in summer and eight in winter. The Devil's tattoo; beating with one's foot against the ground, as done by persons in low spirits.

Taw. A schoolboy's game, played with small round balls made of stone dust, called marbles. I'll be one upon your taw presently; a species of threat.

Tawdry. Garish, gawdy, with lace or staring and discordant colours: a term said to be derived from the shrine and altar of St. Audrey (an Isle of Ely saintess), which, for finery, exceeded all others thereabouts, so as to become proverbial; whence any fine dressed man or woman was said to be all St. Audrey, and by contraction all tawdry.

Tawed. Beaten.

Teagueland. Ireland. Teaguelanders; Irishmen.

Tears of the Tankard. The drippings of liquor on a man's waistcoat.

Tea Voider. A chamber pot.

Teddy my Godson. An address to a supposed simple fellow, or ninny. *Irish.*

Teize. To nap the teize; to receive a whipping. *Cant.*

Temple of Bacchus. Merry-making after getting a liceat. *Oxf. Univ. cant.*

Tenant at Will. One whose wife usually fetches him from the alehouse.

Tenant for Life. A married man; i. e. possessed of a woman for life.

Tender Parnell. A tender creature, fearful of the least puff of wind or drop of rain. As tender as Parnell, who broke her finger in a posset drink.

Ten in the Hundred. An usurer: more than five in the hundred being deemed usurious interest.

Ten Toes. *See* Bayard of ten Toes.

Termagant. An outrageous scold; from Termagantes, a cruel pagan, formerly represented in divers shows and entertainments, where, being dressed *à la Turque*, in long clothes, he was mistaken for a furious woman.

Terra firma. An estate in land.

Tester. A sixpence: from *teston*, a coin with a head on it.

Tetbury Portion. A **** and a clap.

Thames. He will not find out a way to set the Thames on fire; he will not make any wonderful discoveries, he is no conjuror.

Thatch-Gallows. A rogue, or man of bad character.

Thick. Intimate. They are as thick as two inkle-weavers.

Thief. You are a murderer and a thief, you have killed a baboon, and stolen his face; vulgar abuse.

Thief in a Candle. Part of the wick, or snuff, which, falling on the tallow, burns and melts it, and, causing it to gutter, thus steals it away.

Thief Takers. Fellows who associate with all kinds of villains, in order to betray them, when they have committed any of those crimes which entitle the persons taking them to a handsome reward, called blood money. It is the business of these thief takers to furnish subjects for a handsome execution at the end of every sessions.

Thimble. A watch. The swell flashes a rum thimble; the gentleman sports a fine watch.

Thingstable. Mr. Thingstable; Mr. Constable: a ludicrous affectation of delicacy in avoiding the pronunciation of the first syllable in the title of that officer, which, in sound, has some similarity to an indecent monosyllable.

Thingumbob. Mr. Thingumbob; a vulgar address or nomination to any person whose name is unknown, the same as Mr. What-d'ye-call-'im. Thingumbobs; testicles.

THIRTEENER. A shilling in Ireland, which there passes for thirteen pence.

THOMAS. Man Thomas; a man's virile member.

THORNBACK. An old maid.

THORNS. To be or sit upon thorns; to be uneasy, impatient, anxious for an event.

THOROUGH BRED. Derived from a good stock. The following little genuine anecdote may forcibly illustrate this term: the father of a celebrated pugilist, who distinguished himself in 1819, on being asked as to the qualities of his son, answered, "I was always considered a good man myself; and, as to my boy's mother, she and I had a *fall out* one day, when I *floored* her six times successively, but she came again, as if nothing had happened. I then allowed her the *best of* the quarrel; and I think this circumstance will satisfy any amateur that my son is a *game* man, and his *pedigree* sound."

THOROUGH CHURCHMAN. A person who goes in at one door of a church, and out at the other, without stopping.

THOROUGH COUGH. Coughing and breaking wind backwards at the same time.

THOROUGH GO NIMBLE. A looseness, a violent purging.

THOROUGH-GOOD-NATURED WENCH. One who being asked to sit down will lie down.

THOROUGH STITCH. To go thorough stitch; to stick at nothing, over shoes, over boots.

THOUGHT. What did thought do? lay in bed and besh-t himself, and thought he was up; reproof to any one who excuses himself for any breach of positive orders, by pleading that he thought to the contrary.

THREE-LEGGED MARE, or STOOL. The gallows, formerly consisting of three posts, over which were laid three transverse beams. This clumsy machine has given place to an elegant contrivance, called the *new drop*, by which the use of that vulgar vehicle, a cart, or mechanical instrument, a ladder, is also avoided; the patients being left suspended by the dropping down of that part of the floor on which they stand. This invention was first made use of for a peer. *See* DROP.

THREE-PENNY UPRIGHT. A retailer of love, who, for the sum mentioned, dispenses her favours standing against a wall.

THREE TO ONE. He is playing three to one, though sure to lose; said of any one engaged in the amorous congress.

THREPS. Threepence.

THROTTLE. To strangle.

THROTTLE. The throat, or gullet.

THROUGH IT, OR GOT THROUGH THE PIECE. To be acquitted of a charge: either by the judgement of yourself, or from the assistance of judicious friends.

THROW OFF. To talk in a sarcastical strain, so as to convey offensive allusions under the mask of pleasantry, or innocent freedom; but, perhaps, secretly venting that abuse which you would not dare to give in direct terms; this is called *throwing off*, a practice at which the *flash* ladies are very expert, when any little jealousies arise among them. To begin to talk *flash*, and speak freely of robberies past, or in contemplation, when in company with *family people*, is also termed *throwing off;* meaning to banish all reserve, none but friends being present: also, to sing when called on by the company present. *See* CHAUNT.

THRUM. To play on any instrument stringed with wire. A thrummer of wire; a player on the spinet, harpsichord, or guitar.

THRUMS. Threepence.

THUMB. By rule of thumb; to do any thing by dint of practice. To kiss one's thumb instead of the book; a vulgar expedient to avoid perjury in taking a false oath.

THUMMIKINS. An instrument formerly used in Scotland, like a vice, to pinch the thumbs of persons accused of different crimes, in order to extort confession.

THUMP. A blow. This is better than a thump on the back with a stone; said on giving any one a drink of good liquor on a cold morning. Thatch, thistle, thunder, and thump; words to the Irish, like the Shibboleth of the Hebrews.

THUMPING. Great. A thumping boy.

THWACK. A great blow with a stick across the shoulders.

TO PEG A HACK. To mount the box of a hackney-coach, drive yourself, and give the *Jarvey* a holiday. *Cant.*

TIB. A young lass.

TIBBY. A cat.

TIB OF THE BUTTERY. A goose. *Cant.* Saint Tibb's evening; the evening of the last day, or day of judgement: he will pay you on St. Tibb's eve. *Irish.*

TICK. To run o'tick; take up goods upon trust, to run in debt. Tick; a watch. *See Sessions Papers.*

TICKLE PITCHER. A thirsty fellow, a sot.

TICKLE TAIL. A rod, or schoolmaster. A man's penis.

TICKLE TEXT. A parson.

TICKRUM. A license.

TIDY. Neat.

TIFFING. Eating or drinking out of meal time, disputing or falling out: also, lying with a wench. A tiff of punch, a small bowl of punch.

Tilbury. Sixpence: so called from its formerly being the fare for crossing over from Gravesend to Tilbury fort.

Tile. A hat. *Cant.*

Tilt. To tilt; to fight with a sword. To run full tilt against one; allusion to the ancient tilting with the lance.

Tilter. A sword.

Timber Toe. A man with a wooden leg.

Tim Whisky. A light one-horse chaise without a head.

Tinny. A fire; a conflagration.

Tinny-Hunters. Persons whose practice it is to attend fires, for the purpose of plundering the unfortunate sufferers, under pretence of assisting them to remove their property.

Tiny. Little.

Tip. To give or lend. Tip me your daddle; give me your hand. Tip me a hog; give me a shilling. To tip the lion; to flatten a man's nose with the thumb, and at the same time to extend his mouth with the fingers, thereby giving him a sort of lion-like countenance. To tip the velvet; tonguing a woman. To tip all nine; to knock down all the nine pins at once, at the game of bowls or skittles: tipping, at these games, is slightly touching the tops of the pins with the bowl. Tip; a draught: don't spoil his tip. To tip your legs a gallop; to be off.

Tipperary Fortune. Two town lands, Stream's town, and Ballinocack; said of Irish women without fortune.

Tipple. Liquor.

Tipplers. Sots who are continually sipping.

Tipsey. Almost drunk.

Tip-top. The best: perhaps from fruit, that growing at the top of the tree being generally the best, as partaking most of the sun. A tip-top workman; the best or most excellent workman.

Tit. A horse: a pretty little tit; a smart little girl. A tit, or tid bit; a delicate morsel. Tommy tit; a smart lively little fellow.

Tit for Tat. An equivalent.

Titter. A girl. *Cant.*

Tittle-tattle. Idle discourse, scandal, women's talk, or small talk.

Titter-tatter. One reeling and ready to fall at the least touch: also, the childish amusement of riding upon the two ends of a plank, poised upon the prop underneath its centre: called also a see saw.

Tittup. A gentle hand gallop, or canter

Tizzy. Sixpence.

Toad. Toad in a hole; meat baked or boiled in pye-crust. He or she sits like a toad upon a chopping block; a saying of any one who sits ill on horseback. As much need of it as a toad of a side-pocket: said of a person who desires any thing for which he has no real occasion. As full of money as a toad is of feathers.

Toad-Eater. A poor female relation, and humble companion or reduced gentlewoman, in a great family, the standing butt, on whom all kinds of practical jokes are played off, and all ill humours vented. This appellation is derived from a mountebank's servant, on whom all experiments used to be made in public by the doctor, his master; among which was the eating of toads, formerly supposed poisonous. Swallowing toads is here figuratively meant for swallowing or putting up with insults, as disagreeable to a person of feeling as toads to the stomach.

Toast. A health: also, a beautiful woman whose health is often drank by men. The origin of this term (as it is said) was this:—a beautiful lady bathing in a cold bath, one of her admirers, out of gallantry, drank some of the water; whereupon another of her lovers observed, he never drank in the morning, but he would kiss the toast, and immediately saluted the lady.

Toasting Iron, or Cheese-Toaster. A sword.

Tobacco. A plant, once in great estimation as a medicine.

> Tobacco hic
> Will make you well if you be sick.
> Tobacco hic
> If you be well will make you sick.

Toby. To toby a man is to rob him on the highway; a person convicted of this offence is said to be done for a toby. The toby applies exclusively to robbing on horseback; the practice of footpad robbery being properly called the spice; though it is common to distinguish the former by the title of high-toby, and the latter of low-toby.

Toby-Gill, or Tobyman. Properly signifies a highwayman.

Toddle. To walk away. The cove was touting, but stagging the traps he toddled; he was looking out and seeing the officers he walked away.

> "Oft may we hear thy cheerful footsteps sound,
> And see us *toddle in* with heart elate."
>
> *Vide Randall's Diary.*

Todge. Beat all to a todge: said of any thing beat to smash.

Toddy. Originally, the juice of the cocoa tree, and afterwards rum, water, sugar, and nutmeg.

Tog. A coat. *Cant.* To tog is to dress or put on clothes: to tog a person is also to supply them with apparel, and they are said to be well or queerly togged, according to their appearance.

TOGGER. (UPPER) A great coat.

> " And with his *upper togger* gay,
> Prepared to *toddle* swift away."
>
> *Vide Randall's Scrap Book.*

TOGGED OUT TO THE NINES. A fanciful phrase, meaning simply that a person is well or gaily dressed.

TOGMANS. The same.

TOGS. Clothes. The swell is rum togged; the gentleman is handsomely dressed.

TOKEN. The plague: also, the venereal disease. She tipped him the token; she gave him a clap, or pox.

TOL, or TOLEDO. A sword. From Spanish swords made at Toledo, which place was famous for sword blades of an extraordinary temper.

TOLLIBAN RIG. A species of cheat carried on by a woman, assuming the character of a dumb and deaf conjuror.

TOM CONEY. A simple fellow.

TOM LONG. A tiresome story-teller. It is coming by Tom Long, the carrier; said of any thing that has been long expected.

TOMMY. Soft tommy, or white tommy; bread is so called by sailors to distinguish it from biscuit. Brown tommy; ammunition bread for soldiers, or brown bread given to convicts on board the hulks.

TOM OF BEDLAM. The same as Abram man.

TO-MORROW-COME-NEVER. When two Sundays come together; never.

TOM THUMB. A dwarf, a little hop-o'-my-thumb.

TONGUE. Tongue enough for two sets of teeth; said of a talkative person. As old as my tongue, and a little older than my teeth; a dovetail in answer to the question, How old are you? Tongue pad; a scold, or nimble-tongued person.

TONIC. A halfpenny.

TONY. A silly fellow or ninny. A mere tony; a simpleton.

TOOL. The instrument of any person or faction, a cat's paw. *See* CAT'S PAW.

TOOLS. Implements for housebreaking, pistols, &c. Any person convicted under the police act, with any of the above implements about his person, is said to be *fixed for the tools.*

TOOTH. Something for the tooth; i. e. grub. *Cant.*

TOOTH-MUSIC. Chewing.

TOOTH-PICK. A large stick. An ironical expression.

TOP. To cheat, or trick: also, to insult; he thought to have topped upon me. Top; the signal among tailors for snuffing the candles; he who last pronounces that word is obliged to get up and perform the operation. To be topped; to be hanged. The cove was topped for smashing queer screens; he was hanged for uttering forged banknotes.

Top Diver. A lover of women. An old top diver; one who has loved old hat in his time.

Toper. One that loves his bottle, a soaker. *See* Soak.

Top Heavy. Drunk.

Top Lights. The eyes. Blast your top lights. *See* Curse.

Topper. A violent blow on the head: also, a hat. *Cant.*

Topping Cheat. The gallows. *Cant.*

Topping Cove. The hangman. *Cant.*

Topping Fellow. One at the top or head of his profession.

Topping Man. A rich man.

Top Ropes. To sway away on all top ropes; to live riotously or extravagantly.

Top Sail. He paid his debts at Portsmouth with the top-sail; i. e. he went to sea and left them unpaid. So soldiers are said to pay off their scores with the drum; that is, by marching away.

Top Sawyer signifies a man that is a master genius in any profession. It is a piece of Norfolk slang, and took its rise from Norfolk being a great timber county, where the top sawyers get double the wages of those beneath them.

Topsy-turvy. The top side the other way; i. e. the wrong side upwards; some explain it, the top side turf ways, turf being always laid the wrong side upwards.

Torchecul. Bumfodder.

Tormentor of Catgut. A fiddler.

Tormentor of Sheep-skin. A drummer.

Tory. An advocate for absolute monarchy and church power: also, an Irish vagabond, robber, or rapparee.

Toss for Sides. A custom adopted in the prize-ring, to decide which man shall face the sun. The seconds "*shy a copper.*"

Toss Pot. A drunkard.

Totty-Headed. Giddy, hair-brained.

Touch. To touch; to get money from any one: also, to arrest. Touched in the wind; broken-winded. Touched in the head; insane, crazy. To touch up a woman; to have carnal knowledge of her. Touch bone and whistle: any one having broken wind backwards, according to the vulgar law, may be pinched by any of the company till he has touched bone (i.e. his teeth) and whistled.

Tough Yarn. A long story. *Cant.*

Tout. A look-out house, or eminence.

Touters. In the sporting world, men, who, on the sly, obtain the speed and capabilities of race-horses during their training, and then give information to certain persons, who, from such sort of knowledge, bet their money with more certainty.

Touting. (From *tueri;* to look out.) Publicans forestalling guests, or meeting them on the road, and begging their custom; to be met with at Brighton, Margate, &c.: also, thieves or smugglers looking out to see that the coast is clear. Touting ken; the bar of a public-house.

Towel. A oaken towel; a cudgel. To rub one down with an oaken towel; to beat or cudgel him.

Tower. Clipped money. They have been round the Tower with it. *Cant.*

Tower. To overlook, to rise aloft, as in a high tower.

Tower-Hill-Play. A slap on the face, and a kick on the breech.

Town. A woman of the town; a prostitute. To be on the town; to live by prostitution.

Town-Bull. A common whore-master. To roar like a town-bull; to cry or bellow aloud.

Tow-Street. To get a person in a line, to decoy.

Track. To go. Track up the dancers; go up stairs. *Cant.*

Tradesmen. Thieves. Clever tradesmen; good thieves.

Tramp. On the look-out for employment; walking about from place to place. *Cant.*

Translators. Sellers of old mended shoes and boots, between cobblers and shoe-makers.

Transmogriphy, or **Transmigrify.** To patch up, vamp, or alter.

Transnear. To come up with any body.

Tranter. *See* **Crocker.**

Trap. To understand trap; to know one's own interest.

Trapan. To inveigle, or ensnare.

Trapes. A slatternly woman, a careless, sluttish woman.

Traps. Constables, thief-takers. *Cant.*

Trap Sticks. Thin legs; gambs: from the sticks with which boys play at trap-ball.

Traveller. To tip the traveller; to tell wonderful stories, to romance.

Travelling Piquet. A mode of amusement, practised by two persons riding in a carriage, each reckoning towards his game the persons or animals that pass by on the side next them, according to the following estimation:—

A parson riding on a gray horse, with blue furniture;—game.

An old woman under a hedge;—ditto.

A cat looking out of a window;—60.

A man, woman, and child, in a buggy;—40.

A man with a woman behind him;—30.

A flock of sheep;—20.

A flock of geese;—10.

A postchaise;—5.

A horseman;—2.

A man or woman walking;—1.

Tray Trip. An ancient game like Scotch hop, played on a pavement, marked out with chalk into different compartments.

Trencher Cap. The square cap worn by the collegians, at the universities of Oxford and Cambridge.

Trencher Man. A stout trencher man; one who has a good appetite, or, as the term is, plays a good knife and fork.

Treswins. Threepence.

Trib. A prison: perhaps from tribulation.

Trig. A bit of stick, paper, &c. placed by thieves in the key-hole of, or elsewhere about, the door of a house, which they suspect to be uninhabited; if the *trig* remains unmoved the following day, it is a proof that no person sleeps in the house, on which the gang enter it the ensuing night *upon the screw,* and frequently meet with a good booty, such as beds, carpets, &c. the family being probably out of town. This operation is called *trigging the jigger.*

Trig it. To play truant. To lay a man trigging; to knock him down.

Trigrymate. An idle female companion.

Trim. State dress. In a sad trim; dirty: also, spruce or fine; a trim fellow.

Trimming. Cheating, changing side, or beating. I'll trim his jacket; I'll thrash him. To be trimmed; to be shaved: I'll just step and get trimmed.

Trim Tram. Like master, like man.

Trine. To hang: also, Tyburn.

Tringum trangum. A whim, or maggot.

Trining. Hanging.

Trinkets. Toys, baubles, or nicknacks.

Trip. A short voyage or journey, a false step or stumble, an error of the tongue, a bastard. She has made a trip; she has had a bastard.

Tripe. The belly, or guts. Mr. Double Tripe; a fat man. Tripes and trullibubs; the entrails: also, a jeering appellation for a fat man.

Troll. To loiter or saunter about.

TROLLOP. A lusty coarse sluttish woman.

TROLLYLOLLY. Coarse lace, once much in fashion.

TROOPER. You will die the death of a trooper's horse, that is, with your shoes on; a jocular method of telling any one he will be hanged.

TROT. An old trot; a decrepit old woman. A dog trot; a gentle pace.

TROTTERS. Feet. To shake one's trotters at Bilby's ball, where the sheriff pays the fiddlers; perhaps the Bilboes' ball, i. e. the ball of fetters;—fetters and stocks were anciently called the bilboes. Box your trotters; be off.

TROUNCE. To punish by course of law.

TRUCK. To exchange, swap, or barter: also, a wheel such as ships' guns are placed upon.

TRULL. A soldier's or a tinker's trull; a soldier's or tinker's female companion. *Guteli*, or *trulli*, are spirits like women, which show great kindness to men, and hereof it is that we call light women trulls. *Randle Holms's Academy of Armory*.

TRUMP. A good fellow; no flincher; but who displays courage upon every suit. *Cant.* The best card in the pack.

TRUMPERY. An old whore, or goods of no value; rubbish.

TRUMPET. To sound one's own trumpet; to praise one's self.

TRUMPETER. The king of Spain's trumpeter; a braying ass. His trumpeter is dead, he is therefore forced to sound his own trumpet. He would make an excellent trumpeter, for he has a strong breath; said of one having a fœted breath.

TRUMPS. To be put to one's trumps; to be in difficulties, or put to one's shifts. Something may turn up trumps; something lucky may happen. All his cards are trumps; he is extremely fortunate.

TRUNDLERS. Peas. *Obsolete*.

TRUNK. A nose. How fares your old trunk? does your nose still stand fast? an allusion to the proboscis or trunk of an elephant. To shove a trunk; to introduce one's self unasked into any place or company. Trunk-maker like; more noise than work.

TRUSTED ALONE. This bit of *flash* is made use of, in speaking of any knowing or experienced person; meaning, that he is so *deep* as to the tricks of the town, that he may be "trusted *alone*" in any company without danger to himself.

TRUSTY TROGAN, or TRUSTY TROUT. A true friend.

TRYNING. *See* TRINING.

TRY ON. To endeavour. To live by thieving. Coves who try it on; professed thieves.

TUB THUMPER. A Presbyterian parson.

Tucked up. Hanged. A tucker up to an old bachelor or widower; a supposed mistress.

Tu Quoque. The mother of all saints.

Tumbler. A cart: also, a sharper employed to draw in pigeons to game; likewise a posture-master, or rope-dancer. To shove the tumbler, or perhaps tumbril; to be whipped at the cart's tail.

Tune. To beat. His father tuned him delightfully; perhaps from fetching a tune out of the person beaten, or from a comparison with the disagreeable sounds of instruments when tuning. *Obsolete.*

Tup. To have carnal knowledge of a woman. *Vide Othello.*

Tup. A ram: figuratively, a cuckold.

Tup Running. A rural sport practised at wakes and fairs in Derbyshire; a ram, whose tail is well soaped and greased, is turned out to the multitude; any one that can take him by the tail, and hold him fast, is to have him for his own.

Turf. On the turf; persons who keep running horses, or attend and bet at horse-races, are said to be on the turf.

Turk. A cruel, hard-hearted man. Turkish treatment; barbarous usage. Turkish shore; Lambeth, Southwark, and Rotherhithe sides of the Thames.

Turkey Merchant. A poulterer.

Turncoat. One who has changed his party from interested motives.

Turned up. Acquitted, or discharged, for want of evidence. *Cant.*

Turnip-pated. White or fair haired.

Turnips. To give any person *turnips*, is to get rid of him at all events.

Turnpike-Man. A parson; because the clergy collect their tolls at our entrance into and exit from the world.

Turn up. A fight produced from a hasty quarrel. A casual boxing match. It is also to desist from, or relinquish any particular habit or mode of life. To quit a person suddenly in the street is termed, *turning him up*. *Cant.*

Turn up. To desist from, or relinquish any particular habit or mode of life, or the further pursuit of any object you had in view, is called *turning it up*. To *turn-up* a mistress, or a male acquaintance, is to drop all intercourse or correspondence with them. To *turn up* a particular house or shop, you have been accustomed to use, or deal at, signifies to withdraw your patronage, or custom, and visit it no more. To quit a person in the street, whether secretly or openly, is called *turning him up*. To *turn* a man *up sweet*, is to get rid of him effectually, but yet to leave him in perfect good humour, and free from any suspicion or discontent;

this piece of *finesse* often affords a field for the exercise of consummate address, as in the case of *turning up a flat*, after having stripped him of all his money at a play, or a shop-keeper, whom you have just robbed before his face of something valuable, *upon the pinch*, or *the hoist*.

Turn up a Trump. Is to procure a good stake; or in any manner improving your situation in life.

Tuzzy-muzzy. The monosyllable.

Twaddle. Perplexity, confusion, or any thing else: a fashionable term that for awhile succeeded that of *bore*. *See* Bore.

Twangey, or Stangey. A north country name for a tailor.

Tweague. In a great tweague: in a great passion. Tweaguey; peevish, passionate.

Tweak. To pull: to tweak any one's nose.

Twelver. A shilling.

Twiddle-diddles. Testicles.

Twiddle poop. An effeminate looking fellow.

Twig. Handsome: stylish. The cove is togged in twig; the fellow is dressed in the fashion.

Twig. To observe. Twig the cull, he is peery; observe the fellow, he is watching us: also, to disengage, snap asunder, or break off. To twig the darbies; to knock off the irons.

Twig. In good twig; that is, to accomplish an object cleverly. A well-dressed man or woman is said to be in *prime twig*. *Prime twig*, also, signifies high spirits. *Ex. gr.*

> "Never since the renown'd days of *Broughton* and *Figg*,
> Was the fanciful world in such *very prime twig*."
>
> *Crib's Memorial.*

> ———— "Lark, or some *delicious jig*,
> The mind delights in, when 'tis in *prime twig*."
>
> *Vide Rendall's Diary.*

Twiss. A jordan, or pot de chambre. (*Irish.*) A Mr. Richard Twiss, having, in his "travels," given a very unfavourable description of the Irish character, the inhabitants of Dublin, by way of revenge, thought proper to christen this utensil by his name—suffice it to say, that the baptismal rites were not wanting at the ceremony. On a nephew of this gentleman, the following epigram was made:

> "Perish the country, yet my name
> Shall ne'er in *story* be forgot,
> But still the more increase in fame,
> The more the *country goes to pot.*"

At the bottom of the *jordan* was his portrait, and the following specimen of Irish wit:

"Let every one piss,
On lying Dick Twiss."

TWIST. A mixture of half tea and half coffee; likewise brandy, beer, and eggs. A good twist; a good appetite. To twist it down apace; to eat heartily.

TWISTED. Executed, hanged.

TWIT. To reproach a person, or remind him of favours conferred.

TWITTER. All in a twitter; in a fright. Twittering is also the note of some small birds, such as the robin, &c.

TWITTOC. Two. *Cant.*

TWO-HANDED. Great. A two-handed fellow or wench; a great strapping man or woman.

TWO-HANDED PUT. The amorous congress.

TWO THIEVES BEATING A ROGUE. A man beating his hands against his sides to warm himself in cold weather: called, also, beating the booby, and cuffing Jonas.

TWO TO ONE SHOP. A pawnbroker's: alluding to the three blue balls, the sign of that trade: or perhaps to its being two to one that the goods pledged are never redeemed.

TYBURN BLOSSOM. A young thief or pickpocket, who, in time, will ripen into fruit borne by the deadly never-green.

TYBURN TIPPET. A halter: see Latimer's sermon before Edward VI. A.D. 1549. *Rather obsolete in* 1822.

TYE. A neckcloth.

TYE IT UP. To *tye up* any particular custom, practice, or habit, is synonymous with *knifing, stowing, turning* it *up*, or *stashing* it. To *tye it up* is a phrase, which, used emphatically, is generally understood to mean quitting a course of depredation and wickedness. *See* SQUARE and DO THE TRICK.

TYKE. A dog: also, a clown: a Yorkshire tyke.

V

VAGARIES. Frolics, wild rambles.

VAIN-GLORIOUS, or OSTENTATIOUS MAN. One who boasts without reason; or, as the canters say, pisses more than he drinks.

VALENTINE. The first woman seen by a man, or man seen by a woman, on St. Valentine's day, the 14th of February, is generally chosen to this post, and has the sole right to the first night's lodging with the dells, who afterwards are used in common among the whole fraternity. He carries a short truncheon in his hand, which he calls his filchman, and has a larger share than ordinary of whatever is gained by the society. He often travels in company with thirty or forty males and females, abram men, and others, over whom he presides arbitrarily. Sometimes the women and children, who are unable to travel, or fatigued, are by turns carried in panniers by an ass or two, or by some poor jades procured for that purpose.

UPSTARTS. Persons lately raised to honours and riches from mean stations.

UP THE SPOUT. Having clothes or any other articles pledged at the pawnbroker's: in allusion to a long spout, through which the articles, when redeemed, are conveyed from the top to the bottom of the house, in order to expedite business.

UP TO SLUM. To be flash. *Cant.*

UP TO SNUFF. Synonymous with the above phrase; and is often rendered more emphatic by such adjuncts as, "*Up to snuff and two-penny,*" "Up to snuff, and a pinch above it." *Cant.*

UP TO THEIR GOSSIP. To be a match for one who attempts to cheat or deceive; to be on a footing, or in the secret. I'll be up with them; I will repay in kind.

URCHIN. A child, a little fellow: also, a hedgehog.

USED UP. Killed; a military saying, originating from a message sent by the late General Guise, on the expedition at Carthagena, where he desired the commander-in-chief to order him some more grenadiers, for those he had were all *used up.*

W

WABLER. Foot wabler; a contemptuous term for a foot soldier, frequently used by those of the cavalry.

WACK. To share or divide any thing equally, as *wack the blunt,* divide the money, &c.

WADDLE. To go like a duck. To waddle out of 'Change Alley as a lame duck; a term for one who has not been able to pay his gaming debts, called his differences, on the Stock Exchange, and therefore absents himself from it.

WAG. An arch frolicsome fellow.

WAGGISH. Arch, gamesome, frolicsome.

WAGTAIL. A lewd woman.

Waits. Musicians of the lower order, who in most towns play under the windows of the chief inhabitants at midnight, a short time before Christmas, for which they collect a Christmas-box from house to house. They are said to derive their name of waits from being always in waiting to celebrate weddings and other joyous events happening within their district.

Wake. A country feast, commonly on the anniversary of the tutelar saint of the village, that is, the saint to whom the parish church is dedicated: also, a custom of watching the dead, called Late Wake, in use both in Ireland and Wales, where the corpse is deposited under a table, with a plate of salt on its breast; the table is covered with liquor of all sorts, and the guests, particularly the younger part of them, amuse themselves with all kinds of pastimes and recreation: the consequence is generally more than replacing the departed friend.

Walker. A flash expression for telling a lie.

Walking Distiller. One who carries the keg, i. e. a person who is very easy put out of his way: one soon affronted without a cause.

Walking Poulterer. One who steals fowls, and hawks them from door to door.

Walking Stationer. A hawker of pamphlets, &c.

Walking the Plank. A mode of destroying devoted persons or officers in a mutiny or ship-board, by blindfolding them, and obliging them to walk on a plank, laid over the ship's side; by this means, as the mutineers suppose, avoiding the penalty of murder.

Walking up against the Wall. To run up a score, which, in ale-houses, is commonly recorded with chalk on the walls of the bar.

Wall. To walk or crawl up the wall; to be scored up at a public-house. Wall-eyed, having an eye with little or no sight, all white like a plastered wall.

Wall-Flowers. Clothes exposed to sale in the streets. *Cant.*

Wanted. When any of the *traps* or runners have a private information against a *family person*, and are using means to apprehend the party, they say, such a one is *wanted;* and it becomes the latter, on receiving such intimation, to keep *out of the way*, until the *stink* is over, or until he or she can find means to *stash the business* through the medium of *Mr. Palmer*, or by some other means.

Wap. To copulate, to beat. If she wont wap for a winne, let her trine for a make; if she won't lie with a man for a penny, let her hang for a halfpenny. Mort wap-apace; a woman of experience, or very expert at this sport.

WAPPER-EYED. Sore-eyed.

WARE. A woman's ware; her commodity.

WARE HAWK. An exclamation used by thieves to inform their confederates that some police-officers are at hand.

WARM. Rich, in good circumstances. To warm, or give a man a warming; to beat him. *See* CHAFED.

WARMING-PAN. A large old-fashioned watch. A Scotch warming-pan; a female bedfellow.

WARREN. One that is security for goods taken upon credit by extravagant young gentlemen. Cunny warren; a girl's boarding-school: also, a bawdy-house.

WASP. An infected prostitute, who, like a wasp, carries a sting in her tail.

WASPISH. Peevish, spiteful.

WASTE. House of waste; a tavern or alehouse, where idle people waste both their time and money.

WASTE-BUTT. Mr. Waste-butt, the publican; it is observed of most men when they commence publicans, from their habit of drinking with their customers in general, all sorts of liquors, that "they are little better than *waste-butts.*"

WASTE OF READY. Including it in Hoyle's dominions, a course of gambling, loo-tables, &c. *Oxf. Univ. cant.*

WATCH, CHAIN, AND SEALS. A sheep's head and pluck.

WATER BEWITCHED. Very weak punch or beer.

WATER-MILL. The monosyllable.

WATER OF LIFE. Gin.

> "Toast his sweet name in the *water of life.*"
> *Vide Randall's Diary.*

WATERPAD. One that robs ships on the river Thames.

WATER SCRIGER. A doctor who prescribes from inspecting the water of his patients. *See* PISS PROPHET.

WATER SNEAK. Robbing ships or vessels on a navigable river, or canal, by getting on board unperceived, generally in the night. *The water-sneak* is lately made a capital offence.

WATER SNEAKSMAN. A man who steals from ships or craft on the river.

WATERY-HEADED. Apt to shed tears.

WATTLES. Ears. *Cant.*

WEAR IT. Among the flash people, is to lay under the stigma of having turned a *nose*.

WEASEL-FACED. Thin, meagre-faced. Weasel-gutted; thin-bodied; a weasel is a thin long slender animal with a sharp face.

WEDDING. The emptying of a necessary-house, particularly in London. You have been at an Irish wedding, where black eyes are given instead of favours; said to any one who has a black eye.

WEDGE. Silver plate, because melted by the receivers of stolen goods into wedges. *Cant.*

WEED. To pilfer or purloin a small portion from a large quantity of any thing; often done by young or timid depredators, in the hope of escaping detection, as, an apprentice or shopman will *weed* his master's *lob*, that is, take small sums out of the till when opportunity offers, which sort of peculation may be carried on with impunity for a length of time; but experienced thieves sometimes think it good judgement to *weed* a place, in order that it may be *good* again, perhaps, for a considerable length of time, as in the instance of a warehouse, or other depôt for goods, to which they may possess an easy access by means of a false key; in this case, by taking too great *a swag* at first, the proprietors would discover the deficiency, and take measures to prevent future depredation. To *weed the swag* is to embezzle part of the booty, unknown to your *pals*, before a division takes place, a temptation against which very few of *the family* are proof, if they can find an opportunity. A *flash cove*, on discovering a deficiency in his purse or property, which he cannot account for, will declare that he, (or it, naming the article,) has been *wedded to the ruffian*.

WEEPING CROSS. To come home by Weeping-cross; to repent.

WEIGH FORTY. A term formerly used by the police, who are as well versed in *flash* as the thieves themselves and of whom it is said, did often wink at depredations of a petty nature, for which no reward would attach, and to let a thief *reign* unmolested till he commits a capital crime; they then *grab* him, and, on conviction, share (in many cases) a reward of £40, or upwards; therefore those gentry will say, Let him alone at present, we don't *want* him till he *weighs his weight*, meaning, of course, forty pounds.

WELL. To divide unfairly. To conceal part. A cant phrase used by thieves, where one of the party conceals some of the booty, instead of dividing it fairly amongst his confederates.

WELL-HUNG. The blowen was nutts upon the kiddey because he is well-hung; the girl is pleased with the youth because his genitals are large.

WELSH COMB. The thumb and four fingers.

WELSH EJECTMENT. To unroof the house, a method practised by landlords in Wales to eject a bad tenant.

WELSH FIDDLE. The itch. *See* SCOTCH FIDDLE.

WELSH MILE. Like a Welsh mile, long and narrow. His story is like a Welsh mile, long and tedious.

WELSH RABBIT. [i. e. a Welsh rare-bit.] Bread and cheese

toasted. *See* RABBIT. The Welsh are said to be so remarkably fond of cheese, that, in cases of difficulty, their midwives apply a piece of toasted cheese to the *janua vitæ* to attract and entice the young Taffy, who, on smelling it, makes most vigorous efforts to come forth.

WESTMINSTER WEDDING. A match between a whore and a rogue.

WET PARSON. One who moistens his clay freely, in order to make it stick together.

WET QUAKER. One of that sect who has no objection to the spirit derived from wine.

WET-THEE-THROUGH. Gin. *Cant.*

WETTING THE NECK. A drunkard. *Cant.*

WHACK. A share of a booty obtained by fraud. A paddy whack; a stout brawney Irishman.

WHAPPER. A large man or woman.

WHEEDLE. A sharper. To cut a wheedle; to decoy by fawning or insinuation. *Cant.*

WHEELBAND IN THE NICK. Regular drinking over the left thumb.

WHELP. An impudent whelp: a saucy boy.

WHEREAS. To follow a whereas; to become a bankrupt, to figure among princes and potentates; the notice given in the gazette that a commission of bankruptcy is issued out against any trader, always beginning with the word Whereas. He will soon march in the rear of a whereas.

WHET. A morning's draught, commonly white wine, supposed to whet or sharpen the appetite.

WHIDDING. Talking slang. *Scotch cant.*

WHIDS. Words. *Cant.*

WHIDDLE. To tell or discover. He whiddles; he peaches. He whiddles the whole scrap; he discovers all he knows. The cull whiddled because they would not tip him a snack; the fellow peached because they would not give him a share. They whiddle beef, and we must brush; they cry out thieves, and we must make off. *Cant.*

WHIDDLER. An informer, or one that betrays the secrets of the gang.

WHIP-BELLY VENGEANCE, or pinch-gut vengeance, of which he that gets the most has the worst share. Weak or sour beer.

WHIP JACKS. The tenth order of the canting crew; rogues who, having learned a few sea terms, beg with counterfeit passes, pretending to be sailors shipwrecked on the neighbouring coast, and on their way to the port from whence they sailed.

WHIP OFF. To run away, to drink off greedily, to snatch. He whipped away from home, went to the ale-house, where he whipped off a full tankard, and, coming back, whipped off a fellow's hat from his head.

WHIPPER-SNAPPER. A diminutive fellow.

WHIPSHIRE. Yorkshire.

WHIPSTER. A sharp or subtle fellow.

WHIP THE COCK, A piece of sport practised at wakes, horse-races, and fairs, in Leicestershire: a cock being tied or fastened into a hat or basket, half a dozen carters blindfolded, and armed with their cart whips, are placed round it, who, after being turned thrice about, begin to whip the cock, which if any one strikes so as to make it cry out, it becomes his property; the joke is, that, instead of whipping the cock, they flog each other heartily.

WHIPT-SYLLABUB. A flimsy frothy discourse or treatise, without solidity.

WHIRLYGIGS. Testicles.

WHISKER. A great lie.

WHISKER SPLITTER. A man of intrigue.

WHISKIN. A shallow brown drinking bowl.

WHISKY. A malt spirit much drank in Ireland and Scotland: also, a one-horse chaise. *See* TIN WHISKY.

WHISTLE. The throat. To wet one's whistle; to drink.

WHISTLING SHOP. Rooms in the King's Bench and Fleet prisons where drams are privately sold.

WHIT. [i.e. Whittington's.] Newgate. *Cant.* Five rum-padders are rubbed in the darkmans out of the Whit, and are piked into the deuseaville: five highwaymen broke out of Newgate in the night, and are gone into the country.

WHITE BAIT. Silver. *Cant.*

WHITECHAPEL. Whitechapel portion; two smocks and what nature gave. Whitechapel breed; fat, ragged, and saucy. *See* ST. GILES'S BREED. Whitechapel beau; one who dresses with a needle and thread, and undresses with a knife. To play at whist Whitechapel fashion; i.e. aces and kings first.

WHITE FEATHER. He has a white feather; he is a coward: an allusion to a game cock, which having a white feather is a proof that he is not of the true game breed. Speaking of *Randall*, the author of *Randall's Diary* says,

> "He never yet has shown in fight
> The snow-*white feather's damning shade.*"

Recounting a meeting at *Belcher's*, the author of *Crib's Memorial* says they were

> "All high-bred heroes of *the ring*,
> Whose very *gammon* would delight one,
> Who, nurs'd beneath *the Fancy's* wing,
> Show all her *feathers* but the *white one.*"

White Lie. A harmless lie, one not told with a malicious intent, a lie told to reconcile people at variance.

White-livered. Cowardly, malicious.

White Ribbin. Gin.

White Serjeant. A man fetched from the tavern or ale-house by his wife, is said to be arrested by the white serjeant.

White Swelling. A woman big with child is said to have a white swelling.

White Tape. Geneva.

Whitewashed. One who has taken the benefit of an act of insolvency, to defraud his creditors, is said to have been whitewashed.

White Wine. Gin. *Cant.* A name frequently applied to gin in the top circles.

White Wool. Geneva.

Whither-go-ye. A wife: wives being sometimes apt to question their husbands whither they are going. *Obsolete.*

Whittington's College. Newgate: built or repaired by the famous lord mayor of that name.

Whore-monger. A man that keeps more than one mistress. A country gentleman, who kept a female friend, being reproved by the parson of the parish, and styled a whore-monger, asked the parson whether he had a cheese in his house, and being answered in the affirmative, 'Pray,' says he, 'does that one cheese make you a cheese-monger?'

Whore Pipe. The sugar-stick.

Whore's Bird. A debauched fellow, the largest of all birds. He sings more like a whore's bird than a canary bird; said of one who has a strong manly voice.

Whore's Curse. A piece of gold coin, value five shillings and three pence, frequently given to women of the town by such as professed always to give gold, and who, before the introduction of those pieces, always gave half a guinea.

Whore's Kitling, or Whore's Son. A bastard.

Whow Ball. A milk-maid: from their frequent use of the word *whow*, to make the cow stand still in milking. Ball is the supposed name of the cow. *Rural cant.*

Wibble. Bad drink.

Wibling's Witch. The four of clubs: from one James Wibling, who, in the reign of King James I. grew rich by private gaming, and was commonly observed to have that card, and never to lose a game but when he had it not.

Wicket. A casement: also, a little door.

Widow's Weeds. Mourning clothes of a peculiar fashion, denoting her state. A grass widow; a discarded mistress. A widow bewitched; a woman whose husband is abroad, and said, but not certainly known, to be dead.

Wife. A fetter fixed to one leg.

Wife in Water Colours. A mistress, or concubine; water colours being, like their engagements, easily effaced or dissolved.

Wiganowns. A man wearing a large wig.

Wigsby. Mr. Wigsby; a man wearing a wig.

Wild Rogues. Rogues trained up to stealing from their cradles.

Wild Squirt. A looseness.

Wild-goose Chase. A tedious uncertain pursuit, like the following a flock of wild geese, who are remarkably shy.

Willing Tit. A free horse, or a coming girl.

Willow. Poor, and of no reputation. To wear the willow; to be abandoned by a lover or mistress.

Win. A penny.

Wind. To raise the wind; to procure money.

Wind. A man transported for life: among the flash people it is termed, he is *lagged* for his *wind*.

Winder. Transportation for life. The blowen has napped a winder for a lift; the wench is transported for life for stealing in a shop.

Winding-post (To nap the). To be transported.

Wind-mill. The fundament. She has no fortune but her mills: i.e. she has nothing but her **** and ****.

Windfall. A legacy, or any accidental accession of property.

Windy. Foolish. A windy fellow; a simple fellow.

Wings. Arms. *Sea term.*

Wink. To tip one the wink; to give a signal by winking the eye.

Winnings. Plunder, goods, or money acquired by theft.

Winter Cricket. A tailor.

Winter's Day. He is like a winter's day, short and nasty.

Wipe. A blow, or reproach. I'll give you a wipe on the chops. That story gave him a fine wipe: also, a handkerchief.

Wipe. A handkerchief. *Cant.*

Wipe Drawer. A pickpocket, one who steals handkerchiefs. He drew a broad, narrow, cam, or specked wiper; he picked a pocket of a broad, narrow, cambrick, or coloured handkerchief.

Wise Men of Gotham. Gotham is a village in Nottinghamshire: its magistrates are said to have attempted to hedge in a cuckoo; a bush, called the cuckoo's bush, is still shown in support of the tradition. A thousand other ridiculous stories are told of the men of Gotham.

Wiseacre. A foolish conceited fellow.

WISEACRE'S HALL. Gresham College.

WISTY CASTORS. Heavy blows given by scientific pugilists, tending to take the fight out of each other. *Lancashire cant.* A favourite phrase of Bob Gregson.

WITCHER. Silver. Witcher bubber; a silver bowl. Witcher tilter; a silver hilted sword. Witcher cully; a silversmith.

WOBBLE. To boil. Pot wobbler; one who boils a pot.

WOFFLE. To eat or to drink.

WOLF IN THE STOMACH. A monstrous or canine appetite.

WOOD. In a wood; bewildered, in a maze, in a peck of troubles, puzzled, or at a loss what course to take in any business. To look over the wood; to ascend the pulpit, to preach: I shall look over the wood at St. James's on Sunday next. To look through the wood; to stand in the pillory. Up to the arms in wood; in the pillory.

WOOD PECKER. A by-stander, who bets whilst another plays.

WOODCOCK. A tailor with a long bill.

WOODEN HABEAS. A coffin. A man who dies in prison is said to go out with a wooden habeas. He went out with a wooden habeas; i.e. his coffin.

WOODEN SPOON. *(Cambridge.)* The last junior optime. *See* WRANGLER, OPTIME.

WOODEN HORSE. To ride the wooden horse was a military punishment formerly in use. This horse consisted of two or more planks about eight feet long, fixed together so as to form a sharp ridge or angle, which answered to the body of the horse. It was supported by four posts, about six feet long, for legs. A head, neck, and tail, rudely cut in wood, were added, which completed the appearance of a horse. On this sharp ridge delinquents were mounted, with their hands tied behind them; and to steady them (as it was said), and lest the horse should kick them off, one or more firelocks were tied to each leg. In this situation they were sometimes condemned to sit for an hour or two; but, at length, it having been found to injure the soldiers materially, and sometimes to rupture them, it was left off about the time of the accession of King George I. A wooden horse was standing in the Parade at Portsmouth as late as the year 1750.

WOODEN RUFF. The pillory. *See* NORWAY NECKLOTH.

WOODEN SURTOUT. A coffin.

WOMAN OF THE TOWN, or WOMAN OF PLEASURE. A prostitute.

WOMAN AND HER HUSBAND. A married couple, where the woman is bigger than her husband.

Woman's Conscience. Never satisfied.

Woman of all Work. Sometimes applied to a female servant, who refuses none of her master's commands.

Woolbird. A sheep. *Cant.*

Wool-gathering. Your wits are gone a wool-gathering; saying to an absent man, one in a reverie, or absorbed in thought.

Woolley Crown. A soft-headed fellow.

Word Grubbers. Verbal critics: and, also, persons who use hard words in common discourse.

Word Pecker. A punster, one who plays upon words.

Word of Mouth. To drink by word of mouth; i.e. out of the bowl or bottle, instead of a glass.

Work. To work upon any particular game, is to practise generally that species of fraud or depredation; as, he *works upon the crack*; he follows house-breaking, &c. A offender having been detected in the very fact, particularly in cases of coining, colouring base metal, &c. is emphatically said to have been grabbed at work, meaning to imply, that the proof against him being so plain, he has no ground of defence to set up.

Work-bench. A bedstead. *Cant.*

World. All the world and his wife; every body, a great company.

Wranglers. At Cambridge, the first class (generally of twelve) at the annual examination for a degree. There are three classes of honours, wranglers, senior optimes, and junior optimes. Wranglers are said to be born with golden spoons in their mouths, the senior optimes with silver, and the junior with leaden ones. The last junior optime is called the wooden spoon. Those who are not qualified for honours are either in the *gulf*, (that is, meritorious, but not deserving of being in the three first classes,) or among the οι πολλοι, *the many*. *See* Pluck, Apostles, &c.

Wrap Rascal. A red cloak: called, also, a roquelaire.

Wrinkle. A wrinkle-bellied whore; one who has had a number of bastards: child-bearing leaves wrinkles in a woman's belly. To take the wrinkles out of any one's belly; to fill it out by a hearty meal. You have one wrinkle more in your a–se; i.e. you have one piece of knowledge more than you had, every fresh piece of knowledge being supposed, by the vulgar naturalists, to add a wrinkle to that part.

Wrinkle. To utter a falsehood. *Cant.*

Wrinkler. A person prone to lying: such a character is called, also, a gully, which is, probably, an abbreviation of Gulliver, and from hence, to gully signifies to lie, or deal in the marvellous.

WRY MOUTH AND A PISSEN PAIR OF BREECHES. Hanging.
WRY NECK DAY. Hanging day.
WYN. *See* WIN.

X

XANTIPPE. The name of Socrates' wife; now used to signify a shrew, or scolding wife.

Y

YACK. A watch. *Obsolete.*
YAFFLING. Eating. *Cant.*
YAM. To eat or stuff heartily.
YANKEY, or YANKEY DOODLE. A booby, or country lout: a name given to the New Englandmen in North America. A general appellation for an American.
YARMOUTH CAPON. A red herring: Yarmouth being a famous place for curing herrings.
YARMOUTH PYE. A pye made of herrings highly spiced, which the city of Norwich is, by charter, bound to present annually to the king.
YARN. Yarning, or spinning a yarn, is a favourite amusement among flash people, signifying to relate their various adventures, exploits, and escapes, to each other. This is most common and gratifying among persons in confinement or exile, to enliven a dull hour, and probably excite a secret hope of one day enjoying a repetition of their former pleasures. *See* BONED. A person expert at telling these stories is said to spin a fine yarn. A man using a great deal of rhetoric, and exerting all his art to talk another person out of any thing he is intent upon, the latter will answer, 'Aye, aye, you can spin a good yarn, but it won't do;' meaning, all your eloquence will not have the desired effect.
YARUM. Milk. *Cant.*
YEA AND NAY MAN. A quaker, a simple fellow, one who can only answer yes or no.
YELLOW. To look yellow; to be jealous. I happened to call on Mr. Green, who was out; on coming home, and finding me with his wife, he began to look confounded blue, and was, I thought, a little yellow.
YELLOW BELLY. A native of the fens of Lincolnshire; an allusion to the eels caught there.
YELLOW BOYS. Guineas.

Yelp. To cry out. Yelper; a town crier: also, one apt to make great complaints on trifling occasions.

Yelpers. Wild beasts.

Yest. A contraction of yesterday.

Yoked. Married. A yoke; the quantum of labour performed at one spell by husbandmen, the day's work being divided in summer into three yokes. *Kentish term.*

Yokuff. A chest or box.

Yore. To look at a person. *Cant.*

Yorkshire Tyke. A Yorkshire clown. To come Yorkshire over any one; to cheat him.

Youkel. A countryman. *Cant.*

Young One. A familiar expression of contempt for another's ignorance, as, 'ah! I see you're a young one:' 'how d'ye do, young one?'

Yowl. To cry aloud, or howl.

Z

ZAD. Crooked, like the letter Z. He is a mere zad, or, perhaps, zed; a description of a very crooked or deformed person.

Zany. The jester, jack pudding, or merry andrew to a mountebank.

Zedland. Great part of the west country, where the letter Z is substituted for S: as zee for see, zun for sun, &c. &c. This prevails through the counties of Devonshire, Dorsetshire, and Somersetshire.

Zoc, or Soc. A blow. I gid him a zoc; I gave him a blow. *West country.*

Zouch, or Slouch. A slovenly ungenteel man, one who has a stoop in his gait. A slouched hat; a hat with its brims let down, or uncocked.

Zounds. An exclamation. An abbreviation of *God's wounds.*

THE END.

MARCHANT, Printer, Ingram-Court, Fenchurch-Street.

GAN'S LIFE IN LONDON,

Thirty-Six Coloured Plates (the Scenes from
l Life, by I. R. *and* G. CRUIKSHANK)
l numerous Wood-Cuts.

ı original Work, entitled LIFE IN LON-
I ; or, the DAY and NIGHT SCENES of
, Hawthorn, Esq. and his elegant Friend,
ıthian Tom, in their Rambles and Sprees
ıgh the Metropolis. By PIERCE EGAN,
or of "Walks through Bath," "Sporting
dotes," "Picture of the Fancy," "Box-
" &c. Elegantly printed in Royal 8vo.
: £1 : 16*s*. in Boards, or, in Twelve Num-
, (to be had by one or more at a time,)
› 3*s*. each.

They do these things better in France!" said
:NE. "I say not," replies TOM; "LONDON
ıt the World for 'Life.'---Why, it's Carlton-Palace
Charley's Shelter,' and no *chance* to win." "Bravo,"
JERRY; "there never was such times as these, my
ny! Ha! ha!"---NEW CHAFF.

m the above ORIGINAL WORK FIVE Dramas
been produced, and are nightly performed at five
res in the Metropolis, besides, at the Theatre Royal
ı, at Bristol, and several other theatres in various
of the kingdom; and, in America. In the short
of eight months, the above celebrated heroes, TOM,
RY, and LOGIC, have made their bows to upwards of
: Hundred different and delighted audiences, an epoch
ımatic history unprecedented, and which renders any
nent on the popularity of this Original Work unne-
ry.

n these days, when every man who can read calls
nself a man of letters, and all who can write set up for
.hors; when almost every branch of literature has
en stripped, and little remains but to begin at the
;inning again; no small share of praise is due to the
;enious and daring author, who strikes into a new
th, and presents to the public view an object which
s never been seen before, or has been forgotten. THIS
THE GREAT MERIT OF THE AUTHOR OF THE
)OK BEFORE US. The task is a difficult one, and
t few men can execute it. Of the utility of such a
ırk there can be no doubt, while London abounds as it
es with imposture and temptation. As far as it has
oceeded, (the first three numbers only having been
blished,) it is executed with considerable taste and
ıth, and deserves to fill a respectable rank among
ırks of *practical philosophy*. It is one of the most amu-
ıg books lately published; for our own part, but per-
ıps we are partial, we prefer it to many of the sketches
mankind which have appeared since the days of the
ectator. '*Le Franc Parleur*' does not speak half so
ıinly as our hero. '*L'Hermite de la Chaussee d'Antin*'
ıds too retired a life, and the '*Hermit in London*' is
o dandyish and vapid, to compare with him. *Geoffrey*
ıyon presents mere *sketches*, while CORINTHIAN
)M gives finished *portraits*; with all the delicacy and
ecision of GERARD DOUW, he unites the boldness
RUBENS, and the intimate knowledge of TENIERS."
uropean Magazine, November, 1820.

O THE SPORTING WORLD.

3OXIANA; or, SKETCHES of MODERN
GILISM: including every Pugilistic Ex-
.t from the Days of Figg and Broughton,
ın to the Fight between Painter and Spring,
the 1st of April, 1818; with the Age,
ight, Style of Fighting, and Character of
h Pugilist, a variety of Original Anecdotes,
gs, &c.; forming a *complete Boxing Calen-*
and *Book of Reference*. By PIERCE
ıAN. In three large Volumes, 8vo. embel-
ıed with numerous PORTRAITS. Price £2
ɔoards.

'he VOLUMES may be had *separately:*

OL. I. (Dedicated to Captain Barclay), contains every
lle and Anecdote, connected with scientific Pugilism,
ı Figg and Broughton to the period of Cribb's Championship; with an Introduction on the origin, rise, and progress of Pugilism in England. Price 12*s*. boards.

VOL. II. (Dedicated to the Earl of Yarmouth), containing every Battle and Anecdote from Cribb's Championship to the First Battle of Painter and Spring; with an Introduction on the Antiquity of Pugilism, and the mode of using the Cæstus in the Combats of the Ancients, contrasted with the period of Figg and Broughton,---the Scientific Time of Mendoza,---and the improved system of Tactics, illustrated at the present day, by Mr. Jackson, and the advantages of the Gloves considered, as practised with at the Fives-Court: with an Account of the Origin and National Utility of the Pugilistic Club. Price 14*s*. boards.

VOL. III. (Dedicated to the Marquis of Worcester), containing, in addition to the merits of the OLD and NEW SCHOOLS of Boxers, with their peculiar traits, contrasted,---REMARKS on the Re-appearance of Mendoza and Owen in the Prize-Ring. The decline and fall of Scroggins. The *top-of-the-tree qualities* of Randall, and his climax. Turner's practice in the Court of Chancery. The Irish Champion's visit to England. His victory over Oliver, and his Knighthood. Donnelly's return to Ireland. His death from the whiskey fever. Epitaphs, philosophical Oration, plaintive Ballads, Elegies, &c. connected with that *mournful* milling event. The tumble down of the Lancashire Hero. Rise of Spring. Bob, the Giant, twice overcome by Shelton. West-country Dick upon his legs. The Norfolk dumplings jumping out of the pot for joy. The intrepid little Gypsey, that supplies *caper-sauce* gratis, in all his *turn-ups*, to his opponents. Extensive business of the Master of the Rolls. The RUMPSTEAKS *dressed* by *Gas Light*; and the *Cooper* also new hooped by the same blazing quality. The GYBLET-PIE opened to satisfy all the Lovers of *Taste*, and the RASHER *broiled* without a gridiron. The *Sprig of Myrtle* turned Brown. Belcher the first second. Cooper's elegant Fight. Sutton still on the *black* side of the question---and the Champion of England not only having a *hand* still left for any *Customer* that wishes to shake it---the *Cribb* being also in his favour, besides keeping the *Game* alive, &c. &c.

The Third Volume will also be found *rich* in original anecdote, from the CORINTHIAN to the COSTERMONGER; in fact, the Author assures the Sporting World, not a stone has been left unturned to procure them. Likewise some NEW SONGS, incidental to the *Fancy*. Price 18*s*. boards.

"BOXIANA is a book we never tire of; take it up when we will, it puts us into immediate spirits. It is a sufficient justification of Pugilism to say,---Mr. EGAN is its Historian. He combines within himself, as the historian of British Pugilism, all the qualifications possessed by all the historians of British Poetry. He has all the elegance and feeling of a *Percy*---all the classical grace and inventive ingenuity of a *Warton*---all the enthusiasm and zeal of a *Headly*---all the acuteness and vigour of a *Ritson*---all the learning and wit of an *Ellis*---all the delicacy and discernment of a *Campbell*; and, at the same time, his style is perfectly his own, and likely to remain so, for it is as inimitable as it is excellent. The man who has not read "BOXIANA" is ignorant of the power of the English language."
---*Blackwood's Magazine, March,* 1820.

SPORTING ANECDOTES.

SPORTING ANECDOTES, original and selected, (many of them concerning our late King); including numerous Characteristic Portraits of Persons in every Walk of Life, who have acquired Notoriety from their Achievements on the Turf, at the Table, and in the Diversions of the Field: the whole forming *a Complete Delineation of the Sporting World*. By PIERCE EGAN. Embellished with a characteristic Frontispiece, representing eight Varieties of Sporting Amusements, price 9*s*. in boards, or 12*s*. elegantly bound.

"Mr. Egan, the author of 'BOXIANA,' has, in a little Octavo Volume, entitled "SPORTING ANECDOTES," contrived to amass together all the particulars of *Horse*, *Dog*, and *Man*, worthy of being known.---It is a happy composition; full of whim and particular phrases, with a slip of morality in it, like a bit of lemon peel in one's punch, and delightfully flavoured with the choicest lime juice of *slang*. Deeply as we have dived into the jewels of Mr. Egan's book, the store is inexhaustible. Turn which way we will, innumerable sparkling subjects (the epithet is perfectly modern) invite us to take them. But we really, like Sinbad in the Valley of Serpents, must be content with the few invaluable diamonds, of which we have possessed ourselves. They are, and will be, a fortune to us. Ever leaf in the book glitters like a river in the sun. How many interesting characters, anecdotes, and speculations beckon to our minds!---Jack Cavanagh, the ball-player, revels through three pages of genuine Fives-Court prose. Captain Barclay runs his matches,---trains,---and *spars* before us.---Captain O'Kelly, the Duke of Queensbury, Colonel Thornton, Mr. Elwes, Colonel Mellish, and Major Topham, walk by us, not as "the illustrious dead,"---but alive,---ardent,---betting, --- breathing, --- all jollity, *game*, and spirit! Racers, pigeons, pedestrians, fighting-cocks, terriers, trotters, badgers, weasels, pheasants, falconers, fishermen, stoats, stags, foxes, and gentlemen,---swarm, like bees.---Matches against time,---extraordinary snipe shooting,---flights of a pigeon,---all that can be interesting to the naturalist, the pugilist, or the gentleman, is to be met with in Mr. Egan's book. It is the *cleverest* Volume in the World. It has no affectations,---no dispirited passages,---no tame subjects,---no nonsense! It does not run a long-winded subject down,---but is 'every thing by fits, and nothing long.' All persons who have heard of Blumsell, the running painter,---Wheatley, the fighting oilman,---the inimitable walking Powell,---Jack Spires, the racket-player,---the incomparable Dan Crisp,---the wonderful phenomenon mare, Mr. Wells's matchless Pipylenal!---all who have read of Flying Childers,---Snowball, the fleet black greyhound,---Eclipse,---Tom Cribb,---Hambletonian, and Sir Charles Bunbury!---all, we say, who have heard or read of these great names, and who respect perfection and talent wherever it can be found,---let them purchase Mr. Egan's SPORTING ANECDOTES---for they are faithful in the dispensation of fame to Man and Beast."---*Baldwin's London Magazine, August and September*, 1820.

THE ROAD TO A FIGHT.

A PICTURE of the FANCY GOING to a FIGHT at MOULSEY HURST, (measuring in length 14 feet,) containing numerous ORIGINAL CHARACTERS, many of them *Portraits*; in which all the FROLIC, FUN, LARK, GIG, LIFE, GAMMON, and TRYING-IT-ON, are depicted, incident to the pursuit of a PRIZE MILL: dedicated, by permission, to Mr. JACKSON, and the *Noblemen* and *Gentlemen* composing the PUGILISTIC CLUB.

THIS PICTURE commences with the Night before Starting, and depicts the Interior of the CASTLE TAVERN—Amateurs betting—and the DAFFY CLUB in high *Spirits*. Also, the Bustle at Peep of Day, in setting off to the Scene of Action. The Road, in all that variety of *style* and *costume* which the SPORTING WORLD so amply furnishes,—exhibiting the CORINTHIANS in their *bang-up* sets-out of *blood* and *bone*; the SWELLS, NIB SPRIGS, and TIDY ONES, in their Tandems, Gigs, and Trotters; the *Lads* in their Rattlers, Heavy Drags, and Tumblers, including the Bermondsey Boys and Tothilfields Coster-mongers, in all their gradations, down to the *Stampers*, &c. Groups of Sporting Characters assembled at LAWRENCE'S, the Red Lion, Hampton. The Amateurs in boats, crossing the Thames to gain Moulsey Hurst. The grand Climax—the RING, with all its extensive contingencies. The Humours of a BULL BAIT for a Silver Collar, a *let-loose* match? and the *Denouement*.—A peep at the Interior of TATTERSALL'S upon the *Settling-Day*. Throughout the PICTURE, not a *Pink* has been overlooked, nor an *Out-and-Outer* forgotten: the whole forming "*A bit of good truth!*".

A copious and characteristic *Key* accompanies the Picture, written by PIERCE EGAN.

"For I am nothing, if not CHARACTER!"

*** The Price of the Picture, with the *Key*, is 14*s*. *plain*, or £1 *coloured*, neatly [cut] up in a box for the pocket. Also, framed black and gold, and varnished, in which it will be found a very interesting piece furniture for the GENTLEMAN OR SPORTSM[AN] (measuring in length 43 inches, by 15 wi[de]) £1 : 12*s*. *plain*, or £1 : 18*s*. *coloured*.

"Nothing equal to this Picture has appeared since inimitable Hogarth's 'March to Finchley.' In the 'P[icture] of the Fancy,' we find real life, originality of charac[ter], the peculiar traits of a certain class in society of the [pre]sent day, from the nobleman to the match-boy, so mas[terly] portrayed, and with so much *naivete*, that it might be [said] it is without a competitor in the modern school of de[sign] and invention. The above Picture and Key have [been] received with the highest approbation in the Sp[orting] World; but to those persons not connected with th[e pur]suit it represents, it will nevertheless be found a plea[sing] companion for the parlour, from the fund of amuse[ment] which it affords; and in the dressing-room of the ma[n of] the world, or the sportsman's cabinet, it cannot fa[il] proving a welcome resident."---*Sporting Magazine*, 1819.

SPORTSMAN'S VOCAL LIBRARY.

THE SPORTSMAN'S VOCAL LIBRARY, being SONGS of the CHASE; inclu[ding] some also on *Racing*, *Shooting*, *Ang[ling]*, *Hawking*, *Arching*, &c. handsomely printe[d] foolscap 8vo. with appropriate Embel[lish]ments, 2d Edition, price 9*s*. boards.

"This Collection has been made with much judg[ment] and industry. The book is exquisitely printed on fine p[aper] and embellished with two beautiful Engravings, viz. [a] Title and Frontispiece, the joint efforts of Mr. Mar[shall], the Animal Painter; and Mr. John Scott, the Engr[aver]. There is likewise a Tailpiece engraved on wood, repr[esent]ing, in miniature, the joys of the table after a fox-c[hase]." ---*Sporting Magazine*.

TO THE ADMIRERS OF

THE CHASE, THE TURF, THE STUD, THE RING, &c.

Now publishing, in Monthly Numbers, p[rice] 2s. 6d. each, a new Work, entitled,

THE

Annals of Sporting

AND

FANCY GAZETTE;

A MAGAZINE,

Entirely appropriated to

SPORTING SUBJECTS

AND

FANCY PURSUITS;

Containing every Thing worthy of Remark on

HUNTING,	COCKING,	CRICKET,
SHOOTING,	PUGILISM,	BILLIARDS,
COURSING,	WRESTLING,	ROWING,
RACING,	SINGLE STICK,	SAILING,
FISHING,	PEDESTRIANISM,	&c. &c.

Accompanied with

STRIKING REPRESENTATIONS

OF THE

VARIOUS SUBJECTS.

N.B. All the *Plates* connected with FIELD SPO[RTS] will be *coloured after Nature*.

CPSIA information can be obtained
at www.ICGtesting.com
Printed in the USA
LVOW09*1117020817
543551LV00016BA/243/P